# FOREST AND BIODIVERSITY CONSERVATION

ENV BOOKS SERIES

# FOREST
# AND
# BIODIVERSITY CONSERVATION


*Editors*

**Dr. Alka Chauhan**

*Society for Environment, Health, Awareness of Nutrition & Toxicology (SEHAT)*
*1775, Sohan Ganj, Near Clock Tower*
*Delhi-110 007 (India)*

*&*

**Dr. Pawan Kumar 'Bharti'**

*Society for Environment, Health, Awareness of Nutrition & Toxicology (SEHAT)*
*1775, Sohan Ganj, Near Clock Tower, Delhi - 110 007 (India)*
E-mail: *gurupawanbharti@rediffmail.com*



DPH

**DISCOVERY PUBLISHING HOUSE PVT. LTD.**
**INDIA**

*Published by:*
**Namit Wasan**
**DISCOVERY PUBLISHING HOUSE PVT. LTD.**
4383/4B, Ansari Road, Darya Ganj
New Delhi-110 002 (India)
*Phone* : +91-11-23279245, 43596064-65
*Fax* : +91-11-23253475
*E-mail* : discoverypublishinghouse@gmail.com
namitwasan9@gmail.com
sales@discoverypublishinggroup.com
*web* : www.discoverypublishinggroup.com

***First Edition:* 2017**

**ISBN: 978-93-5056-873-6**

**Forest and Biodiversity Conservation**



*Printed at:*
Infinity Imaging Systems
Delhi

# ENV Books Series, India

Calls descriptive and error free chapters for upcoming volumes of books on various environmental issues. Send your manuscripts to envbooks@gmail.com

*Founding Editor* **(*Editor-in-Chief*)**

**Dr. Pawan Kumar 'Bharti'**

*Society for Environment, Health, Awareness of Nutrition & Toxicology (SEHAT-India)*

*1775, Sohanganj, Near Clock Tower, Delhi-7, (India)*

E-mail:*gurupawanbharti@rediffmail.com*

***Other Important Titles by Editor-in-Chief:***

1. **Advances in Biotechnology and Ecological Sciences**
   Bharti, P.K., Chauhan, A. and Ray, J. (eds.)
   (ISBN: 978-93-5056-358-8).
2. **Advances in Agriculture and Ecology**
   Bharti, P.K.; Chauhan, A. and Ezeaku Peter Ikemefuna (eds.)
   (ISBN: 978-93-5056-362-5).
3. **Agriculture and Environmental Biotechnology**
   Bharti, P.K. and Chauhan, A. (eds.)
   (ISBN: 978-93-5056-479-0).
4. **Agriculture Development and Sustainable Environment**
   Ray, J. and Bharti, P.K. (eds.)
   (ISBN: 978-93-5056-759-3).
5. **Agriculture Ecology and Environment**
   Bharti, P.K. and Olubukola O. Babalola (eds.)
   (ISBN: 978-93-5056-480-6).
6. **Agriculture Ecology, Sustainable Development and Agribusiness Management**
   Mehta Piyush; Sharma Pankaj; and 'Bharti' P.K. (eds.)
   (ISBN: 978-93-5056-851-4).
7. **Agriculture, Environment and Nano-science**
   Bharti, Pawan K. (ed.)
   (ISBN: 978-93-5056-760-5).
8. **Agricultural Practices and Crop Disease Control**
   Chauhan Alka and Sharma Anubhuti (eds.)
   (ISBN: 978-93-5056-859-0).

9. **Agro-biodiversity: *Conservation and Sustainable Development***
Sharma, Pankaj; Singh, Narayan; and Bharti, P.K. (eds.)
(ISBN: 978-93-505-782-1).

10. **Agro-forestry and Climate Change**
Bharti, Pawan K. and Singh, Narayan (eds.)
(ISBN: 978-93-5056-514-8).

11. **Agro-forestry and Sustainable Agriculture**
Sharma, Pankaj; Bharti, P.K. (eds.)
(ISBN: 978-93-5056-786-9).

12. **Aquaculture and Fisheries Environment**
Gupta, S.K. and Pawan K. Bharti (eds.)
(ISBN: 978-93-5056-408-0).

13. **Aquatic Biodiversity and Pollution**
Bharti, P.K.; Chauhan, A. and Kaoud, H.A.H. (eds.)
(ISBN: 978-93-5056-359-5).

14. **Aquatic Ecology and Biotechnology**
Bharti, P.K. and Zaki, M.S.A. (eds.)
(ISBN: 978-93-5056-451-6).

15. **Aquatic Environment and Toxicology**
Bharti, Pawan K. (ed.)
(ISBN: 978-93-5056-236-9).

16. **Biodiversity, Biotechnology and Environmental Conservation**
Bharti, P.K. and Bhandari, G. (eds.)
(ISBN: 978-93-5056-750-0).

17. **Biodiversity of Aquatic Ecosystem: *Significance, Threat and Conservation* (2013)**
Bharti, P.K. and Kaoud, H.A.H. (eds.)
(ISBN: 978-93-5056-297-0).

18. **Biological Diversity and Ecology**
Arya, M.K.; Bharti, P.K. and Ritesh Joshi (eds.)
(ISBN: 978-93-5056-785-2).

19. **Bioremediation and Microbial Biotechnology**
Gupta, Sandeep; and Bharti, P.K. (eds.)
(ISBN: 978-93-5056-783-8).

20. **Biotechnological Approaches and Water Ecosystem**
Zaki, M.S.A.; and Bharti, P.K. (eds.)
(ISBN: 978-93-5056-779-1).

21. **Biotechnology, Agro-ecology and Environment**
Chauhan, Avnish and Bharti, P.K. (eds.)
(ISBN: 978-93-5056-757-9).

22. **Biotechnology and Environmental Management**
Arya Arun; Maheswari Raaz K., & Bharti, P.K (eds.)
(ISBN: 978-93-5056-862-0).

23. **Clean Technologies and Environmental Protection**
Chauhan, A.; Sharma, S. and Bharti, P.K. (eds.)
(ISBN: 978-93-5056-731-9).

24. **Climate Change and Agriculture**
Bharti, P.K. and Chauhan, Avnish (eds.)
(ISBN: 978-93-5056-148-5).

25. **Climate Change and Biodiversity**
Bharti, P.K. and Chauhan, Avnish (eds.)
(ISBN: 978-93-5056-360-1).

26. **Climate Change, Disaster Management and Environment**
Chauhan, Alka; Bharti, P.K. (eds.)
(ISBN: 978-93-5056-784-5).

27. **Conservation and Cultivation of Medicinal Plants**
Bharti, P.K. and Singh Narayan (eds.)
(ISBN: 978-93-5056-740-1).

28. **Crop Productivity and Plant Disease Management**
Chauhan, Alka; Bharti, P.K. and Sadana, Deepti (eds.)
(ISBN: 978-93-5056-791-3).

29. **Eco-toxicology and Eco-technology**
Bharti, P.K. and Zaki, M. (eds.)
(ISBN: 978-93-5056-313-7).

30. **Environmental Biotechnology and Application**
Bharti, P.K. and Chauhan, Avnish (eds.)
(ISBN: 978-93-5056-262-8).

31. **Environmental Conservation and Biotechnology**
Chauhan, A. and P.K. Bharti (eds.)
(ISBN: 978-93-5056-512-4).

32. **Environmental Health and Problems**
Bharti, P.K. and Gajananda, Kh. (eds.)
(ISBN: 978-93-5056-263-5).

33. **Environmental Pollution and Biodiversity**
Bharti, P.K.; Chauhan, Avnish and Kumar, P. (eds.)
(ISBN: 978-93-5056-149-2).

34. **Farming Techniques and Crop Production**
Chauhan Alka; Sharma Anubhuti; Ray Jaswant and 'Bharti' P.K. (eds.)
(ISBN: 978-93-5056-855-2).

35. **Fisheries and Toxicology**
Zaki, M.S.A.; Bharti, P.K. and Chauhan, A. (eds.)
(ISBN: 978-93-5056-452-3).

36. **Fish Habitat and Aquaculture**
Bharti, P.K.; Gupta Kr. Sanjay (eds.)
(ISBN: 978-93-5056-744-9).

37. **Food Processing, Management and Nanotechnology**
Chauhan, Avnish; Bharti, P.K. (eds.)
(ISBN: 978-93-5056-796-8).

38. **Freshwater Ecosystem and Xenobiotics**
Bharti, P.K.; Zaki, M. and Chauhan, A. (eds.)
(ISBN: 978-93-5056-299-4).

39. **Heavy Metals and Metalloids in Biosphere:** ***Impacts & Assessment***
Chauhan, Avnish, Gupta, Sandeep; and Bharti, P.K. (eds.)
(ISBN: 978-93-5056-860-6).

40. **Limnology and Aquatic Science**
Sharma, S., and Bharti, P.K. (eds.)
(ISBN: 978-93-5056-735-7).

41. **Medicinal Plants:** ***Distribution, Utilization and Significance***
Sharma, P.; Bharti, P.K. and Narayan Singh (eds.)
(ISBN: 978-93-5056-734-0).

42. **Microbial Applications and Environment**
Bharti, Pawan K. (ed.)
(ISBN: 978-93-5056-515-5).

43. **Microbial Ecology and Habitat**
Bharti, Pawan K. (ed.)
(ISBN: 978-93-5056-514-8).

44. **Microbial Environment and Bioremediation**
Chauhan Alka; K. Rathoure Ashok; and K Maheshwari Raaz (eds.)
(ISBN: 978-93-5056-856-9).

45. **Natural Ecosystem and Climate Change**
Bharti, P.K., and Kh. Gajananda (ed.)
(ISBN: 978-93-5056-745-6).

46. **Pest Management and Agro-Techniques**
Biswas, Asim; Bharti, P.K., Chauhan, Avnish (eds.)
(ISBN: 978-93-5056-794-4).

47. **Prakriti me Aushadhi (*in Hindi*)**
Singh, J.R.; Bharti, P.K. and Bharti, B.
(ISBN: 978-93-5056-200-0).

48. **Seed Technology, Plant Growth and Cropping System**
Tyagi, P.K. and Bharti, P.K. (eds.)
(ISBN: 978-93-5056-738-8).

49. **Seed Treatment, Plant Heath and Agro-technology**
Chauhan, A. and Bharti, P.K. (eds.)
(ISBN: 978-93-5056-810-1).

50. **Soil Characteristics and Agro-ecology**
Avnish Chauhan and Bharti, P.K. (eds.)
(ISBN: 978-93-5056-758-6).
51. **Soil Contamination and Conservation**
Ezeaku, P.I. and Bharti, P.K. (eds.)
(ISBN: 978-93-5056-737-1).
52. **Soil Quality and Contamination**
Bharti, P.K. and Chauhan, Avnish (eds.)
(ISBN: 978-93-5056-361-8).
53. **Sustainable Aquaculture Management**
Gupta, S.K.; Bharti, P.K (eds.)
(ISBN: 978-93-5056-797-5).
54. **Waste Disposal and Management**
Bharti, P.K.; Tabassum, B. and Bajaj, P. (eds.)
(ISBN: 978-93-5056-729-6).
55. **Waste Generation and Utilization**
Bajaj Priya; Tabassum, B., and Bharti, P.K. (eds.)
(ISBN: 978-93-5056-792-0).
56. **Waste Management and Environmental Health**
Tabassum, B., Bajaj Priya, and Bharti, P.K. (eds.)
(ISBN: 978-93-5056-777-7).
57. **Water Resources:** ***Mapping Monitoring and Management***
Tyagi, P.K., Chauhan, Avnish and Bharti, P.K. (eds.)
(ISBN: 978-93-5056-861-3).
58. **Water Resources and Agriculture**
Bharti, P.K. and Ezeaku Peter Ikemefuna (eds.)
(ISBN: 978-93-5056-481-3).
59 **Waste Resources Management:** ***Monitoring and Assessment***
Gupta, Sandeep and Bharti, P.K. (eds.)
(ISBN: 978-93-5056-799-9).

# Preface

A forest is a large area of land covered with trees or other woody vegetation. Hundreds of more precise definitions of forest are used throughout the world, incorporating factors such as tree density, tree height, land use, legal standing and ecological function. According to the widely used United Nations Food and Agriculture Organization definition, forests covered four billion hectares (15 million square miles) or approximately 30 percent of the world's land area in 2006.

Forests are the dominant terrestrial ecosystem of Earth, and are distributed across the globe. Forests account for 75% of the gross primary productivity of the Earth's biosphere, and contain 80% of the Earth's plant biomass.

Forestry is the science and craft of creating, managing, using, conserving, and repairing forests and associated resources to meet desired goals, needs, and values for human and environment benefits. Forestry is practiced in plantations and naturalstands. The science of forestry has elements that belong to the biological, physical, social, political and managerial sciences.

Modern forestry generally embraces a broad range of concerns, in what is known as multiple-use management, including the provision of timber, fuel wood, wildlife habitat, natural water quality management, recreation, landscape and community protection, employment, aesthetically appealing landscapes, biodiversity management, watershed management, erosion control, and preserving forests as 'sinks' for atmospheric carbon dioxide. A practitioner of forestry is known as a forester. Other terms are used a verderer and a silviculturalist being common ones. Silviculture is narrower than forestry, being concerned only with forest plants, but is often used synonymously with forestry.

Forest ecosystems have come to be seen as the most important component of the biosphere, and forestry has emerged as a vital applied science, craft, and technology.

Forestry is an important economic segment in various industrial countries. For example, in Germany, forests cover nearly a third of the land area, wood is the most important renewable resource, and forestry supports more than a million jobs and about billion in yearly turnover.

Forestry in India is a significant rural industry and a major environmental resource. India is one of the ten most forest-rich countries of the world along with the Russian Federation, Brazil, Canada, United States of America, China, Democratic Republic of the Congo, Australia, Indonesia and Sudan. Together, India and these countries account for 67 percent of total forest area of the world. India's forest cover grew at 0.22% annually over 1990-2000, and has grown at the rate of 0.46% per year over 2000-2010, after decades where forest degradation was a matter of serious concern.

Forestry in India is more than just about wood and fuel. India has a thriving non-wood forest products industry, which produces latex, gums, resins, essential oils, flavours, fragrances and aroma chemicals, incense sticks, handicrafts, thatching materials and medicinal plants. About 60% of non-wood forest products production is consumed locally. About 50% of the total revenue from the forestry industry in India is in non-wood forest products category. In 2002, non-wood forest products were a source of significant supplemental income to over 400 million people in India, mostly rural.

Biodiversity refers to the variety of life. It is seen in the number of species in an ecosystem or on the entire Earth. Biodiversity gets used as a measure of the health of biological systems, and to see if there is a danger that too many species become extinct. The United Nations designated 2011-2020 as the "United Nations Decade on Biodiversity".

Biodiversity, a contraction of "biological diversity," generally refers to the variety and variability of life on Earth. One of the most widely used definitions defines it in terms of the variability within species, between species and between ecosystems. It is a measure of the variety of organisms present in different ecosystems. This can refer to genetic variation, ecosystem variation, or species variation (number of species) within an area, biome, or planet. Terrestrial biodiversity tends to be greater near the equator, which seems to be the result of the warm climate and high primary productivity. Biodiversity is not distributed evenly on Earth. It is richest in the tropics. Marine biodiversity tends to be highest along coasts in the Western Pacific, where sea surface temperature is highest and in the mid-latitudinal band in all oceans. There are latitudinal gradients in species diversity. Biodiversity generally tends to cluster in hotspots, and has been increasing through time, but will be likely to slow in the future.

The number and variety of plants, animals and other organisms that exist is known as biodiversity. It is an essential component of nature and it ensures the survival of human species by providing food, fuel, shelter, medicines and other resources to mankind. The richness of biodiversity depends on the climatic conditions and area of the region. All species of plants taken together are known as flora and about 70,000 species of plants are known to date. All species of animals taken together are known as fauna which includes birds, mammals, fish, reptiles, insects, crustaceans, molluscs, etc.

Forests are biologically diverse systems, representing some of the richest biological areas on Earth. They offer a variety of habitats for plants, animals and micro-organisms. However, forest biodiversity is increasingly threatened as a result of deforestation, fragmentation, climate change and other stressors. Tropical, temperate and boreal forests offer a diverse set of habitats for plants, animals and micro-organisms. Consequently forests hold the majority of the world's terrestrial species. However these biologically rich systems are increasingly threatened, largely as a result of human activity.

Forest biological diversity is broad term referring to all the life forms found within forested areas and the ecological roles they perform. As such, forest biological diversity encompasses not just trees but the multitude of plants, animals and micro-organisms that inhabit forest areas and their associated genetic diversity.

In the last 8000 years about 45% of the Earth's original forest cover has disappeared, cleared mostly during the past century. The Food and Agriculture Organization of the United Nations (FAO) recently estimated that about 13 million hectares of the world's forests are lost due to deforestation each year. The annual net loss of forest area between 2000 and 2005 was 7.3 million hectares (equivalent to the net loss of 0.18 percent of the world's forests).

Forest biological diversity is a broad term that refers to all life forms found within forested areas and the ecological roles they perform. As such, forest biological diversity encompasses not just trees, but the multitude of plants, animals and micro-organisms that inhabit forest areas and their associated genetic diversity.

Forest biological diversity can be considered at different levels, including the ecosystem, landscapes, species, populations and genetics. Complex interactions can occur within and amongst these levels. In biologically diverse forests, this complexity allows organisms to adapt to continually changing environmental conditions and to maintain ecosystem functions.

In the annex to decision II/9, the Conference of the Parties recognized that:

"Forest biological diversity results from evolutionary processes over thousands and even millions of years which, in themselves, are driven by ecological forces such as climate, fire, competition and disturbance. Furthermore, the diversity of forest ecosystems (in both physical and biological features) results in high levels of adaptation, a feature of forest ecosystems which is an integral component of their biological diversity. Within specific forest ecosystems, the maintenance of ecological processes is dependent upon the maintenance of their biological diversity."

The present book updates the subject content of forestry, forest ecosystem, biological diversity, endangered species and biodiversity conservation.

The book will be helpful for the researchers, academia working in the field of forestry, forest ecosystem, biological diversity, endangered species and biodiversity conservation and management.

**–Editors**

(envbooks@gmail.com)

# Contents

Pages: 1-26

**FOREST AND BIODIVERSITY CONSERVATION**

*Edited by:* **Dr. Alka Chauhan** and **Dr. Pawan Kumar 'Bharti'**

**ISBN: 978-93-5056-873-6**

*Edition:* **2017**

*Published by:* **Discovery Publishing House Pvt. Ltd., New Delhi (India)**

# 1 Assessment of Spatio-temporal Patterns of Forest Disturbance and Regrowth in Shifting Cultivation Areas of Dima Hasao District, Assam Using Time-series Satellite Images

*D.Nandi[1]; P.C. Sahu[2] and P. Longmailai[3]*

## ABSTRACT

Shifting cultivation is the traditional method of cultivation practiced in Dima Hasao district of Assam, northeast India. Forest dynamics are characterized by disturbances and recovery, key processes affecting the shifting cycle. Thus,spatially and temporally explicit knowledge of these processes and their drivers are critical for understanding shifting cultivation. Here we used a new method that uses time series satellite data to estimate changes in shifting cultivation associated with forest disturbances and recovery. The study area was selected is a typical shifting cultivation region in Dima Hasao district. Map were developed from 105 Landsat Operational Land Imager, Landsat Thematic Mapper and Enhance Thematic Mapper + images and were assessed for validity point using TimeSyncR, a time series validation and interpretation tool. We develop disturbances and regrowth map of forest from the result of TimeSyncR, describe previously at pixel scale. The objectives of this study was to examine the abrupt and frequent trends associated with a range of spectral indicator (NVI,EVI,NDMI,N37I & NBR) of forest recovery and regrowth in shifting cultivation. Taken together these results indicate that spectral indices characterized the gradual increase and decrease over the period 1997 to 2015. These manifestations are best achieved using the TimeSync interpretation tool that can detect both abrupt and longer-duration processes within the Landsat archive.

[1] Department of Remote Sensing and G.I.S, North Orissa University, Baripada (Orissa, (India)

[2] Department of Geology, M.P.C. Autonomous College, Baripada - 757 003 (Orissa) (India)

[3] Department of Remote Sensing and G.I.S, North Orissa University, Baripada, (Orissa) (India)

# INTRODUCTION

## Forest Disturbance and Re-Growth

Forest disturbances are the events that caused the change in the shape, structure and compositions of a forest ecosystem, beyond the growth and death of individual organism. In other words, it can be defined as the temporary change in environment condition that leads to pronounced change in our ecosystem. Disturbances can often vary in frequency and intensity, sometimes resulting in the removal of large amounts of biomass and include natural disasters such as fire, landslides, wind, and volcanic eruptions, outbreaks of insects, fungi, and other pathogens. Apart from that, devastating effects of human impact on the environment such as clear cutting, forest clearing (Shifting Cultivation) can also be considered as the major disturbances in the forest ecosystem. Disturbance forces can have profound immediate effects on ecosystems and can, accordingly, greatly alter the natural community. Because of these and the growing impacts on populations, these effects can continue for an extended period of time. Not all disturbances are destructive or negative to the overall forest ecosystem. Many natural disturbances allow for renewal and re-growth and often release necessary nutrients. Small-scale disturbances are the key to creating and maintaining diversity and heterogeneity within a forest. Small-scale disturbances are events such as single-tree blow downs, which create gaps that let light through the canopy to the under-storey and forest floor. This available light allows early-succession shade-intolerant species to colonize and maintain a population within the dominant forest, leading to the complex spatial mosaic forest structure recognized as old-growth. This process is referred to as patch dynamics or gap dynamics and has been described across many types of forests, including tropical, temperate, and boreal. Since a disturbance in the forest (deforestation) has a huge temporal impact on natural habitats and the ecosystem, reforestation or forest re-growth will soon occur which have been wiped out or depleted due to the human activity in the forest like clearing or cutting down the forest for shifting cultivation (jhum cultivation), setting up industries etc. Forest recovery and re-growth are key processes in forest ecosystem dynamics. Recovery is the re-establishment of a new forest stand or regeneration of a partially disturbed stand following a previous disturbance.

## Shifting Cultivation

Shifting cultivation is an important form of primitive agriculture land use. In this system forest area is cleared by slash and burn technique. Till 1950's shifting cultivation, under its diverse forms of slash-and-burn system was a traditional method of cultivating tropical highland and mountain soils, mostly for providing a minimum subsistence to the peasantry (Singh, 1997). For primitive cultures, the cultivation was a remarkable innovation which is based on the revolutionary transition from forest based food gathering to agriculture based food production. The cycle of rotation was also long having enough time to regenerate the soil. This is how a nomadic cropping system for self-sufficient subsistence economy developed with labor efficient systems.

Shifting cultivation is one of the earliest forms of agricultural system years back when man began to change its mode of life from food gathers and hunters to cultivators. It is a primitive form of agriculture, which is believed to have originated in the Neolithic period around 7000 B.C. (Subramanyam and Sambamurty, 2000). The understanding of human being towards shifting agriculture started long before, if not synchronized with pioneer shifting cultivation. Nomenclatures of shifting cultivation are given as 'Jhum' or 'Jhuming'cultivation in North-East India. It is variably termed as rotational bush fallow agriculture, swidden cultivation, or slashes and burn cultivation, and is an ancient form of agriculture still common in many parts of the humid tropics (Raman, 2001). Shifting agriculture involves clearing a patch of forest land, but retaining useful trees & plants, cultivating it for 2 to 3 years and then abandoned it for 10-20 years and allowed to revert to their natural vegetation while the cultivator moves on to another plot. The period of cultivation is usually terminated when the soil shows signs of exhaustion or, more commonly, when the field is overrun by weeds. The length of time that a field is cultivated is usually shorter than the period over which the land is allowed to regenerate by lying fallow. This technique is often used in Less Economically Developed Countries or Low Income Countries. Shifting cultivation has gradually become the scientific debate focus of the development of agro-forestry in the humid countries (Dove *et al*, 1983). It is highly diverse land use system. Shifting cultivation spreads from mountains to lowland ecosystems and from tropical forests to grasslands (Spencer, 1966).

**Spatial and Temporal Pattern of Shifting Cultivation**

Assessing the spatial and temporal patterns of disturbances enables determination and recovery, their long-term and potential effect on forest land due to shifting cultivation. The increase in human population, particularly in the developing countries, has put tremendous pressures on land. The extension of crop lands, for increasing food production, has been directly responsible for the reduction in areas under forests and grass lands. According to one estimate, about 40% of the land surface of the earth was converted into crop lands and permanent pastures by early 1990s. More than 6% area under tropical forests was converted to shifting cultivation between 1980 and 1990 across all tropical countries. About 10% of forest land was converted to shifting cultivation in Asia during the 1980-1990(Singh *et al*, 1995). Ecologically, these regions are far worse than realized. Apart from losing vegetation and biomass due to the practice of shifting cultivation, many other ecological factors too have been affected. Due to shifting cultivation practice on slopes, down-stream siltation of the water bodies is apparent in many districts. Protection and repair of drainage basins for conservation of ecological resources including water need large amounts of financial input. The shifting cultivation areas normally receive moderate to high rainfall. Due to splash forces generated from the rain drops, the erosion of precious top soil occurs. Thus, the major factors which influence the rate of soil erosion are the rainfall, the topography of the terrain, and the kind of vegetation and soil conditions. Today, shifting cultivation has disappeared from many other areas of the world. On a global scale, however, the system still constitutes the basis for the livelihood of an estimated 300-500 million people in Central Africa, South America, Oceania, and Southeast Asia, and is practiced on about 30% of all arable land but providing food to only 8% of the world population. In India, shifting cultivation has been trapped in a low-level and unstable equilibrium owing to two equally unviable paradigms that operate at the policy and institutional levels. The dominant perspective is that shifting cultivation is a wasteful and ecologically dysfunctional system, detrimental to forests and soil, and hence needs to be eradicated by inducing cultivators to adopt other forms of livelihood. The current practice of shifting cultivation in eastern and north eastern regions of India is an extravagant and unscientific form of land use. The evil effects of shifting cultivation are devastating and far-reaching in degrading the environment and ecology of these regions. Frequent shifting from one land to the other has affected the ecology of these regions. The area under natural forest has declined; the fragmentation of habitat, local disappearance of native species and invasion by exotic weeds and other plants are some of the other ecological consequences of shifting agriculture.

**Role of Geospatial Technology**

Remote Sensing data and their derivatives provide unique and appropriate input information to assess changes in shifting area across different spatial & temporal scale.The net change of forest land can be determined by the rate of shifting land change at fine spatial & temporal scale. Only satellite data can adequately captures its dynamics over large area. Using time series of remote sensing data both continuous and sudden forest change phenomena can be assessed, quantified and monitored (Kenny *et al*, 2007). The Landsat satellites provide a unique, continuous record of earth observation at ample spatial and spectral resolution since 1972 and, hence are well-suited for long-term forest change analyses (Cohen *et al*, 2004; Kennedy *et al*, 2010). Moreover, since the recent opening of the Landsat archive by the United States Geological Survey (USGS), new methodological approaches have emerged that make use of annual Landsat time series (Huang *et al.*, 2010; Kennedy *et al.*, 2010).

Several studies have already used remote sensing to map patterns of deforestation and to analyze the rates of forest cover change in the tropics and elsewhere (Hall *et al.*, 1991; Roughgarden *et al.*, 1991; wood and Skole,1998). Satellite image classification, change analysis (Armeteras *et al.*, 2006; Mas *et al.*, 2004) and econometric modeling are used to identify the rates, hotspots and drivers of deforestation in global hotspots of biodiversity and tropical deforestation. Monitoring of change (deforestation or reforestation) is frequently perceived as one of the most important contributions of remote sensing technology to study of global ecological and environment change (Apan *et al*, 1998; Roughgarden *et al.*, 1991). Temporal changes analysis from a GIS database reveals differences between the two dates and quantification of these changes. However, in temporal changes analysis, inherent features such as scale, classification scheme, accuracy and mapping methods need to be taken into account (Comber *et al.*, 2003; Fuller *et al.*, 2003; petit and lambin, 2002). In India, NRSA for the first time carried out country wide mapping of forest cover using Landsat MSS data in 1972-75 and later in 1980-82 (NRSA,1983). Subsequently, FSI,an operational agency in India started mapping forest cover in the country using remote sensing data. The biennial forest assessment was started by FSI at 1:250,000 scale and later at improved scale beyond 1:50,000. The forest is classified in four density classes (FSI, 2001). In the recent years, improvements in sensor technology an mapping techniques has changed the classification scheme, which also now includes mapping the trees outside the government-owned forest areas and community forests (FSI, 2003). (Joshi *et al.* (2006) mapped vegetation cover/land use map of India using IRS-1D WIFS data. It reports 36 classes with a focus on 16 forest cover types, which are in strong agreement with the forest cover types described byChampion and Seth (1968) a first ever vegetation mapping in India. Attempt has been made to assess forest cover in northeast India using temporal IRS-1C WIFS data for monitoring the phonological fluxes of forest landscape of northeast India (Roy and Joshi, 2002). The Normalized Difference Vegetation Index (NDVI) is evaluatedfor monitoring seasonal changes in vegetation. A hybrid approach (unsupervised and supervised) of classification provided better results with the overall accuracy of different classes as 82.15%. The present assessment of forest cover in the northeast region is 42.24% of the total geographical area whereas the estimation made by FSI is found 64.31% of the geographical area.

## OBJECTIVES

1. To examine the forest recovery and re-growth in shifting cultivation area within the observation period (1997 to 2015) using Time-Series Satellite Images.
2. The objectives of this study was to examine the abrupt and gradual trends associated with a range of spectral indicator (NVI, EVI, NDMI, N37I & NBR) in shifting cultivation region using TimeSyncR.
3. To quantify forest loss & gain associated with this process.

## LITERATURE REVIEW

### Studies Related to Shifting Cultivation

Laos based on time series satellite image s(Inoue *et al.*) 2010 Assessed land use and carbon stocks in Slash–and–burn ecosystems in tropical mountain. The study area was selected in a typical slash-and-burn region in the northern part of Laos. The chrono-sequential changes of land-use such as the relative areas of community age and cropping(C) + fallow(F) pattern were derived from the analysis of time series satellite images. The Chrono-sequential analysis showed that a consistent increase pf S/B area during the past three decades and a rapid increase after 1990. Approximately 37% of the whole area was with the community age of 1-5 years, whereas10% for 6-10 years in 2004. The ecosystem carbon stock at a regional scale was estimated but synthesizing the land-use patterns and semi-empirical carbon stock model derived from in situ measurements where the community age was used as a clue to the linkage. The ecosystem carbon stock in the region was strongly affected by the land-use patterns; the temporal average of carbon stock in 1C+10F cycles. The study approach proved to be useful especially in such regions and low data-availability and accessibility. This study revealed the dynamic change of land-use and ecosystem carbon stock in the tropical mountain of Laos as affected by land-use. Results suggested the significant potential of carbon sequestration through changing land-use and ecosystem management scenerios. These quantitative estimates would be useful to better understand and manage the land-use and ecosystem carbon stock towards higher sustainability and food security in similar ecosystem.

G molinario *et al.* (2015) showed the forest cover dynamics of shifting cultivation in the Democratic Republic of Congo using a remote sensing-based assessment for 2000-2010. The spatial contextualization of forest cover loss is therefore necessary to understand its impacts and plan its management. They characterized forest clearing using spatial models in a Geographical Information System, applying morphological image processing to the Forested 'Afrique Central Evalueepar Tele-detection product. This process allowed creating forest fragmentation maps for 2000, 2005 and 2010, classifying previously homogenous primary forest into separate patch, edge, perforated, fragmented and core forest subtypes. Subsequently, they used spatial rules to map the established rural complex separately from isolated forest perforations, tracking the growth of these areas in time. Results confirm that the expansion of the rural complex and forest perforations has high variance throughout the country, with consequent differences in local impacts on forest ecology and habitat fragmentation. Between 2000 and 2010 the rural complex grew by 10.2% (46 182 ha), increasing from 11.9% to 13.1% of the total land area (1.2% change) while perforated forest grew by 74.4% (23 856 ha), from 0.8% to 1.5%. Core forest decreased by 3.8% (54 852 ha), from 38% to 36.6%

of the 2010 land area. Of particular concern is the nearly doubling of perforated forest, a land dynamic that represents greater spatial intrusion of forest clearing within core forest areas and a move away from the established rural complex.

DeFries *et al.* (2007) indicated that the land-use dynamics resulting from shifting cultivation or other temporary clearing may not produce net emissions over the long-term. Forest clearing for shifting cultivation releases less carbon than does permanent forest clearing because the fallow period allows some regrowth (Watson *et al.*, 2000). On average, carbon stocks would remain at some intermediate level associated with regrowth (Ramankutty *et al.*, 2007), depending on forest type and the length of fallow (Fearnside, 2000; Watson *et al.*, 2000). Successive interventions or repeated agriculture-fallow cycles, however, can affect species composition, reduce carbon storage capacity, and act as a precursor to the establishment of more permanent non forest land cover (Eaton & Lawrence, 2009; Peres *et al.*, 2006) Therefore, under shifting cultivation, considering fallows as new deforestation could overestimate related emissions (DeFries *et al.*, 2007), whereas considering them as another type of croplands might underestimate emissions, as carbon density in fallow is higher than in most croplands (Tschakert *et al.*, 2007).

In the context of REDD+, one common challenge to monitoring emissions that arise from shifting cultivation is the absence of clear guidance. Mertz (2009) showed that shifting cultivation systems are particularly difficult to capture because of the complex spectral signature of fields, fallows of various lengths, and the frequent inclusion of permanent farming. Multiyear assessments using a time series of satellite imagery have been suggested as an adequate means of tracking complex land-cover dynamics that include clearing and regrowth. Such assessments increase the possibility of detecting small-scale intervention (Matricardi *et al.*, 2007; Asner *et al.*, 2005; Stone & Lefebvre, 1998; Broadbent *et al.*, 2006), and using subpixel information (Souza *et al.*, 2003; Brandt & Townsend, 2006; Matricardi *et al.*, 2010).

**Studies Related to Forest Recovery and Regrowth**

Forests are the most widely distributed terrestrial vegetation type, and thus plays an important role in providing the environmental context and shaping the dynamics of regional and global ecosystem processes (Wulder, 1998; Westoby, 1989). The return of vegetation and initiation of succession processes, often called recovery, is a critical component of landscape dynamics (Frolking *et al.* 2009; Kennedy *et al.* 2012). Vegetation recovery is a process, not a state; as such, tools and measures that allow for capturing and relating this regeneration and related increase in structural complexity are required (Shatford, Hibbs, and Puettmann 2007). In his analysis of global forest trends using the Food and Agriculture Organization's Forest Resource Assessment data set, Grainger (2008) has identified forest regrowth as an important source of uncertainty. Kennedy *et al.*(2012) showed the spatial and temporal pattern of forest disturbance and regrowth within the area of the Northwest forest plan. They developed approaches to create disturbance and regrowth maps for forests within the area of the NWFP from the results of LandTrendr, a temporal segmentation algorithm described previously only at the pixel scale. Maps were developed from 674 Landsat Thematic Mapper and Enhanced Thematic Mapper + images distributed across 22 separate scene area, and were assessed for validity at 2360 points using TimeSync, a time-series validation and interpretation tool. Maps were then used to address six core monitoring questions focusing on the distribution of disturbance across time, ownership categories, and eco-regions. Forest was disturbed at rates that varied by ownership category and state, ranging from 9% to >39% of forest area over the period 1985 to 2008, with highest cumulative disturbed area on private and native lands in Washington and Oregon and lowest disturbed area on federal protected lands in Washington. Effects of court injections and subsequent implementation of NWFP lowered forest disturbance rates, particularly in Oregon and also caused decreases in the relative magnitude of disturbance on those lands relative to private lands. Protected land also experienced high rates of chronic disturbance, vegetation regrowth rates showed sustantialvariaion among ownership categories. Taken together, these results emphasized the forest management policies do have manifestations at the landscape scale, but that detection of these manifestations is best achieved with mapping approaches that can detect both abrupt and longer-duration processes within the Landsat archive. Monitoring coniferous forest biomass change using a Landsat trajectory-based approach was done by Knorn *et al.* (2013). They presented a new method that uses satellite data to estimate changes in forest aboveground biomass associated with forest disturbance and recovery at annual time steps. Yearly maps of aboveground biomass between 1985 and 2010 based on Landsat time series and field data were created. Then, they applied a trajectory-based segmentation and fitting algorithm to the yearly biomass maps to reconstruct the forest disturbance and recovery history over the last 25 years. They tested the method over a coniferous forest region in the Beskid Mountain (Poland) of the Western Carpathian Mountains, which experienced long-term environmental changes. Overall, 55% of the total coniferous forest experienced a loss of biomass over the observation period, while 30% showed severe or complete removal of forest biomass. At the same time, 11.2% of the reforested or regenerated on previously damaged forest stands. The total coniferous biomass dropped by 15% between 1985 and 2010, indicating negative balance between the losses and the gains. Disturbance hotspots indicates high insect station labels in many areas and reveal strong interaction between biomass loss and climate conditions. Our study demonstrates how spatial and temporal estimates of biomass help to understand regional forest dynamics and derive degradation trends in regard to regional climate change.

## Time Series Analysis Using Remote Sensing

Time series remote sensing is ideally suited for systematic and transparent capture and description of recovery processes for forested ecosystems. From a remote sensing perspective, vegetation recovery has been defined for specific applications or objectives (Buma 2012; Frolking *et al.* 2009; Oliver and Larson 1996). For example, previous studies have defined recovery as: a factor of time since last disturbance (Kennedy *et al.* 2012); spectrally using time series trends (Hermosilla *et al.* 2015a; Schroeder *et al.* 2011; Kennedy, Yang, and Cohen 2010); and the required time to meet certain forest management-based conditions such as potential height, canopy cover, or stocking (LePage and Banner 2014; Franklin *et al.* 2002). Additionally, the structural attributes of vegetation recovery can be characterized using synthetic aperture radar (Saatchi and Moghaddam 2000), light detection and ranging (Bolton, Coops, and Wulder 2015), and passive stereo optical remote sensing (Persson *et al.* 2013). Although all these definitions are valid, the objectives of any study considering time series spectrally based recovery trajectories must be carefully considered, articulated, and linked in a meaningful way to the spectral values or indices used. Additionally, it is critical that the limitations associated with each definition and related methods applied are sufficiently described. Subtle differences among spectrally based recovery indicators can affect the conclusions of a study. Many remote sensing based definitions of recovery have used the normalized differenced vegetation index (NDVI) (Tucker 1979; Cuevas-Gonzalez *et al.* 2009; Sader *et al.* 1989). Although NDVI is particularly sensitive to changes in foliar condition and is commonly used in disturbance detection applications (Nemani and Running 1997), it has demonstrated limitations as an indicator of recovery (Sader *et al.* 1989; Huete *et al.* 1997) largely because forbs, grasses, and other non-woody pioneer vegetation will immediately colonize a disturbed site and rapidly return the site to pre-disturbance NDVI levels (Buma 2012; Schroeder *et al.* 2011). Thus, NDVI provides limited capacity for characterization of structural attributes, which are often more important indicators for biodiversity, habitat availability, and carbon (Pflugmacher *et al.* 2014; Banskota *et al.* 2014). An improved understanding of the information content of particular vegetation indices suggests the use of indices that include short-wave infrared wavelengths (Cohen and Goward 2004; Schroeder *et al.* 2011).

## Time Series Analysis of Satellite Imagery to Identify Shifting Areas

After years of having been collected and archived, medium scale satellite imagery (e.g. Landsat and SPOT) is now available for many parts of the tropics in year-on-year time series for more than 10 years in some cases. Increasingly the utility of these data for analyzing land cover and land cover change is being considered. Budreski *et al.* (2007) use a 14 years time-series of Landsat images for the Amazon region to produce yearly maps showing cleared, revegetated, and primary forest areas. They show how the yearly analysis aids in distinguishing re-vegetated from primary forest areas. Leisz and Rasmussen (in press) demonstrated how to make land cover maps that accurately delineate stages of regrowth on a field after it has been cultivated by using year-on-year medium-scale satellite imagery in conjunction with a rule based classifier that uses rules derived from observed vegetation succession for a region. The stages of regrowth correspond to stages of fallow vegetation in a swidden system. Heinimann (2006) used a robust dichotomous classification approach to land cover change. Multitemporal Landsat imagery is classified into regrowth and clearing, based on biomass indices and using object and rule based classification system. At certain scale of observation the resulting spatio-temporal pattern of clearing/regrowth can be seen as indicator for shifting cultivation.

Earth observation (EO) instruments play an important role in the assessment and monitoring of forest dynamics in a spatially and temporally continuous fashion. Among the current and historic constellation of EO satellites, the Landsat series of stands out for three primary reasons. First, the Landsat program offers the richest and longest running historical archive (40 years) of systematically collected remotely sensed data (Goward *et al.*, 2006), providing otherwise unavailable opportunities for improved understanding of mechanisms and extents of past forest changes and recovery. Second, the unique combination of imagery with a 30 m or similar spatial resolution collected with temporal repeat frequency of 16 days makes Landsat data well suited for detecting changes on the Earth's surface across relatively short time intervals (Coppin and Bauer, 1996; Gillanders *et al.*, 2008; Wulder *et al.*, 2008). Third, due to a new data policy implemented in 2008, all new and archived Landsat data held by the United States Geological Survey (USGS) are available free-of-charge in a pre-preprocessed ready for analysis standard format (Woodcock *et al.*, 2008; Wulder *et al.*, 2012), ultimately increasing the opportunity to utilize multi-temporal images representing a period of time, a large spatial area, or both (Hansen and Loveland, 2012).

The availability of large volumes of free Landsat imagery, coupled with advances in image processing methods and computational capacity have stimulated widespread use of Landsat time series (LTS) in many applications including classification and assessment of changes in forested ecosystems (e.g., Kennedy *et al.*, 2007), prediction of forest biophysical parameters (Knorn *et al.*, 2013) ). To effectively understand how disturbance impacts composition, structure, and function of forests, it is beneficial to quantify disturbances at a time step relevant to the affected processes (for example, annually, Masek *et al.*, 2013) and using long term data sets to, as possible, capture instances and trends related to forest disturbances and recovery (Frolking *et al.*, 2009). Hence, time series data comprised of image stacks over a longer duration and greater temporal frequency can provide a more comprehensive understanding of the complexity of forest disturbance and dynamics than a pair of Landsat images used in a bi-temporal change detection approach (Cohen *et al.*, 2010; Wulder *et al.*, 2012).

Data from daily viewing sensors such as MODIS and AVHRR are well suited for time series analyses at regional and global scales, but are less equipped to capture and analyze finer-scale disturbances that are relevant from management and monitoring perspectives (Walker *et al.*, 2012). The key advantages of Landsat are a spatial resolution that is appropriate for capturing anthropogenic impacts (Townshend and Justice, 1988).Vrises *et al* (2015) used based landsat time series to monitor forest changes in tropical forest. They used BFAST Monitoring Method to detect changes over humid & dry tropical Forests using dense landsat time series. Various data like, Landsat, SAR, MODIS, community-data based etc. are used. R package is tested over several tropical forest sites. They monitor regrowth of forest using MOSUM as an indicator of how post-distriburance time series compares in structure to stable history period. They observed the repeated disturbances using-BFAST Monitoring & MOSUM regrowth methods:-As this method progress,they found that BFAST Monitor can capture range of forest change in Vietnam. It shows how the forest area has changed & disturbed over the years and the forest has been regrowth. The MOSUM show the repeated disturbances of the forest within 2004 to 2015 in a series of time. Lehmann *et al* (2013) showed the forest cover trends from time series Landsat data or the Australian Continent. In this stage they identified the subtle change in vegetation cover by calculating the trends of a vegetation density index over time. They apply such an index-trends approach, which has been developed and applied to time series Landsat imagery in rangeland and woodland environments, to continental-scale monitoring of disturbances within forested regions of Australia. This paper describes the operational methods used for the generation of National Forest Trend (NFT) information, which is a time-series summary providing visual indication of within forest vegetation changes (disturbance and recovery) over time at 25m resolution. This result is based on a national archive of calibrated Landsat TM/ETM+ data from 1989 to 2006 produced for Australia's National Carbon Accounting System (NCAS). The NCAS was designed in 1999 initially to provide consistent fine-scale classifications for monitoring forest cover extent and changes (i.e. land use change) over the Australian continent using time series Landsat imagery. NFT information identifies more subtle changes within forested areas and provides a capacity to identify processes affecting forests which are of primary interest to ecologists and land managers. The NFT product relies on the identification of an appropriate Landsat-based vegetation cover index (defined as a linear combination of spectral image bands) that is sensitive to changes in forest density. The time series of index values at a location, derived from calibrated imagery, represents a consistent surrogate to track density changes. To produce the trends summary information, statistical summaries of the index response over time (such as slope and quadratic curvature) are calculated. These calculated index responses of woody vegetation cover are then displayed as maps where the different colors indicate the approximate timing, direction (decline or increase), magnitude and spatial extent of the changes in vegetation cover. These trend images provide a self-contained and easily interpretable summary of vegetation change at scales that are relevant for natural resource management (NRM) and environmental reporting.

Mapping Mountain Pine Beetle Mortality through growth trend analysis of Time-Series Landsat data (north-central Colorado) was done by Liang *et al.* (2014). They present a forest growth trend analysis method that integrates Landsat temporal trajectories and decision tree techniques to derive annual forest disturbance maps over an 11-year period. The temporal trajectory component successfully captures the disturbance events as represented by spectral segments, whereas decision tree modeling efficiently recognizes and attributes events based upon the characteristics of the segments. Validated against a point set sampled across a gradient of MPB mortality, 86.74% to 94.00% overall accuracy was achieved with small variability in accuracy among years. In contrast, the overall accuracies of single-date classifications ranged from 37.20% to 75.20% and only become comparable with our approach when the training sample size was increased at least four-fold. This demonstrates that the advantages of this time series work flow exist in its small training sample size requirement. The easily understandable, interpretable and modifiable characteristics of our approach suggest that it could be applicable to other eco-regions.

Meigs *et al.,* (2011) used a Landsat time series approach to characterize bark beetle and defoliator impacts on tree mortality and surface fuels in conifer forests. This presents a remote sensing framework to (1) characterize spectral trajectories associated with insect activity of varying duration and severity and (2) relate those trajectories to ground-based measurements of tree mortality and surface fuels in the Cascade Range, Oregon, USA. A Landsat time series change detection algorithm (Land Trends) was used to investigate two study landscapes broadly applicable to conifer forests and dominant insect agents of western North America. They distributed 38 plots across multiple forest types (ranging from mesic mixed-conifer to xeric lodge pole pine) and insect agents (defoliator [western spruce budworm] and bark beetle [mountain pine beetle]). Insect effects were evident in the Landsat time series as combinations of both short- and long-duration changes in the Normalized Burn Ratio spectral index. Western spruce budworm trajectories appeared to show a consistent temporal evolution of long-duration spectral decline (loss of vegetation) followed by recovery, whereas mountain pine beetle plots exhibited both short- and long-duration spectral declines and variable recovery rates. Although temporally variable, insect-affected stands generally conformed to four spectral trajectories: short duration decline then recovery, short- then long-duration decline, long-duration decline, long-duration decline then recovery. When comparing remote sensing data with field measurements of insect impacts, they found that spectral changes were related to cover-based estimates (tree basal area mortality [R2 adj=0.40, F1,34=24.76, Pb0.0001] and down coarse woody detritus [R2 adj=0.29, F1,32=14.72, P=0.0006]). In contrast, ADS changes were related to count-based estimates (e.g., ADS mortality from mountain pine beetle positively correlated with ground-based counts [R2 adj=0.37, F1,22=14.71, P=0.0009]). Fine woody detritus and forest floor depth were not well correlated with Landsat or aerial survey-based change metrics. By characterizing several distinct temporal manifestations of insect activity in conifer forests, this study demonstrates the utility of insect mapping methods that capture a wide range of spectral trajectories. This study also confirms the key role that satellite imagery can play in understanding the interactions among insects, fuels, and wildfire.

Yin *et al.* (2014) used MODIS time series for Mapping annual land use and land cover changes to understand dynamic land systems. In this study, they selected a study region in Inner Mongolia (China), they developed and tested an automated approach for mapping land use and land cover changes at annual time intervals using data from the Moderate Resolution Imaging Spectro-radiometer (MODIS). Their approach characterizes changes between land cover types based on annual time series of per-pixel land cover probabilities. They used the temporal segmentation algorithm MODTrendr to identify trends and changes in the probability time series that were associated with land cover/use conversions. Accuracy assessment revealed good performance of our approach (overall accuracy of 92.0%). The method detected conversions from forest to grassland with a user's accuracy of 94.0±2.0% and a producer's accuracy of 95.6±1.6%. Conversions between cropland and grassland were detected with a user's and a producer's accuracy of 65.8±4.8% and 72.2±9.2%, respectively. They here present for the first time an approach that combines probabilities derived from machine learning (random forest classification) with time series based analysis (MODTrendr) for land cover/use change analysis at MODIS scale.

## STUDY AREA

### Location

The selected study area is located in the central part of Dima Hasaodistrict.TheDimaHasao district is situated at southern part of Assam (25 N 2 4 N-92 E 92 1 E) and is bounded by Nagaland & Manipur state in the east, Cachar district of Assam in the south, Meghalaya state and part of Karbi-anglong district in the west, and another part of Karbi-Anglong and Nagaon district in the north. It occupies an area of 4,888km$^2$. It is the third largest district of Assam followed by Karbi-Anglong and Sonitpur district.

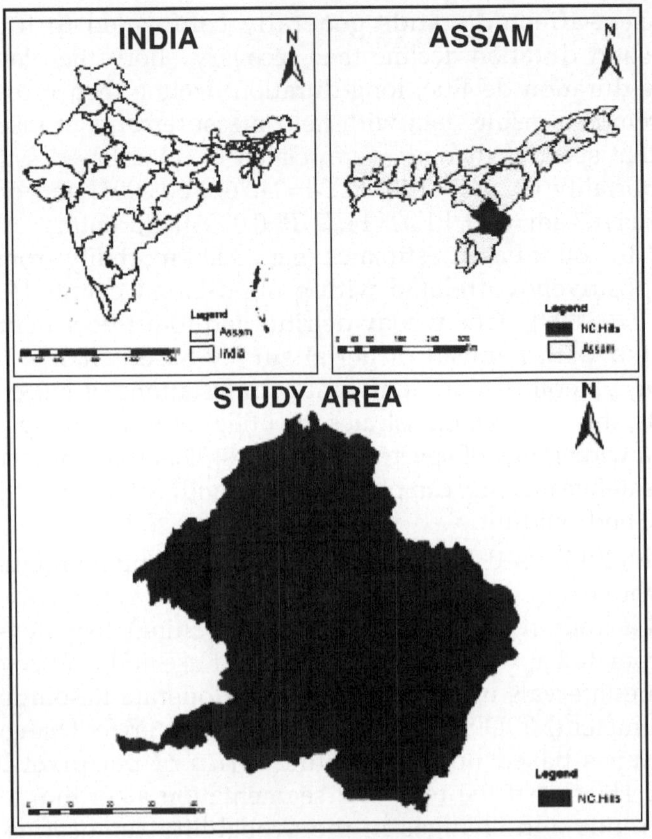


**Fig. 1.1: Location Map of the Study Area**

## Topography

District topography shows the positional features of the District, the major portion of the district is covered by hills. The main range is "Borail" of which Thumjang is the highest peak of 1866m and Hempeupet is the second highest peak of 1748m. The other main range is "khartheng"range. Topographically, the District can be divided under three distinct regions. This are:

- The low-lying areas
- The high Hills of Eastern and Western portions
- The Plateau area.

The low-lying areas are the valleys of Diyung, Langting, Mahur and Jatinga rivers. These areas are inhabited by Dimasas. The high Hills are the areas covered by Borailhills ranges. The JemeNagas, Hmars, the Kukis are the inhabitant of this region. The plateau of Gunjung, Khorongma and Garampani areas these region have the average height of about 2500feets above the mean sea levels. The inhabitants are Dimasas, Biates, Khelmas and Karbies.

## Soil

Soil in the north part is sandy loam and gradually becomes lateritic towards the south. The upper slopes have coarse and gritty soil, which shallow in depth. Middle and lower slopes have alluvial soil. The red forests soils are deep and fertile and slightly acidic with PH ranging between 6 and 7. Though the main features of soil and rocks have been described above, there are local variations depending on micro climatic factors.

## Climate

The district can be divided into three distinct zones South to North. The Southern part of Borailrange receives considerable high precipitation. The northern part falls in the rain shadow of the range and consequently precipitation is much lower. The northern part of the district around Langting is one of the driest and hottest parts of Assam. The central part has a cool and equable climate. Cyclonic disturbances and storms occur frequently in Surma valley but seldom visit Dima Hasao district. This is due to shielding effect of Borail Range. Thunderstorm is quite frequent during summer months. Mist and fog occur duing winter. Frost is unknown, even in depression. Light to moderate winds blow from North or northeast, expect during monsoon when the wind blows from southwest.

## Temperature

Winter starts from middle of the November. Both day and night temperature starts falling. The mean maximum and minimum temperature are 25.9° C and 17.5° C respectively at Haflong January is the coolest month with maximum and minimum temperature being 20.7° C and 10.7° C respectively. The lowest temperature recorded at Haflong is 5.4° C. The summer starts from March onwards and day and night temperature rising. The average temperature in summer month is 27. 7° C, with highest recorded 34. 7° C. August and September are the hottest month of the year.

## Rainfall

The typical sub-tropical monsoon climate prevalent in the area is characterized by the excessive moisture content of air throughout the year. The area receive pre monsoon shower during April, which is accompanied by thunder storms and hail force winds. This spell of pre monsoon shower is followed by a brief dry days and monsoon starts from the end of May or beginning of June. The amount of the rainfall is highest in the month of July and August. Southernmost part of the district gets the highest rainfall in the district. Rainfall and the number of rainy days decrease from south to north.

**Table 1.1: Average rainfall and number of rainy days in different parts of the district**

| Location | Mean Annual Rainfall (mm) | Average Number of Rainfall Days |
|---|---|---|
| Jatinga Valley | 4,767 | 249 |
| Harangajao | 3,787 | 135 |
| Haflong | 2,278 | 118 |
| Maibang | 1,458 | 84 |

**Humidity**

The mean annual relative humidity is 34.25% and 77.75% in the morning and afternoon respectively. During monsoon the relative humidity is about 80% and above; and between February and April relative humidity in the afternoon is about 60%.

**Flora**

Nature has endowed the hill tracts of the district with flora and fauna of great variety. The evergreen, semi-evergreen and deciduous forests growing in harmony with a host of other herds, shrubs, climbers and grasses which impart unique vegetative features to this region. Favorable climate conditions, rainfall, temperature, humidity, topography have helped the tropical vegetation to grow luxuriantly in the area. The characteristic vegetation of the area consists of tree species of evergreen. Though a large part of the area is covered with vegetation, only a small fraction of it has constituted into Reserved Forests of proposed Reserve Forest (16%) still vast tract remains as Unclassed State Forest cover N.C. Hills district is 87% (FSI2003). Depending upon the pre-dominant species, the natural forest of the Dima Hasao, fall under the following category of subtypes:

1. Cachar Tropical evergreen Forests (IB/C3)
2. Cachar Tropical semi-evergreen Forest (2B/C3)
3. Northern Tropical, Sub-tropical Broad leaved Hill Forest forests (8B/C2)
4. Tropical Moist Mixed Deciduous Forests- 8B Ghogra Oak type
5. Cane Brakes
6. Secondary Moist Bamboo Brakes (2B/Ca)

Cachar Tropical evergreen Forests type is generally found on the lower slopes of the northern and eastern aspects. The Forest is largely composed of evergreen species. Cachar tropical semi-evergreen occurs in hill tops. The forests have both evergreen and deciduous species. Northern Sub-tropical Broad leaved Hills Forests, originally forest cover of Board leaved evergreen species have mostly been cleared and altered by repeated felling, burning and Jhum cultivation. These are now considerable areas of open grasslands with scattered trees. In some patches almost pine, oak forests and found along with schism wallichii species. The tree growths in these Forests are three different storeys, though they look monolithic from distant. The major species are Artocarpuschaplasa (Cham), Micheliachampaca (Titasopa), Mansoniadepikae (Badam), Schimawallichii (Makrisal), Phoebegoalparensist (Bonsum), Adinacordifloa (Galdu), Gmelinaarborea (Gamari), Duabangaspecies (Khokan) Bhelu (Tetramelesmudiflora), Albezziaprocera (Koroi),Terminalia (Bohera etc.), Middle storey consists of trees like Eugeniaspecies (Jam), Callicarpaspecies (Kum), Emblicaofficinalis (Amla), Albezziaspecies (moj), Holarhenaantidysentrica (Dudhuri) etc. The under storey consists of Eupatorium Odoratum (AsomLota), Imperata Cycindrica, Flemingia species, Leea species, Lantanacamara Zizyphusspecies (Bonbogari), Clerodendron species (Dhatpattitu ), Litsea species, Phrtninum species (Kaupat), Murrayakoenijii (Narsingha) etc. Besides these, the forests are made impregnable with multitude of tree climbers. DimaHasao Forests is rich in non-wood Forests products (NWEP). NWEP are forest products of consumption, other timber, firewood etc. These products include oil-bearing seeds, leaf edible fruits, bark yielding tannin and dye, bamboos, medicinal plants etc. These products not only meet the commercial requirements but are an important source of employment to people living in and around forest.

**Fauna**

The Favorable topographical climatic and edaphic conditions have caused forest to grow luxuriantly in Dima Hasao district. The forest in the hill tract is habitat for great variety of wild animals and avifauna, which are representative of wild life of the oriental Zoogeographic realm. Among the larger forms of mammals' elephants, wild buffaloes, tiger, leopard, various kinds of deers, sambhar, wild dog, capped languor and other primates deserves special mention. Many of these animals groups are representative of wild animals typical of the eastern part of sub Himalayan Zoological zone. In addition to the large animals also found in the area Himalayan Black Bear, sloth bear, many varieties of lesser cats, mountain goats, wild pigs, jackal, many variety of squirrel, including flying squirrel etc. As many as even varieties tortoise have been identified within Hajong Lake in Langting-Mupa Reserve Forest. The avifauna includes many colourful birds living in forests and in swamps. Birds frequently spotted in the area are-Great Himalayan Horn Bill Imperial and great pigeon, Emerald dove, Hill partridges, Jungle flow, Hoope, Pheasants, king fisher, white breast water hen, Heron, Egrets Paradise fly catcher etc. The Forests are home of variety of reptiles including python, king cobra, monitor lizard, tortoise and host of other snakes and several insects and butterflies.

## DATA USED AND METHODOLOGY

### Satellite Data

Landsat 8 OLI: Landsat 8 was launched on February 11, 2013. Landsat8 satellite has two main sensors: the Operational Land Imager (OLI) and the Thermal Infrared Sensor (TIRS). OLI will collect images using nine spectral bands in different wavelengths of visible, near-infrared, and shortwave light to observe a 185km wide swath of the Earth in 15-30 meter resolution covering wide areas of the Earth's landscape while providing sufficient resolution to distinguish features like urban centers, farms, forests and other land uses.

## SOFTWARE USED

1. ArcGIS 10.1
2. ERDAS IMAGINE 2014
3. R, RSTUDIO 3.1
4. TymeSyncR package

### ArcGIS

is a geographic information system (GIS) for working with maps and geographic information. It is used for creating and using maps; compiling geographic data; analyzing mapped information; sharing and discovering geographic information; using maps and geographic information in a range of applications; and managing geographic information in a database.

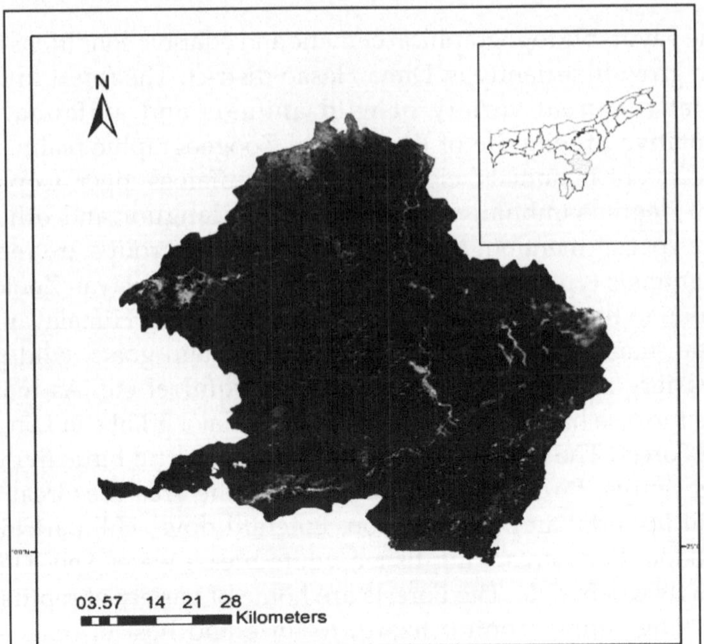


**Fig. 1.2: FCC Satellite Image of Dima Hasao District**

***ERDAS Imagine*** is a remote sensing application with raster graphics editor abilities designed by ERDAS for geospatial applications. The latest version is 2015. Imagine is aimed mainly at geospatial raster data processing and allows users to prepare, display and enhance digital images for mapping use in geographic information system (GIS) and computer-aided design (CAD) software. It is a toolbox allowing the user to perform numerous operations on an image and generate an answer to specific geographical questions.

***Rstudio*** is a free and open-source integrated development environment for R, a programming language for statistical computing and graphics. RStudio is written in the C++ programming language and uses the Qt framework for its graphical user interface

***TimeSync*** is a Landsat time series visualization tool and web application that can be used to characterize the quality of map products derived from Landsat time series derive independent plot-based estimates of change, explore the value of Landsat time seriess for understanding and visualizing change on the earth surface. TimeSync R is a package loosely based on the TimeSync method for interpreting satellite image for calibration & validation of change method and product described only at the pixel scale.

## METHODOLOGY

### Phase 1: Data Aquired

In this study all the satellite images -Landsat 8 OLI, Landsat 7 ETM+ and Landsat 5 TM are freely downloaded from USGS.

### Phase 2: Layer Stacking

The satellite images in zip format are unzip (assemble in an individual file format). We assemble the data using layer stack in ERDAS. The file containing the data layer are selected in order, beginning with band 1. It is very important to place the data in correct order band 1 followed by band 2 etc. Enter a new file name consider using a naming conversion that incorporate the image data in.imgformat this process will take several minutes. We can monitor the progress will actually consist of two files, the main data file has a file extension of.img and the associated "pyramid" file has an extension of.rrd. RGB is a visible band and NIR, SWIR band are used in this study for finding out the indices in Erdas. We experiment with the image by creating several false color images. Change the displayed bands from the RGB-321 combination above to RGB-432 and it creates a color infra-red image (CIR) similar to that used in CIR photography. This combination uses the Near Infrared band of data in the satellite image and vegetation will appear red. Vegetation is highly reflective in this part of the spectrum so this display is a very powerful way to examine changes in vegetation. Another useful band combination is an RGB-742 display. Vegetation will appear green. It is a useful way to separate urban from vegetated areas. These techniques do not change the data, just the display, allowing you to learn more about the earth's surface.

**Phase 3:Atmospheric Correction**

Many atmospheric correction methods have been proposed for use with multi-spectral satellite imagery (Hadjimitsis *et al.*, 2004). Such methods consist of image-based methods, methods that use atmospheric modeling and, finally, methods that use ground data during the satellite overpass. These data can be converted to Top of the Atmosphere (ToA) reflectance using rescaling factors and parameters found in the metadata file (MTL.txt) provided with the data. The Landsat 8 OLI sensor is more sensitive so these data are rescaled into 16-bit digital number (DNs) with a range from 0 and 65536. Also these data have been converted to reflectance, rather than radiance, so DNs can be manually converted to Reflectance in a single step. We generate a model using a formula in ERDAS.The Landsat Thematic Mapper (TM) and Enhanced Thematic Mapper Plus (ETM+) sensors capture reflected solar energy, convert these data to radiance, then rescale this data into an 8-bit DN with a range between 0 and 255. It is possible to manually convert these DNs to ToA Reflectance using a two-step process. The first step is to convert the DNs to radiance values using the spectral radiance scaling specific to the individual scene you are working with. The second step converts the radiance data to ToA reflectance. For each scene you need to know the distance between the sun and earth in astronomical units, the day of the year (Julian date), and solar zenith angle.

**The Spectral Radiance Scaling Method**

$L\lambda$= ((LMAX$\lambda$-LMIN$\lambda$)/QCALMAX))*((QCAL-QCALMIN)+LMIN$\lambda$

Where:

$L\lambda$ is the cell value as radiance QCAL = digital number LMIN$\lambda$= spectral radiance scales to QCALMIN LMAX$\lambda$ = spectral radiance scales to QCALMAX QCALMIN = the minimum quantized calibrated pixel value (typically = 1) QCALMAX = the maximum quantized calibrated pixel value (typically = 255)

**To Convert Radiance to ToA Reflectance**

$\rho\lambda=\pi*L\lambda*d2/ESUN\lambda*\cos\theta s$

Where: $\rho\lambda$ = Unit less plantary reflectance $L\lambda$= spectral radiance (from earlier step) d = Earth-Sun distance in astronomical units ESUN$\lambda$ = mean solar exoatmospheric irradiances $\theta s$ = solar zenith angle

The solar zenith angle can be calculated using the University of Oregon Solar Position Calculator.

**Phase 4: Indices**

After the atmospheric correction of data, we applied 5 indices for each individual image in ERDAS: the Normalized Difference Vegetation Index (NDVI), Normalized Burn Ratio (NBR), N37I, (NDMI) and Enhanced Vegetation Index (EVI). The details of these indices are described below:

***A brief description of indices used in this study is given below:***

(a) **NDVI** The NDVI is the most common and known vegetation index and has been proposed by Rouse *et al.* (1974). It is computed as: NDVI = (NIR-R)/(NIR+R). Ranges from -1 to 1 Never (Rarely?) divide by zero.Indicates amount of vegetation, distinguishes veg from soil, minimizes topographic effects, etc. A good index. Does not eliminate atmospheric effects.

(b) **EVI** The **enhanced vegetation index** (**EVI**) is an 'optimized' vegetation index designed to enhance the vegetation signal with improved sensitivity in high biomass regions and improved vegetation monitoring through a de-coupling of the canopy background signal and a reduction in atmosphere influences. EVI is computed following this equation:

EVI=G*(NIR-)/(NIR+C1*RED-C2*BLUE+L)

where NIR/red/blue are atmospherically-corrected or partially atmosphere corrected (Rayleigh and ozone absorption) surface reflectance, L is the canopy background adjustment that addresses non-linear, differential NIR and red radiant transfer through a canopy, and C1, C2 are the coefficients of the aerosol resistance term, which uses the blue band to correct for aerosol influences in the red band. This equation is process in model maker (ERDAS), then we prepared an excel sheet, we then create a file in Notepad++ in.bcf format, then open Erdas file - batch - open batch command file - ok

(c) **NDMI** Another approach was developed by Goodwin *et al.* (2008) and was shown to be quite accurate in identifying MPB attack in northern British Columbia using Landsat imagery acquired over a twenty-five year period. In this research, the authors use the Normalized Difference Moisture Index (NDMI) derived from Landsat spectral bands 4 and 5 and calculated using the following equation:

NDMI = [Band 4 – Band 5]/[Band4 +Band 5]

This index contrasts the near-infrared (NIR) band 4, which is sensitive to the reflectance of leaf chlorophyll content to the mid-infrared (MIR) band 5, which is sensitive to the absorbance of leaf moisture.

(d) **NBR:** NBR was originally developed for use with Landsat TM and ETM+ bands 4 and 7, but it will work with any multispectral sensor with a NIR band between 0.76-0.9 ìm and a SWIR band between 2.08-2.35 ìm. The Normalized Burn Ratio (NBR) was defined to highlight areas that have burned and to index the severity of a burn using Landsat TM imagery. The formula for the NBR is very similar to that of NDVI except that it uses near-infrared band 4 and the short-wave infrared band 7. NBR=(NIR-SWIR)/(NIR+SWIR) The NBR equation was designed to be calculated from reflectance, but it can be calculated from radiance and digital number (DN) with changes to the burn severity table below.

(e) **N37I** The concept of indices for long-term ionospheric predictions relies on the assumption that the important characteristics of the ionosphere, such as the critical frequencies of the various layers and the MUF factor M (3000) F2, depend in a systematic way on certain measurable quantities concerned with solar radiation. It should however be noted that the correlation between these indices and the actual ionospheric characteristics does not necessarily imply a causal relationship, but rather an indication of associated phenomena.

**Phase 6 :TimesyncR**

We prepared a point shape file in ERDAS - sample like shifting patches including forest, river and settlement.Take this point sample as x,y coordinate. We need to focus on a single pixel to convert the coordinates to a Spatial Polygons representing the outline of that pixel. To display a plot of the time series of each of the indices, set plot to TRUE. This will show all three indices as stacked time series plot each at a time. For more informative plot labels, set plotlab. Set the range of pixel within -1 to 1.

## RESULTS AND DISCUSSIONS

In this study, 105 Landsat 8 OLI, Landsat 7 ETM+, Landsat 5 TM scenes were analyzed to create a set of cloud-free image at a spatial resolution of 30 m. Remote sensing offers considerable potential for supporting shifting monitoring, because it provides long-term and repetitive observation over large areas. Among the most cited studies, the Landsat-based detection of Trends in Disturbance and Recovery (TimeSyncR) tool allows the spectral trajectories of land surface changes to be extracted from yearly Landsat time series stacks. The derivation of reference data has been developed and integrated in a software package known as TimeSync. Trends in recovery varied depending on the indicator. This result may indicate the return of vegetation and initiation of succession processes is at least partially dependent on shifting cultivation zone, but the indices are also correlated. For example, NBR shows the abrupt incline and abrupt decline trend in shifting patches within the year 1997-1998 and the value went below 0.2.5 which indicate high post fire regrowth and even shows the high value (>0.66). There is a quite gradual increase and decrease within the year 1998 and 2015 with a value ranges within 0.2 to 0.6 which indicate low severity burn ti high severity burn. It is important to note that the number of pixels recovered is a number of pixels recovered is function of number of years since disturbance. Therefore, the number of pixels recovered is necessarily biased towards shorter recovery times in the time series. The majority of pixels detected as disturbed had observable trends of vegetation recovery within the year of disturbance. NBR have been shown to be related to structural components of vegetation, NDVI and EVI are more sensitive to levels of chlorophyll. NDMI is sensitive to the reflectance of leaf chlorophyll content to the mid-infrared (MIR) band, which is sensitive to the absorbance of leaf moisture. NBR are known to represent the recovery of non-leafy structural attributes of vegetation beyond the initial flush of grasses, herbs, and shrubs. The curves of non-recovered pixels for NDVI likely represent variation of spectral recovery across a gradient of disturbance severity. By contrast, the linear curves of NBR are likely an artifact of continually increasing near-infrared reflectance as leaf cover accumulates within the disturbed pixel. Thus, the results indicate that the NBR are expected to be more suitable for tracking vegetation succession following disturbance when compared to NDVI. Based on knowledge of succession processes (Oliver 1980), the signal from visible and near-infrared wavelengths is expected to quickly saturate following disturbance due to the rapid colonization of early pioneer and shade-intolerant species. Recovery rates among the shifting zones suggest that there may be subtle spectral differences in succession processes. For example, the frequency of recovered pixels for NDVI, NDMI and the EVI provided improved opportunities to observe differences between the shifting zones in the 16 years disturbance. Recovery rates among the shifting zones during later succession (*i.e.* ≥ 16 years disturbance) were also best observed using NDVI, EVI, NDMI, N37I and NBR. The results should be interpreted with some caution because recovery was not distinguished for different disturbance types. It was evident that the choice of recovery indicator was important for different types of disturbance. Additionally, disturbance legacies are evident in the recovery rates from visual assessment of harvesting and fire. Recovery is remarkably heterogeneous within fires, which is primarily evident with the mid-infrared spectral band and NBR indices.

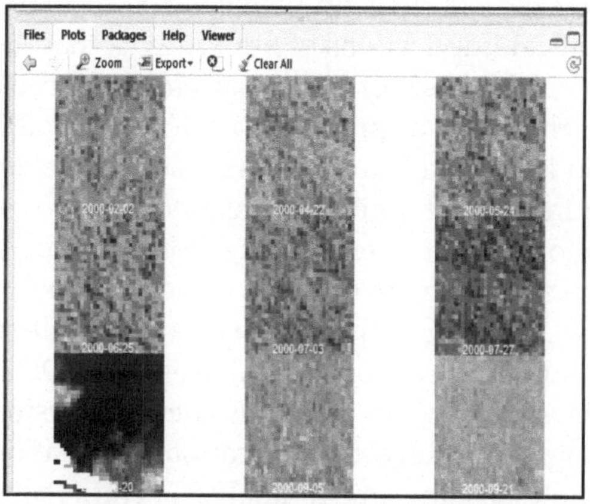


**Fig. 1.3: Image Process in R Studio**

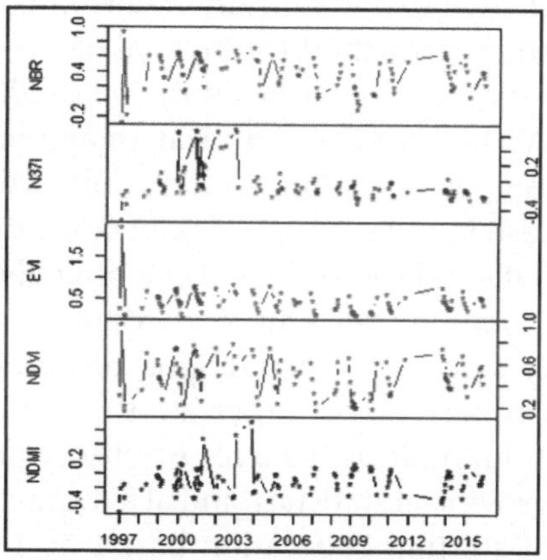


**Fig. 1.4: Trend of Shifting Cultivation**

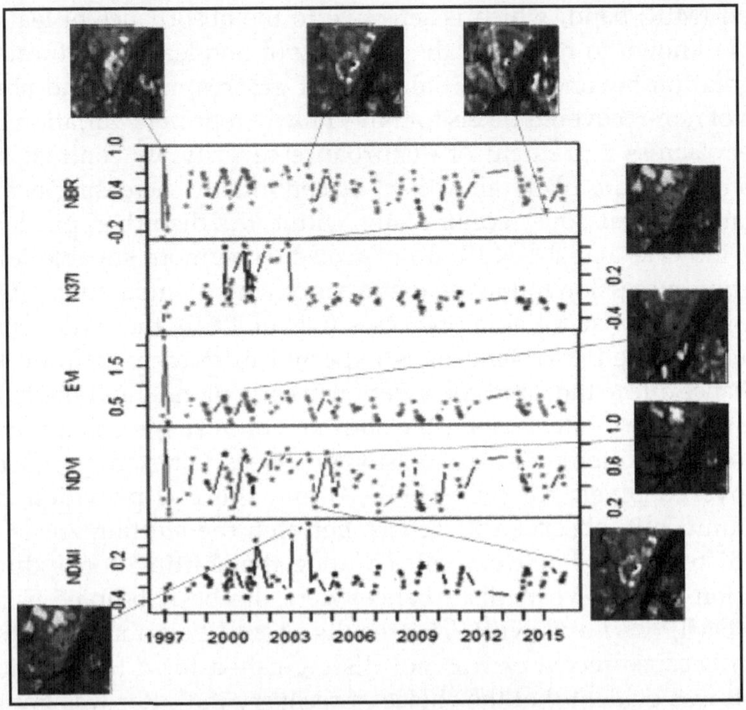


**Fig. 1.5: Patches of Shifting Cultivation**

The work presented here adds to the literature that applies a tool based to area under shifting cultivation. Our approaches differ from similar previous studies in that we used Landsat image, as agent in the tool, where shifting change is dynamically determined by the relationship between the recovery and regrowth of forest. One of the central implications of our study is that the agent unit must be chosen carefully on the basis of particular circumstances. We believe that Landsat image are the most appropriate units of decision making regarding shifting cultivation in Dima Hasao, but this may not be the case in other socio-cultural contexts. In tropical regions, infrequent cloud-free data and the fast recovery of vegetation can hamper the detection of changes in forest cover. Our study demonstrates that TimeSyncR tool is indeed capable of producing encouraging results for pursuing this research strategy further. Unlike in most other studies, we evaluate our model results using MODIS data, multiple sources of observation data, both at the aggregate level using provincial statistics, and at a more disaggregate level using location information of shifting cultivation based on remote sensing image analysis. The results seem to validate the basic underlying mechanism of the model that determines land-use patterns based on the balance between crop demand and supply. Furthermore, by comparing model results and observed data at different resolutions, we find that the tool.

## CONCLUSION

To map disturbances and recovery trend we applied TimeSyncR, a package loosely based on the TimeSync method. We showed the effectiveness of this method to map abrupt and gradual forest change. A near-annual time series provided detailed information on stand-replacing disturbances, long term degradation and forest regeneration. The main advantage of a near-annual time series approach over bi-temporal study on mapping disturbances is, that the first enables detecting long-term trends, while the latter could miss or under-estimate those. Putting our findings in a regional context, we found very complex disturbance history in the study area. Massive forests lose and gain between 1997 and 2015, triggered by the coincidental effect of shifting cultivation. On the one hand, gradual disturbances were dominating in the study region, indicating the increasing and decreasing role of shifting cultivation. In this paper, we analyzed the implications of considering 5 spectral indices (EVI, NDVI, NDMI, NBR, and N37I) to estimate forest recovery rates of DimaHasao district using Landsat time series. The results indicated the spectral indices characterized different component of forest recovery. Recovery time was remarkably heterogeneous within different disturbance type was dependent on the indicator. Fire were particularly heterogeneous using NDVI as a recovery indicator, but NBR and the mid-infrared spectral band showed improvement in distinguishing area that took the longest to recover. We note that imagery is often used in isolation and supplementing optical observations with active remote sensing measurements that can provide structure information could enhance estimation of re-growth with disturbance history from Landsat. Regardless, the results presented here can advance the assessment and monitoring of forest recovery for large area mapping initiatives and improve our understanding of post-disturbance forest dynamics in Dima Hasao.

## *REFERENCES*

Banskota, Asim Kayastha, Nilam Falkowski, Michael J. Wulder, Michael A. Froese, Robert E. White, Joanne C(2014): Forest Monitoring Using Landsat Time Series Data: A Review, pp: 362-384

Brady, N.C. (1996): Alternatives to Slash-and-burn: A Global Imperative. *Agric. Ecosyst. Environ.* 58, pp: 3-11.

Comte, I.; Davidson, R.; Lucotte, M.; de Carvalho, C.J.R.; de Assis Oliveira, F.; Da Silva, B.P.; Rousseau, G.X.( 2012): Physicochemical Properties of Soils in the Brazilian Amazon Following Fire-free Land Preparation and Slash-and-burn Practices. *Agric. Ecosyst. Environ. 156*, pp: 1108-115.

Das, Er Sujit Choudhury, Er Subhrajyoti Roy, Ar Arpita, (2012): The Success Story of Rehabilitation of Jhumias in Tripura- A Study on Baramura-Deutamura Range, pp: 25-29.

Dove, M.R. (1983): Theories of Swidden Agriculture and the Political Economy of Ignorance. *Agrofor. Syst., 1*, pp: 85-99.

Fallis, A.G, (2013): Journal of Chemical Information and Modeling, 1689-1699.

Gen, Tor (2006): Gunnar, Remote Sensing of Complex Land use Change Trajectories – A Case Study from the Highlands of Madagascar, pp: 219-228.

Goldammer, J.G. (1988): Rural Land-use and Wildland Fires in the Tropics. *Agrofor. Syst.*, *6*, pp: 235-252.

Imbernon, Jacques, (1998): ASB Technical ReportIs.

Inoue, Y.; Kiyono, Y.; Asai, H.; Ochiai, Y.; Qi, J.; Olioso, A.; Shiraiwa, T.; Horie, T.; Saito, K.; Dounagsavanh, L. (2010): Assessing Land-use and Carbon Stock in Slash-and-burn Ecosystems in Tropical Mountain of Laos based on Time-series Satellite Images. *Int. J. Appl. Earth Obs. Geoinf.*, 12, pp: 287-297.

Jepsen, M.R. Leisz, S.Rasmussen, K.Jakobsen, J.MØller Jensen, L.Christiansen, L. (2006) Agent based Modelling of Shifting Cultivation Field Patterns, Vietnam, pp: 1067-1085.

Jeus, Maria Henriques, Pedro Laranjeira, Pedro, (2012): The Impact of Shifting Cultivation in the Forestry Ecosystems of Timor-Leste, pp: 0-16.

Kennedy, Robert E. Yang, Zhiqiang Cohen, Warren B. Pfaff, Eric Braaten, Justin Nelson, Peder, (2012): Spatial and Temporal Patterns of Forest Disturbance and Regrowth within the Area of the Northwest Forest Plan, pp: 117-133.

Kimura, Daiji (1998): Land use in Shifting Cultivation: The Case of the Bongando (Ngandu) in Central Zaire, pp: 179-203.

Kumar, Ashish Marcot, Bruce G Roy, P S, (2006): Spatial Patterns and Processes for Shifting Cultivation Landscape in Garo Hills, India, pp: 4-11.

Li, PengFeng, Zhiming Jiang, Luguang Liao, Chenhua Zhang, Jinghua (2014): A Review of Swidden Agriculture in Southeast Asia, pp: 1654-1683.

Pelletier, Johanne Codjia, Claude Potvin, Catherine (2012): Traditional Shifting Agriculture: Tracking Forest Carbon Stock and Biodiversity Through Time in Western Panama, pp: 3581-3595.

Ranjan, R Upadhyay, V P (1999): Ecological Problems due to Shifting Cultivation, pp: 1246-1250.

Samek, Jay H, Shifting Cultivation in Oudomxay and Luang Prabang, Lao PDR (2006): A Spatial and Temporal Assessment of the Forest-farm-fallow Landscape Mosaic using Remote Sensing and GIS.

Schuck, E.C.; Nganje, W.; Yantio, D. (2002): The Role of Land Tenure and Extension Education in the Adoption of Slash and Burn Agriculture. *Ecol. Econ.* pp: 43, 61-70.

Van Vliet, N.; Mertz, O.; Heinimann, A.; Langanke, T.; Pascual, U.; Schmook, B.; Adams, C.; Schmidt-Vogt, D.; Messerli, P.; Leisz, S.; *et al.* (2012): Trends, Drivers and Impacts of Changes in Swidden Cultivation in Tropical Forest-agriculture Frontiers: A Global Assessment. *Glob. Environ. Chang.* Vol. 22, pp: 418-429.

Wada, Yumiko Rajan, Krishnan S. Shibasaki, Ryosuke (2007): Modelling, the Spatial Distribution of Shifting Cultivation in Luangprabang, Lao PDR, 261-278.

Woods, M, Rural (2009): Geography, pp: 429-441.

Pages: 27-40

**FOREST AND BIODIVERSITY CONSERVATION**

*Edited by:* **Dr. Alka Chauhan** and **Dr. Pawan Kumar 'Bharti'**

**ISBN: 978-93-5056-873-6**

*Edition:* **2017**

*Published by:* **Discovery Publishing House Pvt. Ltd., New Delhi (India)**

# 2 Biotechnological Approaches for Biodiversity Conservation and its Impacts on Biodiversity

*Showkat Ahmad Bhat*[1]; *Mashooq Ahmad Dar*[2]
*Tehseen Hassan*[3] *and Hilal Ahmad Wani*[3]

## ABSTRACT

Biodiversity is the level of variation of life forms. It is the entirety of genes, species and ecosystems of a region. In recent years ever increasing loss of biodiversity has posed a serious threat to the survival of mankind. Damage of the habitat of plants and animals, introduction of exotic species, over exploitation of animals and plants, over population of human and over consumption of natural resources are the root causes of all biodiversity loss. Climatic change, again a consequence of human activities, has very adverse effects on biological diversity. Global warming affects plants, animals and microorganisms, both by changing their habitats and by direct effects of temperature. In addition, inadequate knowledge, inefficient use of information and economic system and policies which fail to value the environment are also responsible for the loss of biological diversity. There is anurgent need for the conservation of biodiversity. Biotechnology offers new means of conserving biodiversity. Conservation may be *in situ* or *ex situ*, either in the natural or semi-natural habitat, or in some purpose-built environment. Biotechnology including tissue culture, micro-propagation, marker assisted breeding, conventional breeding, transgenic crops, and genomics, are all quite useful for conserving and propagating biodiversity in many unique ways.

**Keywords:** Biodiversity, Biotechnology, Conservation.

[1] Division of Veterinary Biochemistry, Faculty of Veterinary Sciences & Animal Husbandry, Sheri Kashmir University of Agricultural Science & Technology (SKUAST-K), Srinagar, (J & K) (India)

[2] Department of Biochemistry, University of Kashmir.

[3] Department of Biochemistry, Government Medical College, Srinagar, (J & K) (India)

## INTRODUCTION

Biological diversity or biodiversity is the degree of variations of life forms. It includes variation among animals, plants, microorganisms, the genetic variation among them and all their complex assemblages of communities and ecosystems. Biodiversity is the totality of genes, species and ecosystems of a region. The term 'biodiversity' was first used by Dasmann in 1968. There are three levels of biodiversity-genetic, species and ecosystem diversity. Genetic diversity refers to the variations of genes within the species. It includes all the different genes contained in all individual plants, animals, fungi and microorganisms. It occurs within a species as well as among species. Species diversity refers to the variety of species within a region. Ecosystem diversity refers to all the different habitats and biological communities within individual ecosystem. According to Raven (1992) the number of species of plants, animals and eukaryotic micro-organisms is probably around 10 million, but only 1.4 million have been characterized and given a name by scientists. Distribution of biodiversity depends and varies according to the climate, altitude, soil structure and presence of other species in an area.

## IMPORTANCE OF BIODIVERSITY

Biological diversity is the very basis of human survival and economic development as it provides food, housing, clothing, medicine and industrial raw material and offers a potential for providing many more, yet unknown benefits to mankind. Production efficiency, exploitation and conservation of animal genetic resources are crucial notonly for the global economy, but also for the environment. A wide range of industrial materials are directly obtained from biological resources. Rubber, oil, fiber, building material, timber and paper all are obtained from biological resources. Biodiversity supports a variety of natural ecosystem processes and services. Ecological services like photosynthesis, air and water purification, recycling of nutrients, pollination and prevention of soil erosion are provided by biodiversity. Biodiversity plays very important role in human health. About 80% of the world population depends on medicines obtained from nature (Behera *et al.*, 2008). A large number of drugs are obtained directly or indirectly from biological sources. A wide range of industrial materials are directly obtained from biological resources. Biodiversity is also the source of non-material benefits like spiritual and aesthetic values, knowledge system, culture diversity and spiritual inspiration. It is a source of inspiration to musicians, painters, writers and other artists. Hobbies like gardening and animal keeping are possible because of biodiversity. In recent years, ever-increasing loss of biodiversity has posed a serious threat to the survival of mankind. The main causes of biodiversity loss are: habitat.

## LOSS OF BIODIVERSITY

In recent years, ever-increasing loss of biodiversity has posed a serious threat to the survival of mankind. The main causes of biodiversity loss are:

habitat destruction, invasive species, pollution, population, over-exploitation and climatic changes. Destruction of the habitat is the biggest threat to biodiversity. The ever-increasing spread of cities and the accompanying expansion of agriculture must be held largely responsible. Habitats can also be damaged by flooding, lack of water, climate changes, salination etc., all phenomena which may be both natural and man-made. Habitat extinction compels the species to move where they find it difficult to adapt and this may ultimately lead to their extinction. Invasion by exoticplants and animals is the second important factor responsible for biodiversity loss. Imported plant species threaten then ativeones by being highly competitive and often by lacking local predators, such as insectsor birds. Over-exploitation, in the form of hunting of animals and plants for their commercial value, is a major reason for reduction inbiodiversity. Overpopulation of human and overconsumption of natural resources are the root causes of all biodiversity loss. The world population now stands at 7 billion and is expected to reach 9 billion in 2045. A broadrange of agricultural genetic diversity needs to be availableand utilized in order to feed this s growing population. (Lidderan and Sonnino, 2012). Genetic pollution i.e. uncontrolled hybridization, introgression and genetic swamping can lead to threatening and replacementof endemic species. As soon as a better variety is developed, the same is distributed far and wide and brought in use. As aresult the local/endemic species are discarded and their specific genes are lost. Climatic change has very adverse effects on biological diversity. Since all organisms are adapted to a particular range of physical and chemical conditions, rapid climatic changes could lead to higher number of diseases, landslide and forest fire, which may result in destruction of animals and plants. Climate changeis an added threat to biodiversity that significantly impact genetic resources for food and agriculture (GRFA) and food production. Global warming affects plants, animals and microorganisms, both by changing their habitats and by direct effects of temperature. Climatic changes also affect species at cellular level and can alter the genetic makeup of the cell.

## CONSERVATION OF BIODIVERSITY

Biodiversity conservation is of global concern which requires a holistic approach. Recognizing the need of conservation of biodiversity, the United Nations prepared Convention on Biodiversity (CBD) and adopted it in 1992. This was the first time that a large majority of States agreed to a legally binding instrument for biodiversity conservation and the sustainable use of biological resources. The CBD isa comprehensive approach to biodiversity conservation of both wild and domesticated species. It aims at conservation at the genetic, species and ecosystem levels.There are various methods to conserve biodiversity. Both *in situ* and *ex situ* methods of biodiversity conservation are equally important. It is now recognized that *ex situ* techniques can be efficiently used to complement *in situ* methods, and they may represent the only option for conserving certain highly endangered andrare species (Ramsay *et al.*, 2000). The choice of one or the other technique, or a combination of both, depends on the particular case. The maintenance and protection of natural habitats are the *in situ* methods of conservation. Preserving the habitat is the most important issue in the conservation of biodiversity. Destruction of habitat should be immediately checked and steps should be taken to restore the habitat of animals and plant species. Since chemical pesticides are responsible for a large number of animal deaths occurring every year, minimizing the use of chemical pesticides is another technique for the survival of biodiversity. Conservation of biodiversity through establishment of protected areas like National Park, Wild life sanctuary, Biosphere Reserves, Marine Reserves etc. are very effectivein controlling the loss of biodiversity. Special care should betaken for the species which are threatened and at the verge of extinction. Efforts should be made to protect the indigenous genetic diversity. There is an urgent need to check the unsustainable exploitation of the biological diversity. This should be improved through appropriate legal and institutional system. Preserving diversity through genebank, seed bank and *in vitro* storage are effective methods for biodiversity conservation. In gene banks, the plant and animal materials are conserved and are available forbreeding, reintroduction, research and other purposes. This method is useful for long living perennial trees and shrubs. Seed banks are the most efficient and effective method for sexually reproducing seeds under long term storage. There are a number of seed banks in the world with specialization in the nature of the collection, geographical area, taxonomic groups, wild plants, forestry trees etc. There are a large number of species for which seed banking cannot be used asa method of conservation. Some plants such as banana donot produce seeds and are propagated vegetatively. Some species such as potato or sugarcane include both sterilegenotypes and genotypes which produce orthodox seeds. However, these seeds are generally highly heterozygous and are thus of limited interest for the conservation of particular genotypes. Similarly, some fruit and forest tree species, produce recalcitrant seeds, i.e. seeds that cannot bedried to sufficiently low moisture level to allow their storage at low temperature (Roberts, 1973). For such plants other methods of conservation are used. Restriction on the introduction of exotic species is another approach in biodiversity conservation. There should be restriction on introduction of exotic species without proper investigation.

## APPLICATIONS OF BIOTECHNOLOGY AND ITS EFFECT ON BIODIVERSITY

### Applications of Biotechnologies for Conservation

Though it is generally believed that biotechnology has adverse effects on biodiversity, but in fact biotechnology offers new means of improving biodiversity. Seed banks are the most efficient and effective method of *ex situ* conservation for the majority of endangered species. In seed banks, genetic fingerprints are used to establish the origin of a seed or the relatedness of one plant variety to another. Tissue culture techniques are of great interest for the collection, multiplication and storage of plantgermplasm (Bunn *et al.*, 2007). Such techniques allow propagating plant material with high multiplication rates in an aseptic environment. Micropropagation refers to *in vitro* mass production of plant propagules from any plant part or cell. Such propagules are used to raise whole plants. Through micropropagation, elite clonal material can be very rapidly multiplied. DNA barcoding is a technique in which species identification is performed by using DNA sequences from a small fragment of the genome, with the aim of contributing to a wide range of ecological and conservation studies in which traditional taxonomic identification is not practical. Some of the biotechnological methods used for production and conservation of animal genetic resources are:

## CRYOPRESERVATION

Cryopreservation is the technique currently available to ensure the safe and cost-efficient long-term conservation of species. Materials such as cells, tissues, gametes, oocytes, DNA samples etc. are stored in a genetic databank for future use. There are two types of techniques: classical and new cryopreservation techniques. Classical techniques involve freeze-induced dehydration, where as new techniques are based on vitrification. Classical cryopreservation techniques involves low cooling down to a defined prefreezing temperature, followed by rapid immersion in liquid nitrogen. Vitrification based procedures offer practical advantages in compare is on to classical freezing techniques. Like ultra-rapid freezing, they are more appropriate for complex organs (shoottips, embryos), which contain a variety of celltypes, each with unique requirements under conditions offreeze- induced dehydration. A successful protocol for long-termconservation of two endangered plants viz. Mantisiaspathulata and M. wengeri has been devised through cryopreservation of immature seeds (Das Bhowmik *et al.*, 2011). In case of poultry, as many as 30% of poultry breedsare threatened with extinction and 9% have already gone extinct. A good technique of cell culture and freezing methods will give a broad perspective for unlimited storage of genetic recourses, which in the future can be useful for there storation of extinct species/breeds (Sawicka *et al.*, 2011). Cryopreservation is an effective method used in the conservation of poultry breeds.

## *IN-VITRO* PRODUCTION OF EMBRYOS

*In vitro* embryo production is another way in biodiversity conservation. Methods used in the production of embryos *in vitro* include splitting and cloning of embryos, marker-assisted selection, sexing of embryos and transfer of new genes into an embryo. Embryo Culture and Transfer technique is used to introduce fertilized embryos into surrogate mothers. Sometimes closely related speciescan be used to produce the offspring of an endangered species.

## TRANSGENIC FARM ANIMALS

Production of transgenic crops and animals is another application of biotechnology in biodiversity conservation. Transgenic crops are more likely to increase agricultural biodiversity and help maintain native biodiversity rather than to endanger it. Such crops may prove to be very useful to the farmers and can be of commercial value. However, the practical benefits and risks of the crops need to be assayed in the field and their products scrutinized. In case of animals, several lines of transgenic farm animals have been produced, but none have been commercialized. Some lines are made for the pharmaceutical industry to produce drugs in their milk. Others may show improved resistances towards certain infections. Biotechnological methods have many advantages to conventional captive breeding procedures. Since the animals need not to be moved around, less stress is experienced and the problem of space for keeping the animals is also solved since samples can be taken in thewild. Storage of genetic resources will help to preserve biodiversity and counter the effect of genetic drift on small populations. Even if an animal dies, its genes will still beavailable for future breeding work. The methods of biotechnology can be applied to the study of virtually any biological phenomenon and will in some cases have practical applications for maintaining biodiversity. Conversely, threats to biodiversity by biotechnology also need to be considered.

## BIOTECHNOLOGY FOR THE ACQUISITION OF KNOWLEDGE

In the context of this paper there are two quite different applications of biotechnology or of molecular biology that are relevant. The first is to use biotechnology as a tool for acquiring knowledge, whilst the second is to use biotechnology to directly intervene in plant and animal breeding, in particular to transfer genetic information from one sort of organism to a particular crop or to a farm animal to make it transgenic. Today biological research can hardly be conducted without using biotechnology in one way or another. Taxonomy uses molecular markers to identify individual strains of organisms or to identify species, much in the same way as is also done in for ensicmedicine to identify criminals. This is useful for *ex situ* conservation of plants and microorganisms. In seedbanks, genetic fingerprints are used to establish the origin of a seedor the relatedness of one plant variety to another. A rational classification of most microorganisms has only become possible with these biotechnological methods. This is important to the many collections of micro-organisms that exist around the world. Biotechnology has also proven useful for following genetic markers in plant and animal breeding. Here animal or plant varieties are crossed by conventional, sexual means. Byanalysing a few cells of the newly born calf or of the newly sprouted crop, one can predict some of the expected properties of the progeny, by looking at the presence or absence of certain forms of genes. This enables one to predict a phenotypic property, which will only show up later in life, for instance certain characteristics of a cow's milk or the crop's expected resistance to an infectious plant disease. Using *in vitro* fertilisation of animals, the laboratory test can be done even before the embryo is implanted. This is called preimplantation diagnostics. These applications of biotechnology are in general not controversial. Here the public perception is similar to the application of modern biotechnology in medicine, for instance to industrially produced pharmaceuticals, vaccines and diagnostics. It may be noted that the world-wide sales of biotechnology products in 1999 was worth around 13 billion dollars in the medical field and only 1.6 billion in agriculture. The availability of genome sequences will be a boost to research. The first two complete plant genome sequences determined were those of Arabidopsis and rice. The 120 million base pair (MBP) of the small brassica Arabidopsis were sequenced by an international academic consortium and the data made publicly available as reported by both Adam and also Dennis and Surridge. The 430 MBP sequence of rice was completed only a few weeks later by an industrial group lead by Syngenta and will be available by contract to other researchers as reported by Dickson. Syngenta intends to make the data available free of charge for research directly benefiting subsistence farmers. The public sector sequencing of rice through an international consortium is expected to be completed in 2004. It will hopefully become common practice for companies to make their basic discoveries publicly available, to everyone's benefit. The Monsanto company too has opened up some of its rice sequencing data. Direct gene transfer to crops and farm animals Since all genes consist of DNA and the information in this DNA molecule is read in thesame way in all organisms in order to make proteins, it is in principle possible to take any (single) gene from any organism and transfer it into any other organism so that the recipient should produce a protein normally made only in the donor. The resulting organism is called transgenic. From the time this simple strategy was devised it took molecular biologists about twenty years until the first transgenic plants were made in 1985. Ten years later the first transgenic crop appeared in supermarkets in the USA, the "FlavrSavr" tomato. In 2000 there were world-wide about 45 million hectares planted with commercial transgenic crops. Most transgenic crops planted commercially in 2000 were in the US, Canada, Argentina, with smaller amounts in China, Australia, South Africa, Mexico and Spain. Soybean and corn ranked first and second, making up 57% and 22% of the total area planted with GMOs. Cotton and canola accounted for about 5.3 and 2.8 million ha each, whilst only small areas of transgenic potato, squash and papaya were grown commercially. As small areas of transgenic potato, squash and papaya were grown commercially. As regards the traits, herbicide tolerance was dominant with 74%, while insect resistance was 19%. According to the ISAAA the amounts of virus resistant crops was quite small. Compared to 1999 there was an increase of

10% in the area planted with GMOs. For cornthere was a decrease, presumably because of an anti-GMO-wave that started in Europein early 1999, Soya and cotton showed an increase. The reason US farmers have adopted the transgenic crops surprisingly quickly is because of the economic benefits they offer. In most surveys done by different researchers indifferent parts of the US, the yields were the same or somewhat higher with the newseeds. The most noticeable difference to the farmers was the saving on herbicides. The US National Center for Food and Agricultural Policy cited an annual saving of 220 million $ to soybean farmers. Gianessi and others also found the new crops needed less frequent sprayings and allowed "no till" management. These benefits mostly offset the initial higher cost of the transgenic seeds, but it is also so that farm profits, with or without modern biotechnology, vary a great deal from year to year and region to region. Clearly these economic considerations only hold for countries with economic structures similar to those of the US, but not to LDCs.It is important to remember that a large number of transgenic crops are still in the development stage and will only come onto the market in a few years from now. They are likely to show benefits for the consumers and some may be of particular interest to farmers in tropical countries. Two rice varieties with anticipated consumer benefits are those containing Vitamin A or an increased level of iron in the product have been developed by Potrykus and Beyer. Despite traditional preventative measures (distribution of free vitamin A, encouragement to eat more fruit and vegetables) 130 million youths are vitamin A-deficient, 1 - 2 million die annually as a consequence of vitamin A-deficiency and 500'000 turn blind irreversibly every year. A bowl of 300 g of this cooked rice is thought by Gura to be enough to overcome to a significant degree the vitamin Adeficiency. Similarly iron-deficiency, particularly prevalent in pregnant women, can potentially be alleviated by rice containing an increased amount of iron in its endosperm. Such rice varieties have bee successfully developed in the laboratory, but are far from commercialisation, for both scientific and political reasons.

## NATIVE BIODIVERSITY AND BIOTECHNOLOGY

Biodiversity in the wild has been massively reduced in the industrialised countries over along period of time, in Europe for example over several millennia. Hardly any ecosystem is the same here as it was before humans started to clear forests and develop farming. When we look out of the window we see houses, roads and meadows, whilst three thousand years ago the area was covered in beech and oak forests. Even Europe'sforests are more like manicured gardens than virgin forests, despite the mystical "naturalness" attributed to our forests, at least in Germanic countries. North America stillhas far more native, untouched ecosystems, either in the form of protected areas or inless hospitable regions like the North of Canada. Biodiversity has already diminished on a massive scale in the industrialised countries. Despite many conservation efforts about half of the tropical humid forests have already been destroyed. How then can the rest be preserved, given that the regional population is increasing rapidly, as for instance in sub-Saharan Africa, where a near doubling of the population is expected in the next 25 years? Already today, the per capita food supply in sub-Saharan countries is only 2100 kilocalories compared to 3500 kilocalories in the industrialised countries, so there will be a huge pressure to provide more food as seen by Ndiritu. Even if some food is imported, the vast majority has to be produced regionally ornationally, both for reasons of economy and ecology (e.g. poverty reduction, transport and distribution costs). Yields of cereals have gone up very considerably in the last forty years. In the LDCs thisis primarily a result of the Green Revolution. However, the annual growth increases incereal yields have slowed down from about 3% to 1% per year as shown by Pinstrup-Andersen and others. For the LDCs they were 2.8% in 1967-1982, 1.9% in 1982-1994 and only 1.2% in 1993-2020. These lower yield increases of recent years mean that productivity will probably not keep up with demand in the LDCs. The consequence on biodiversity is devastating and means that more land will be required for farming. This land will primarily come from areas with high native biodiversity, in particular the aforementioned tropical humid and dry forests. Conway concludes that the single most promising way to avoid habitat destruction is to increase farm yields in a process that has been called the second green revolution. Several components will be required to increase productivity: better training and education of farmers (in particular women), more favourable economic and political climate, availability of micro-credits etc. In addition, technical contributions will be necessary too. One such contribution is improved seed, produced either by traditional crop breeding or by modern biotechnology. Reliance will have to be more on the latter, since traditional breeding seems to have reached a yield plateau. So agricultural biotechnology, which is viewed controversially in the public debate, may contribute markedly to conserve biodiversity by preventing the appropriation of native biodiversity-richl and for farming purposes. It should be noted, however, that this technology – like allothers – is no panacea. Pinstup-Andersen and Cohen believe that each application needs to be studied carefully in a case by case manner, like any other new technology. A valid concern is the possible effect of Bt-crops and similar plants on non-target insects. The Bt-crops contain an gene coding for an insecticidal protein originally produced by the soil bacterium Bacillus thuringensis. They were developed to make the plants resistant to a particular, highly damaging pest and have been quite successful in reducing pesticide input when infestation rates are high. In laboratory studies Losey showed that the pollenfrom Bt-corn could kill larvae of the Monarch butterfly, when a large amount of pollen was sprayed on the larvae's favourite food plant, called milkweed.

Subsequent field studies by Sears showed that the Bt-corn caused little or no damage to the Monarch in real agricultural settings. This shows that the impact of transgenic crops on non-targetorganisms cannot be studied only in the laboratory, but requires farm land experimentation. A more limited concern, that largely touches Northern Europe, is the conservation of native plants and animals, in particular birds, in farmed areas. The birds' habitats are fields, hedges, roadsides and fallow land where they depend for food on insects and seeds produced by weeds in or near the crops. These seeds are particularly important in the winter months. Computer models by Watkinson suggest that more intense weed control measures may lead to smaller amounts of seeds being available to birds. This effect seems plausible under certain conditions, but depends on weed management regimes rather than on the presence or absence of transgenic plants and therefore is notan issue of biotechnology. Herbicide tolerant beets may allow farmers to tolerate weeds for a longer time and fight them only after sowing. This is made possible by a post emergence herbicide treatment. More efficient weed management may also make it possible to set aside more land, comments Hodgson. If the lack of food results in a reduction in the bird population, this may according to Johnson lead to an increased number of harmful insects in the fields. It must be remembered that farming the landserves quite different purposes, particularly in Northern Europe. The primary goal isobviously the production of food, but secondary goals, such as conservation of biodiversity and giving city dwellers opportunities for outdoor activities, are also important. For the latter purpose, setting aside more farmland would be helpful. In order to do this, political will and financial incentives are a prerequisite.

## AGRICULTURAL BIODIVERSITY AND BIOTECHNOLOGY

Possibly not only wild plants, but also old landraces might be threatened by transgeniccrops. It needs to be recalled that vertical gene transfer by pollen has always occurred between different old landraces and between different new varieties of crops. Despite this, varieties of apples or cereals have been stable over many years and specific traits have not disappeared. Pollen has always flown. What has become far more precise is the method of analysis. Thanks to gene probes and to GMOs it has become much easier to follow gene flow, since one is no longer dependent on visible traits, but can follow aspecific gene. Nevertheless, it is important to preserve landraces and native relatives of crops for their intrinsic value as well as for having starting material for future crop breeding. Can newly introduced transgenic crops transfer genes vertically to native wild plants and thereby change important characteristics of the wild plants? Vertical gene transfer between cultivars and wild plants has always occurred within the limits of species, if the two types of plants were in close proximity and flowered at the same time. No new problems can be expected from transgenic plants, except if the gene transferred from the GMO to the wild plant significantly increased the fitness of the recipient. This seems rather unlikely a priori, but needs to be studied experimentally as suggested by Ammann, both in the laboratory and the field. Herbicide resistance transfer from a herbicide tolerant, transgenic crop to a close relative can occur in the field, as has been shown for canola by Mikkelsen in Denmark. However, this would be of major significance only if the recipient weed was controlled by this herbicide in this farm setting. Small farmers in many LDCs use a remarkable number of land races of many different crops. These are often well adapted to the local climate and topography, and are used toproduce foods for different cultural purposes. In the Andes region of South America, dozens of different varieties of potatoes are grown, often side by side on small plots. In Europe different varieties of potatoes are used for the industrial production of chips and for preparing Rösti in the home. Will the traditional landraces disappear when, and if, transgenic crops are introduced by farmers in LDCs? To judge by the European past, the answer will be largely yes, not because of any biological hazard emanating from the GMOs, but because farmers need to produce economically and sell their products. Many old varieties of apples have disappeared in Europe because of the preferences of the food retailers and consumers, who buy just a few varieties. The rapid consolidation in the retailers and consumers, who buy just a few varieties. The rapid consolidation in the global seed market too is a concern for the maintenance of agricultural biodiversity: adecreasing number of companies controls the global seed and agrochemical markets. Anti-trust legislation needs to prevent the formation of overly powerful monopolies. This concern is not a consequence of the introduction of agricultural biotechnology, but aconsequence of globalisation. New technologies have in many areas, not only biotechnology, made large companies more powerful and more visible. It may be possible that modern breeding methods based on molecular genetics will per se reverse the trend of variety losses, since the insight in genomics may bring back respect for landraces and the need to conserve them.

## SOCIAL CONSEQUENCES

The introduction and spread of new technologies generally have social consequences with winners and losers. For biotechnology this has led to intense public debate on many different facets, among them ethical, economic, legal and emotional.

## ECONOMIC CONSIDERATIONS

One may wonder under what economic conditions biotechnology will benefit agricultural productivity, prevent the expansion of farm land and thereby help the preservation of biodiversity. It is worth remembering that the green revolution, which improved wheat and rice production in Asia, was initiated through work done in the public sector, namely in the Philippines at the International Rice Research Institute (IRRI) and in Mexico at the Centro Internacional de Mejoramiento de Maiz y Trigo (CIMMYT), both institutions which belong to the Consultative Group of International Agricultural Research (CGIAR). Today, innovative research in agricultural biotechnology is largely done by a few large companies, with smaller contributions from the public sector. That companies strive for intellectual property rights (IPR) through patenting or other protective mechanisms is understandable and largely unavoidable, if innovation is to be maintained. However, provisions need to be made, so that the agricultural research institutions of LDCs obtain easy access to the patented materials and procedures as well as to knowledge they need in order to improve the position of poorer farmers as proposed for instance by IRRI. A very limited number of transfers of specific patents has already occurred, such as from Monsanto to the Kenyan Agricultural Research Institute for producing virus-resistant sweet potatoes discussed by MacIlvain or another to IRRI for the promoter genes used in golden rice reported by Normile. This approach, including the possibility of forced licensing, is more practicable than wanting to overthrow the world's patenting system with the slogan "No patents on life". The patenting system does, however, need to be adapted in order to do justice to the complexity of living organisms. It may be noted in passing that the first patent granted for a living organism was given to Louis Pasteur in 1873 for aspecific type of yeast. A new issue arising in the field of IPR is the attempt to protect traditional, indigenous knowledge and preserve biodiversity through new international legislation as reported for instance by Girsberger. This legal instrument is still in an embryonic state of development. At the level of the individual human being, the lack of food appears to be, and is, largely a problem of distribution: there is not sufficient food available, where it is needed. In addition, the poor simply do not have the money to buy sufficient food. Since in LDCs most of the poor still live on the land, it is there, that more income has to be generated, so that there is not only enough for survival, but a surplus which can be sold on the market. Increasing agricultural productivity is the most effective way to do this and should, according to economists such as Lipton, embrace modern biotechnology as an important component.

## ETHICAL CONSIDERATIONS

The issues involved in the interaction between biodiversity and biotechnology have far reaching consequences and need to be subject to an open and knowledge-based dialogue in society. The heated public debate, seen primarily in Europe in the last couple of years and which in some circles led to near hysteria, is according to Leisinger not sufficient to solve the underlying problems. The dialogue needs to include many different stakeholders, including farmers of LDCs, diverse scientists, policy makers and communicators. Cultural values involved in farming and food production need to be taken into consideration, just as much as the emotional side of eating and drinking. A significant aspect of ethical behaviour is openness. Transparent information is required both from scientists in non-commercial settings as well as from industry. Although competition from fellow researchers and from industries does not allow immediately divulging all research results, both groups should make concessions to the interested public and to policy makers. This should be done by scientists personally and would help improve mutual confidence. Several large projects in biotechnology like HUGO, the Human Genome Organisation, have an "ELSI" component, dealing with ethical, legal and societal implications of biotechnology. This shows that some scientists realise that science cannot be seen asa human activity taking place in a void, without any connection to social and political realities. Ethicists stress that it is the responsibility of scientists to be actively concerned with these issues and that they should take special responsibility incommunicating with non-specialists to explain what they know as well as what they don't know. Matrices of criteria have been set up for instance by Mepham to make it possible to ask relevant questions. Who and what may be affected by agricultural biotechnology, what properties like wellbeing, autonomy or justice may or may not be infringed upon. The questions put forward by ethicists need to answered on the basis of concrete scientific knowledge, using comparisons with other, established agricultural practices. Ethicists will have critical and thought provoking questions. However, their answers and attitudes will have critical and thought provoking questions. However, their answers and attitudes may vary considerably. If they are positive as Comstock, ethicists will suggest pursuing research and application with appropriate caution. There is no easy answer to what the word "appropriate" means, beyond answering questions in a case by case manner to balance benefits and risks. Actively shaping the future and attempting to solve problems always involves risk. It will be important to see ethics not as a stable set of principles but rather a discursive process, which will be apt to cope up with the growing speed of new developments as discussed by Ammann and Ammann. The Nuffield Council of Bioethics recently came to the conclusion that "The moral imperative for making GM crops readily and economically available ... is compelling", if well-informed governments of LDCs want to introduce them. This imperative should be taken seriously and treated with urgency: every day 20'000 children die of malnutrition and 30'000 ha of humid tropical forest are destroyed.

## CONCLUSION

Though the biotechnological methods of biodiversity conservation offer many advantages to conventional procedures but these technologies have various social consequences. How will biotechnology benefit agricultural productivity, prevent the expansion off arm land and thereby help the preservation of biodiversityis a matter of debate. Biotechnology applications must be integrated with ongoing conventional breeding and development programs in order to succeed. Additionally, the generation, adaptation, and adoption of biotechnologies require a consistent level of financial and human resources and appropriate policies need to be inplace.

## *REFERENCES*

Behera K.K., Sahoo S. and Patra S., 2008. Floristic and Medicinal uses of some Plants of Chandakadenudated Forest Patches of Bhubaneswar, Orissa, India. Ethnobot. Leaflets,: 1043-1053.

Bunn E.,Turner S.R., Panaia M. and Dixon K.W., 2007. The Contribution of *in vitro* Technology and Cryogenic Storage to Conservation of Indigenous Plants. AustJ Bot.,: 345-355.

Das Bhowmik S.S., Kumaria, S. and Tandon, P., 2011. Long-term Conservation Through Cryopreservation of Immature Seed of and; two Endangered Plants of North-east India. Cryo Letter, (6): 498-505. Dasmann R.F., 1968. A Different Kind of Country. MacMillan Company, New York.

Lahaye, R., Vander Bank, M., Bogarin, D.,Warner, J., Pupulin, F., Gigot, G., Maurin, O., Duthoit, S., Barraclough,T.G. and Savolainen, V. (2008) DNA Barcodingthe Floras of Biodiversity Hotspots. Proc Natl Acad Sci USA., (8): 2923-2928.

Lidde, P. and Sonnino A., 2012. Biotechnologies for the Management of Genetic Resources for Food and Agriculture. Adv Genet.,: 1-167.

Ramsay M.M., Jackson A.D. and Porley R.D., 2000. Apilot Study for the *ex situ* Conservation of UK Bryophytes. In: BGCI (ed) Eurogard-II Europeanbotanic Garden Congress. EBGC, Las Palmas deGran Canaria: 52-57.

Raven P.H., 1992. Botanical Garden, Missouri, Biotechnology and Genetic Resources, US-ECTask Force on Biotechnology Research, [A Broadoverview of Existing Biodiversity].

Roberts H.F., 1973. Predicting the Viability of Seeds. Seed SciTechnol.,: 499-514.

Sawicka D., Brzeziñska, J. and Bednarczyk M. 2011. Cryoconservation of Embryonic Cells and Gametesas a Poultry Biodiversity Preservation method. Folia Biol (Krakow), 59 (1-2):1-5.

Pages: 41-75

**FOREST AND BIODIVERSITY CONSERVATION**
*Edited by:* **Dr. Alka Chauhan** and **Dr. Pawan Kumar 'Bharti'**
**ISBN: 978-93-5056-873-6**
*Edition:* **2017**
*Published by:* **Discovery Publishing House Pvt. Ltd., New Delhi (India)**

# 3 Preferences of Flower Colour in Butterfly Fauna of the Western Ghats, India

*Maryjane Nikitha; N.A., Arvind and S. Rajashekara**

## *ABSTRACT*

In the present study, the data collated were confined only to the butterflies of the Western Ghats region of India. A database with 1045 records was analyzed those butterfly belonging to 208 number of species belonging to all five families and 133 number of plant species was recorded from the Western Ghats. It also included the attributes (variables) of both butterflies and the host-plants. The most preferred flower colour, flower type and host-habit were determined using the species matrix both at the community and family levels. The relationships between the variables were tested using statistical tools.

The study has shown that at the community level more than half the number of the butterfly species preferred white coloured flowers followed by yellow and pink. At the family level, different butterfly families have different colour preferences. Nymphalids preferred pink/yellow flowers, Hesperiids preferred pink flowers, Lycaenids and Pierids preferred white flowers, and Papilionids preferred red flowers, showing diversity in the flower colour preference behavior of butterflies. Most of the butterfly species preferred to feed on clustered flowers (flower type-inflorescence). A majority of the butterfly species preferred host-plants which are shrubs and herbs, rather than trees and climbers. *Lantana camara* was determined to be the most preferred host-plant followed by asters such as*Tridax procumbens* and *Chromoleana odorata*.

It was confirmed through the correlation and regression analysis that there exists an association between the proboscis length of butterflies and

* Centre for Applied Genetics, Department of Studies in Zoology, Bangalore University, Jnana Bharathi Campus, Bengaluru – 560 056 (India)

size of the flowers. There also exists some extent of association between the sizes of butterflies and flowers. But no associations were found between the butterfly and inflorescence sizes and also between the butterfly size and number of florets in the inflorescence.

**Scope:** Butterflies are diurnal adult flying stage of insects belonging to the order of Lepidoptera (scaly winged) along with the moths. Adult butterflies are large, often times brightly coloured, and conspicuous and has fluttering flight. The earliest known butterfly fossils date back to mid Eocene epoch, 40-50 million years ago. Like other holometabolous insects, the butterfly's life cycle consists of four stages- egg, larva, pupa and adult. The butterflies are placed under six families in the order-Lepidoptera. The first five families –Papilionidae (Swallowtails), Pieridae (Whites and Sulphurs), Nymphalidae (Brush-foots), Lycaenidae (Blues/Gossamer-wings), and Riodinidae(Metalmarks) – are called the true butterflies. The last family, Hesperiidae (Skippers), is sometimes considered separately.

Butterflies are fragile and almost defenseless creatures. They rely on a variety of strategies to protect them from hungry predators. Their main predators include birds, spiders, reptiles, other insects (e.g., wasps, flies, and mites), and small mammals. Most butterflies and moth protect themselves from predators by using camouflage. Some butterflies and moths blend into their environment so well that is it almost impossible to spot them when they are resting on a branch. Some butterflies look like dead leaves (like the Indian leaf butterfly or Evening Brown), others look like the bark of a tree (e.g., the carpenter moth). It is a fact that ants love to eat caterpillars. However, the caterpillars of the blue butterflies have evolved a symbiotic relationship that is mutually beneficial. Most blue butterfly caterpillars have glands on the 11th and 12th segments, which secrete a sugary solution, like honeydew. The ants harvest the honeydew from the caterpillar and in return protect them from other predators. This co-evolution has resulted in butterflies laying eggs, in places where ants are in abundance (Devries 1990).

The Butterflies react to disturbances and changes in habitat; hence, they act as ecological indicators (Mac Nally and Fleishman 2004; Fleishman. 2004). They may get severely affected by the environmental variations and changes in the forest structure, as they are closely dependent on plants (Pollard 1991; Blair 1999). Thus, minor changes in their habitat may lead to either migration or local extinction (Blair 1999; Kunte 2000; Mennechez. 2003). Because of their dependence on the plants, butterfly diversity may reflect overall plant diversity in the given area (Padhye *et al*. 2006).The choice of plants as nectar sources by butterflies depends on various factors, including innate colour preferences (Ilse 1928; Jolivet 1986; Weiss 1997; Pariset and Racheli 1998; Dosa 1999). Innate colour preferences for feeding have been reported for a relatively broad taxonomic range of butterflies including nymphalids, papilionids, satyrids and pierids; and differ between butterfly genera and even between species.

**Current Scenario:** Around 18, 000 species of butterflies are found in the world and 1, 500 species in India (Table 3.1). About 15-20% of the butterfly species are found to be endemic to the Indian Region, which makes this an important region for butterfly diversity and conservation. The Western Ghats are home to around 334 species of butterflies and 11% of them are found to be endemic. The butterflies occur in wide range of shapes and sizes. The world's smallest known butterfly species is the Blue Pygmy (*Brephidium exilis*), is found in Southern California and has a wingspan of less than 2 cm. The largest species is the New Guineas Queen Alexandria's Birdwing (*Ornithoptera alexandrae*) has a wingspan twelve inches long. The Goliath Birdwing butterfly is the second-largest butterfly in the world. Whereas in India, the Southern Birdwing (190mm) is the largest and the Grass Jewel and Tiny Grass Yellow (15mm) are the smallest butterflies.

**Table 3.1: Number of butterfly species documented in the World, India and the Western Ghats**

| Sl. No. | Butterfly Families | Number of Species | | | |
|---|---|---|---|---|---|
| | | World | India | Western Ghats | Endemic to Western Ghats |
| 1. | Papilionidae | 556 | 84 | 19 | 5 |
| 2. | Pieridae | 1215 | 81 | 34 | 3 |
| 3. | Nymphalidae | 6440 | 439 | 97 | 12 |
| 4. | Lycaenidae | 4089 | 318 | 101 | 3 |
| 5. | Riodinidae | 1366 | 16 | 1 | 0 |
| 6. | Hesperiidae | 3592 | 225 | 83 | 10 |
| | **Total** | **17,258** | **1163** | **335** | **33** |

## INTRODUCTION

Angiosperm plants have evolved to attract animals for pollination and seed dispersal. In most cases the visual and olfactory senses i.e., colour and scent are very important for guiding visitors. This interaction between flowering plants and their pollinators are the result of a long co-evolutionary history evolved over several millennia. This interaction has helped to shape the attributes of both plant and its animal pollinator. Indirect information about the sensory capabilities of pollinators can be inferred from the existence of 'pollination syndromes', suites of floral traits that can be used to characterize groups of flowers favoured by different types of pollinators (Proctor and Yeo 1975; Faegriand Pijl 1979). Most animals make use of color information, including wavelength, spectral purity and intensity, as they explore their environments. Butterflies in particular rely on light in a variety of behavioral contexts, and the range of their light perception, which in some taxa extends from ultraviolet through red, is among the broadest known in the animal kingdom (Silberglied 1984; Briscoe and Chittka 2001). Colour vision is an important component of intra- and inter-specific interactions in butterflies (Crane 1955; Silberglied 1984), as well as in the recognition and use of floral food sources.

Colours and patterns that butterflies see are invisible to man. Colour of flowers appears differently to butterflies, because of their sensitivity to Ultra Violet (UV) light. Flowers have ultra-violet patterns that are invisible to humans but which can be recognised by butterflies as a different signature. These UV patterns guide butterflies to the source of nectar in much the same way that runway lights guide an aircraft in to land.Butterflies are often considered to be opportunistic foragers that visit a wide variety of available flowers (Sharp *et al.* 1974; Dosa 1999). However, their choice of flowers is not random and they often exhibit distinct flower preferences, which can differ between butterfly species (Jennersten 1984). Generally the visitation of butterflies to the flowers is influenced by the flower colour, structure and scent (odour). Although, butterflies have often shown an amazing range of flower color preference between the various species, yet as a general rule, flowers that are white, pink, purple, red, yellow and orange attract most of the butterflies. Blue to green flowers are universally the least favorite flower color for this group of insects. Some evidence indicates that butterflies may learn which color flowers tend to produce their favorite types of nectar, using color as a visual cue when hunting for these plants. But the effectiveness of butterfly foraging also depends in part the structure of the flower such as corolla depth, clustering of flowers, but also on proboscis length, which limits the range of flowers from which nectar can be extracted (Porter *et al.* 1992; Corbet 2000).

The mechanisms that are used by butterflies for flower visitations are largely unknown even today despite there are large body of work. For example, we do not know which visual cues attract butterflies to flowers or if butterflies possess memory limitations that force them to restrict their visits to a few flower types (both colour and structure), displaying a flower constant behavior. Flower preference refers to the net over-visitation of one flower type over another, whereas flower constancy refers to the propensity to sequentially visit the flower type last visited, bypassing alternative equally rewarding types. These distinct flower-visiting behaviors can affect plant reproductive success and gene flow in different ways.

By observing colourful butterflies feeding on colourful flowers, it is easy to believe that these animals might have colour vision. However, a number of attempts in the past several decades to demonstrate colour vision in butterflies have not been fully successful in scientific terms (Silberglied 1984). Since, the butterflies react to disturbances and changes in habitat; they often act as ecological indicators (Mac Nally and Fleishman 2004; Fleishman *et al.* 2004). They may get severely affected by the environmental variations and changes in the forest structure, as they are closely dependent on plants (Pollard 1991; Blair 1999). Thus, minor changes in their habitat may lead to either migration or local extinction (Blair 1999; Kunte 2000; Mennechez *et al.* 2003). Because of their dependence on the plants, butterfly diversity may reflect overall plant diversity in the given area (Padhye etal. 2006). Hence, it is highly essential to study their feeding preferences in order to devise new strategies to conserve them be it in natural environment or in man-made habitats such as urban landscapes where the threats are very high. The main objectives of the study are:

(a) To determine which coloured flowers attract the butterflies for feeding.

(b) To determine the flower/plant attributes like flower structure and morphology and host-habit that influence their visitation.

## MATERIALS AND METHODS

### Study Area

The Western Ghats(WG) of India run parallel to the west coast of India between 8°N - 22°N, ending in south of Gujarat State, traversing a length of about 1600km. It spreads over an area of about 160,000 km$^2$, this mountain range contains remaining tropical rain forests (evergreen forests) on its slopes. WG consists of hills from 1000 to 2000m asl altitude, between 8°N - 13°N and 18°N - 19°N. The Nilgiris, Palnis and Anamalais are the only stretches of this mountain range with altitude over 2000m asl. The northern portion of the range is at lower elevations than the southern region. Western Ghats receives much of its rain from the south-west monsoon, hence June to October are generally wettest season. However, the northern portion of the range is generally dryer than the southern portion, as the southern portion also receives north-eastern/return monsoon during November and December. Average annual rainfall on the Western Ghats is 2500 mm. Mean temperature ranges between 20° to 24° C, frequently shooting beyond 30° C during summer (April-May) and sometimes falling to almost 0° C during winter in the high altitude hilly regions. Climate is the major factor that affects the floral and faunal composition of a region. Butterflies being cold-blooded are easily affected by changes in climate.

The Western Ghats is home to hundreds of species of rare, endemic and exotic species of colourful butterflies, some of them extremely rare. Some species are so rare that they are found nowhere else in the world. The region boasts of approximately 334 species of butterflies, out of which 11% are reported to be endemic. They come in a variety of sizes with two pairs of large wings. The color pattern varies from species to species and has a definite role to play in the protection of the species. Human activity has resulted in destruction of host plants threatening the survival of butterflies. The hydro-electric projects have inundated major butterfly habitats in the region (Gadgil 2012).

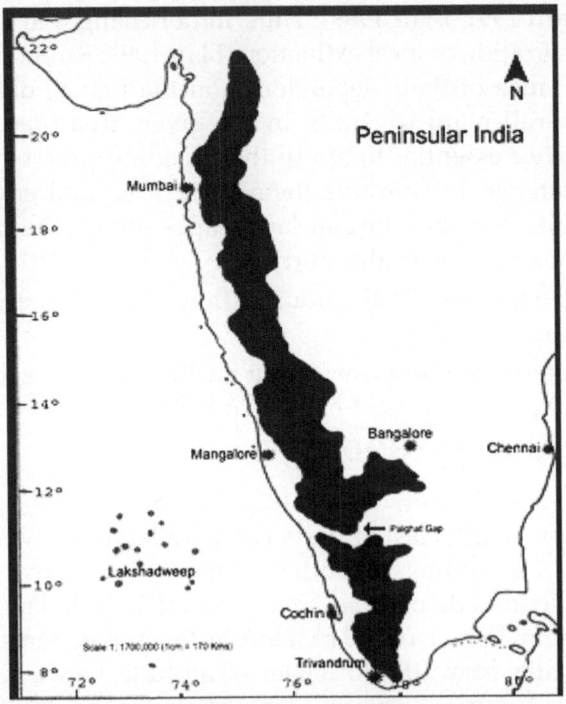


**Fig. 3.1: The Location of Western Ghats on a Map**

## Data Collection and Compilation

Data of the butterflies feeding on the flowers were collated into a database from various sources (Table 3.2). Websites were manually searched for the photographs showing the butterflies feeding on nectar from the nectaries of a flower. Only images of butterflies with their proboscis inserted into the flowers were used to build the database. Images of butterflies photographed in the Western Ghats region were selected. The butterflies found in the photograph were identified with the help of field guides (Antram 1924; Kunte 2000; Kehimkar 2008). Taxonomic details and morphological attributes of the butterflies were gathered using the field guides and the data was used in building the database. The Scientific and Common names of butterflies along with the family they belong were also included in the database. The attributes of Butterflies recorded were:

(a) Wing Span (mm);

(b) Body Length (mm);

(c) Proboscis Length (mm);

(d) Weight of Butterfly;

(e) Proboscis index; and

(f) Wing Load index.

All the information gathered on the butterflies was tabulated in a MS Excel Spreadsheet according to the sequence they were recorded.

**Table 3.2: Different sources of information on butterfly feeding used in this study**

| Sl. No. | Photographic Database | Sources |
|---|---|---|
| 1. | India Nature Watch | http://www.indianaturewatch.net/view_cat.php?tag=western-ghats<br>http://www.indianaturewatch.net/view_cat.php?tag=sahyadri |
| 2. | I Found Butterflies-Indian Foundation for Butterflies | http://www.ifoundbutterflies.org/ |
| 3. | Flickr | https://www.flickr.com/search/?q=butterflies%20of%20western%20ghats |
| 4. | Project Noah, EMRI | https://www.projectnoah.org/missions/8702945 |
| 5. | India Biodiversity Portal | http://indiabiodiversity.org/checklist/show/27 |
| 6. | Tripod | http://indiabutterflies.tripod.com/ |

Apart from this the details of the flower in which the butterfly was found to be feeding were recorded (Table 3.3).The scientific name of the host- plant and the family it is placed under and the habit of the host-plant (herb, shrub, climber or tree) were included in the database. The details on the floral attributes like the flower colour, flower type (solitary, inflorescence or aster), flower size, inflorescence size, number of florets in inflorescence and the flowering season were collated into the database.All the information gathered on the host-plants tabulated in a MS Excel Spreadsheet beside the respective butterflies recorded.

**Table 3.3. List of plant attributes used for in the study**

| Flower Colours | Plant Habits | Flower Types |
|---|---|---|
| Green | Climber | Solitary |
| Blue | Herb | Inflorescence |
| Red/Yellow | Shrub | Aster |
| Lilac | Tree | |
| Orange | | |
| Cream | | |
| Pink/Yellow | | |
| Purple | | |
| Red | | |
| Pink | | |
| Yellow | | |
| White | | |

The plants were identified using the following sources:

## A. Databases:

I. Southeastern Flora: Southeastern US Plant Identification Resource

II. Sahyadri: Western Ghats Biodiversity Information System Flora Database.

III. India Biodiversity Portal

IV. USDA-Natural Resources Conservation Service

**B. Books:**

I. Isaac Kehimkar (2001) - Common Indian Wild Flowers

Thus, a database with 1045 records was built and the format of the database is shown in the Figure 3.2. A total of 208 species of butterflies and 133 species of plant hosts were collated and used for further analysis.

**Data Analysis**

From the data compiled, the attributes of the host plant were considered as independent variables and the attributes of the butterflies were considered as dependent variables. The Independent variables studied are Plant habit, Flower colour, Flower type, Flower size, Inflorescence size and Number of florets in inflorescence. The Dependent variables are Butterfly Size, Proboscis length, Number of Butterfly Species recorded and Number of unique occurrences (records) of butterfly species.

The Data compiled was analyzed using the following tools:

*(i)* The species matrix was created using Pivot Table in MS Excel. The Pivot table is a data summarization tool found in data visualization programs like spreadsheets. It was used to process the data; i.e. to determine the most preferred flower colour, flower type, plant habit and also to determine whether the butterflies prefer native or exotic plant hosts. This tool was used to count the number of butterfly species preferring each of the flower colour, flower type and plant habit.The Pivot table was also used to determine which butterfly family prefers which coloured flower and the top ten plant species preferred by the butterflies. The results were depicted on a pivot chart.

*(ii)* The correlation and regression analysis were used for assessing the relationship between different factors (variables), and for graphically representing the results in a meaningful way. The correlation and regression analysis was performed to determine the relationships between the following variables:

(a) Proboscis length and flower size;

(b) Butterfly Size and flower size;

(c) Butterfly size and inflorescence size; and

(d) Butterfly size and number of florets in inflorescence

*(iii)* Chi-Square Testis used to compare counts (numbers) of things that fall into different categories. The Chi-square Test is commonly used to compare observed data with data we would expect to obtain according to a specific hypothesis. The test is always testing the null hypothesis, which states that there is no significant difference between the expected and observed result. It also states that there is no significant difference between the attributes.

| Sl. No. | Butterfly | Butterfly Family | Plant | Plant Family | Habit | Flower Colour | Flower Type | Flower Size (cm) | Infloescence Size (cm) | # Florets in Inflore-scence | Flowering Season | Wing Span (mm) | Proboscis Length (mm) | Body Length (mm) | Avg. Wing Span (mm) | Weight (mg) | Proboscis Index | Wing Load Index |
|---|---|---|---|---|---|---|---|---|---|---|---|---|---|---|---|---|---|---|
| 1. | Common Grass Yellow | Pieridae | *Clerodendrum paniculatum* | Verbenaceae | Shrub | Red | Inflorescence | 1.3 | 45 | 55 | Mar-Sept | 40-50 | 11.1 | 13 | 31.5 | 23.7 | 0.85 | 0.75 |
| 2. | Common Emigrant | Pieridae | *Clerodendrum paniculatum* | Verbenaceae | Shrub | Red | Inflorescence | 1.3 | 45 | 55 | Mar-Sept | 55-80 | 16.7 | 20.7 | 64.1 | 141.4 | 0.81 | 2.21 |
| 3. | Indian Skipper | Hesperiidae *serratum* | *Clerodendrum* | Verbenaceae | Shrub | Purple | Inflorescence | 4 | 30 | 80 | Aug-Oct | 20-27 | 7.6 | 7.2 | 20.7 | 22.2 | 1.06 | 1.07 |
| 4. | Danaid Eggfly | Nymphalidae | *Mappia foetida* | Icacinaceae | Tree | White | Inflorescence | 0.9 | 3 | 10 | Jan-Dec | 70-85 | 14.4 | 22.4 | 85.5 | 276 | 0.64 | 3.23 |
| 5. | Mottled Emigrant | Pieridae | *Clerodendrum viscosum* | Verbenaceae | Shrub | White | Inflorescence | 1.2 | 20 | 30 | Mar-Sept | 50-70 | 16.4 | 22.2 | 58.7 | 129.9 | 0.74 | 2.21 |
| 6. | Southern Birdwing | Papilionidae | *Clerodendrum paniculatum* | Verbenaceae | Shrub | Red | Inflorescence | 1.3 | 45 | 55 | Mar-Sept | 140-190 | 50 | | 165 | | | |
| 7. | Southern Birdwing | Papilionidae | *Pentas* | Rubiaceae | Herb | Red | Inflorescence | 2.5 | 5 | 20 | Mar-May | 140-190 | 50 | | 165 | | | |
| 8. | Red Helen | Papilionidae | *Pentas* | Rubiaceae | Herb | Red | Inflorescence | 2.5 | 5 | 20 | Mar-May | 110-130 | 33.3 | | 120 | | | |
| 9. | Blue Mormon | Papilionidae | *Pentas* | Rubiaceae | Herb | Pink | Inflorescence | 2.5 | 5 | 20 | Mar-May | 120-150 | 37.9 | 36.6 | 149.7 | 665 | 1.04 | 4.44 |
| 10. | Red Helen | Papilionidae | *Clerodendrum paniculatum* | Verbenaceae | Shrub | Red | Inflorescence | 1.3 | 45 | 55 | Mar-Sept | 110-130 | 33.3 | | 120 | | | |
| 11. | Blue Mormon | Papilionidae | *Clerodendrum paniculatum* | Verbenaceae | Shrub | Red | Inflorescence | 1.3 | 45 | 55 | Mar-Sept | 120-150 | 37.9 | 36.6 | 149.7 | 665 | 1.04 | 4.44 |
| 12. | Blue Tiger | Nymphalidae | *Aster sp.* | Asteraceae | Shrub | Red | Aster | 0.2 | 3 | 45 | Jan-Dec | 90-100 | 12.6 | 26.3 | 91.4 | 378.8 | 0.48 | 4.14 |
| 13. | Southern Birdwing | Papilionidae | *Mussaenda galbrata* | Rubiaceae | Shrub | Orange | Solitary | 4 | | | Apr-Nov | 140-190 | 50 | | 165 | | | |
| 14. | Red Helen | Papilionidae | *Mussaenda galbrata* | Rubiaceae | Shrub | Orange | Solitary | 4 | | | Apr-Nov | 110-130 | 33.3 | | 120 | | | |
| 15. | Blue Mormon | Papilionidae | *Mussaenda galbrata* | Rubiaceae | Shrub | Orange | Solitary | 4 | | | Apr-Nov | 120-150 | 37.9 | 36.6 | 149.7 | 665 | 1.04 | 4.44 |
| 16. | Malabar Tree Nymph | Nymphalidae | *Semecarpus kathalekanensis* | Anacardiaceae | Tree | White | Inflorescence | 1 | 30 | 45 | Jun-Jul | 120-140 | | | 130 | | | |
| 17. | Blue Mormon | Papilionidae | *Lantana camara* | Verbenaceae | Shrub | Pink/Yellow | Inflorescence | 1.2 | 4 | 15 | Jan-Nov | 120-150 | 37.9 | 36.6 | 149.7 | 665 | 1.04 | 4.44 |
| 18. | Common Rose | Papilionidae | *Lantana camara* | Verbenaceae | Shrub | Pink/Yellow | Inflorescence | 1.2 | 4 | 15 | Jan-Nov | 80-110 | 16.8 | 22.3 | 86 | 324.8 | 0.75 | 3.78 |
| 19. | Common Mormon | Papilionidae | *Lantana camara* | Verbenaceae | Shrub | Pink/Yellow | Inflorescence | 1.2 | 4 | 15 | Jan-Nov | 90-100 | 22.8 | 23.1 | 94.3 | 275.5 | 0.99 | 2.92 |

**Fig. 3.2: Database Format for Butterfly in an Excel Spreadsheet**

**Fig. 3.3: Some Examples of the Photos Collected that were used for the Building Database**

**Table 3.4. Database format for recording butterfly data**

| Sl. No. | Common Name | Scientific Name | Family | Proboscis Length (mm) | Body Length (mm) | Wing Span (mm) | Weight (mg) |
|---|---|---|---|---|---|---|---|
| 1. | Southern Birdwing | *Troides minos* | Papilionidae | 50.0 | 48.5 | 165.0 | 750 |
| 2. | Lime Butterfly | *Papilio demoleus* | Papilionidae | 23.7 | 25.8 | 84.9 | 328.1 |
| 3. | Common Crow | *Euploea core* | Nymphalidae | 11.9 | 25.8 | 89.2 | 238.5 |

**Table 3.5: Database format for recording host plant data**

| Sl. No. | Name of Plant Species | Plant Family | Habit | Flower Colour | Flower Type | Flower Size (cm) | Inflorescence Size (cm) | No. Flowers in Inflorescence | Flowering Season |
|---|---|---|---|---|---|---|---|---|---|
| 1. | *Lantana camara* | Verbenaceae | Shrub | Orange | Inflorescence | 1.2 | 4.0 | 15 | Jan-Nov |
| 2. | *Catharanthus roseus* | Apocynaceae | Herb | Pink | Solitary | 4.0 | - | - | Jan-Dec |
| 3. | *Duranta erecta* | Verbenaceae | Shrub | Purple | Inflorescence | 1.5 | 7.0 | 5 | Jan-Dec |

The Chi-Square Test of independence was used to find out whether the different butterfly families were dependent on the preferences of: a) Flowercolour; b) Flower type and c) Plant(host) habit. The analysis was performed manually and the contingency table was created by considering number of records of butterfly species in each family in different flower colour, flower type, plant habit and native/exotic plant species.

*(iv)* Student's t-test is used for comparing the means of two samples (or treatments), even if they have different numbers of replicates. In simple terms, the t-test compares the actual difference between two means in relation to the variation in the data (expressed as the standard deviation of the difference between the means). It was used in this study for comparing the means of preferences of butterflies of samples: (a) climbers and herbs; and (b) climbers and shrubs.

(*v*) The main purpose of Analysis of Variance (ANOVA) is to check any significant difference between groups of some variables found or not. It was used to determine the significant difference between flower types, plant habits and the number of butterfly species preferring them.

## RESULTS

Weanalyzed the 1045 number of records belonging to 208 number of butterfly species belonging to five families of butterflies (Annexure I)and 133 number of plant species (Annexure II).

**Preferences of butterflies for flower colour, plant habit and flower type:**

**(a)** ***Colour preference at community level***

The analysis revealed that the most of butterfly species prefer white coloured flowers (57.69%) to the remaining coloured flowers. White coloured flower is followed by the yellow colour (43.75%), pink (40.86%), red (35.57%) and purple (30.76%). Blue (1.44%) and Green (0.96%) showed the least preferred coloured flowers (Figure 3.4).

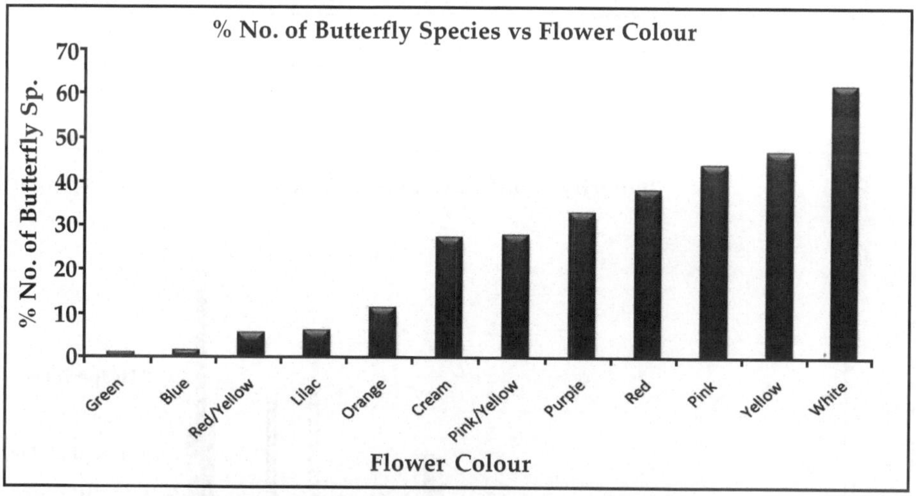


**Fig. 3.4: Histogram Representing the Preference of Flower Colours by most of Butterfly Species**

**(b)** ***Colour preference at family level***

Among therecorded five butterfly families, the most of Lycaenidspecies preferred white coloured flowers and the least preference was purple flowers, and also, none of the Lycaenids showed any preferencefor lilac, orange and blue coloured flower (Table 3.6 and Figure 3.5). The most of Nymphalids preferred to feed on the pink/yellow coloured flowers followed by white, yellow and red flowers. Whereas they preferred lilac and orange flowers the least and never fed on blue coloured flowers. Most of Hesperiids preferred the pink coloured flowers followed by white, yellow and purple coloured flowers. They also rarely preferred orange, cream or blue and never preferred lilac coloured flowers. Papilionids preferred red coloured flowers over all the other coloured flowers and never preferred blue, lilac and cream coloured flowers. Lastly the Pierids preferred white coloured flowers followed by pink, yellow and red coloured flowers. They preferred Lilac coloured flowers the least and never preferred blue and orange flowers (Figure 3.5).A significant difference was found between the colouredpreference of flowers among the different families of butterflies ($\chi^2$ = 88.36, *P=0.000*).

**Table 3.6: Flower colour preferences of the butterfly species belonging to different families in percentage**

| Butterfly Family | Flower Colour | | | | | | | | | |
|---|---|---|---|---|---|---|---|---|---|---|
| | Blue | Red/ Yellow | Lilac | Orange | Cream | Purple | Red | Yellow | Pink/ Yellow | Pink | White |
| Hesperiidae | 0.481 | 0 | 0 | 0.481 | 0.481 | 3.365 | 1.44 | 3.365 | 1.923 | 6.25 | 5.769 |
| Lycaenidae | 0 | 0 | 0 | 0 | 2.404 | 0.962 | 2.88 | 3.846 | 1.442 | 1.44 | 9.615 |
| Nymphalidae | 0 | 0 | 0.481 | 0.481 | 1.442 | 1.442 | 4.80 | 4.808 | 6.731 | 1.92 | 5.769 |
| Papilionidae | 0 | 0 | 0 | 0.481 | 0 | 0.481 | 4.80 | 0.961 | 1.442 | 0.48 | 0.480 |
| Pieridae | 0 | 0.481 | 0.481 | 0 | 0.962 | 1.442 | 2.40 | 2.404 | 1.923 | 2.88 | 3.846 |

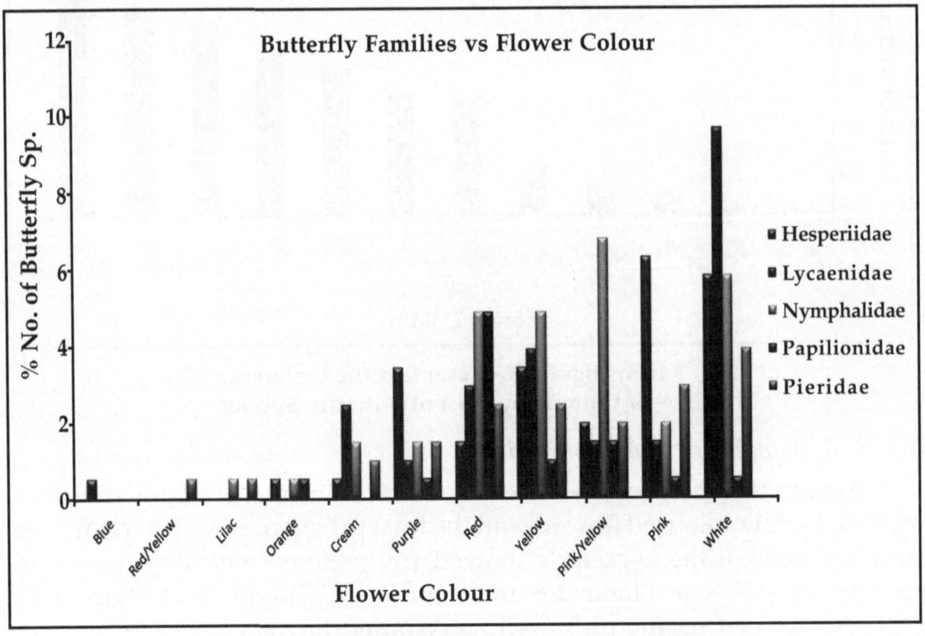


**Fig. 3.5: Histogram showing the Preferred Flower Colours by the different Families of Butterfly**

### (c) *Flower Type*

Most of the butterfly species fed on clustered flowers or inflorescence (Figure 3.6). Nearly 78.84% of the species prefer to feed on the florets of the inflorescence followed by 56.73% of species preferring aster type flowers (have florets smaller in size than that of inflorescence). The least preferred ones are solitary flowers (32.69%) by butterflies.A significant difference was found between the flower type and the number of butterflies preferred for these flowers (ANOVA, F=11.8426; p=1.06E-05). Similarly, there is a significant difference in the preference between families among the different flower type and families of the butterflies ($\chi^2$= 28.728; *P= 0.000*). Furthermore, Papilionid butterflies tend to prefer solitary and inflorescence over asters. And for all other families of butterflies, the inflorescence is most preferred and solitary flowers are least preferred (Figure 3.7).

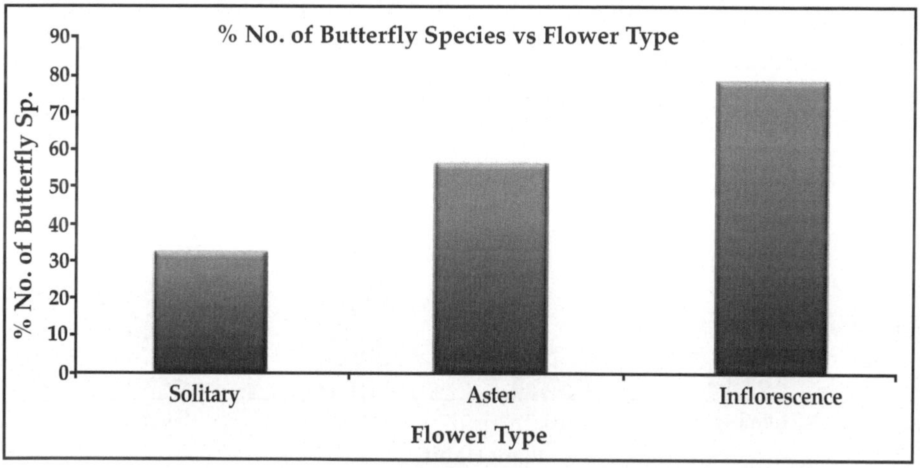


**Fig. 3.6: Preference of Butterflies over the Types of Flowers**

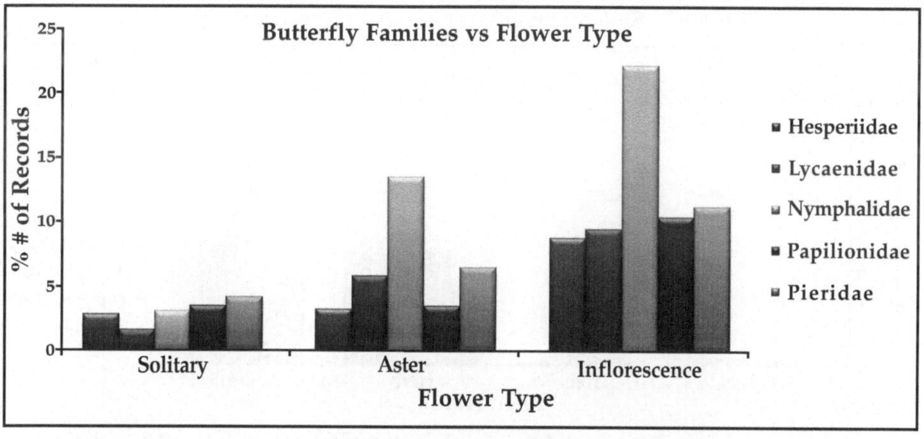


**Fig. 3.7: Type of Flower Preference by the Different Butterflies belonging to the Five Families in Terms of Percent Number of Record/Observations**

### (d) *Plant Habit*

Three quarter of the butterfly species preferred plants which are shrubs. 75.48% of butterfly species prefer shrub habit type of the host plant species to feed on them. The second largest preferred plant-habit type was herb, which is preferred by 69.23 % of the butterfly species. The butterflies did not prefer tree (15.86 %) or climber (12.01 %) type plant hosts very often (Figure 3.8). A significant difference has been occurred between the plant habit and number of butterfly species found utilizing the plants (ANOVA, *F=6.512, P=0.000*). However, the significant difference is also found between the climber and herbs (*T-Test; T=-3.063, P=0.002*) and climber and shrubs (*T-Test; T=-2.99, P=0.003*). Different families of butterflies prefer different plant habit. For example, the Papilionidae and Nympahilidae prefer shrubs to herbs and climber, Lycaenidae tend to favor herbs over shrubs and species belonging to Hesperiidae and Pieridae, did not differ in their preference between herbs and shrubs ($x^2$= *33.343, P=0.000*; Figure 3.9).

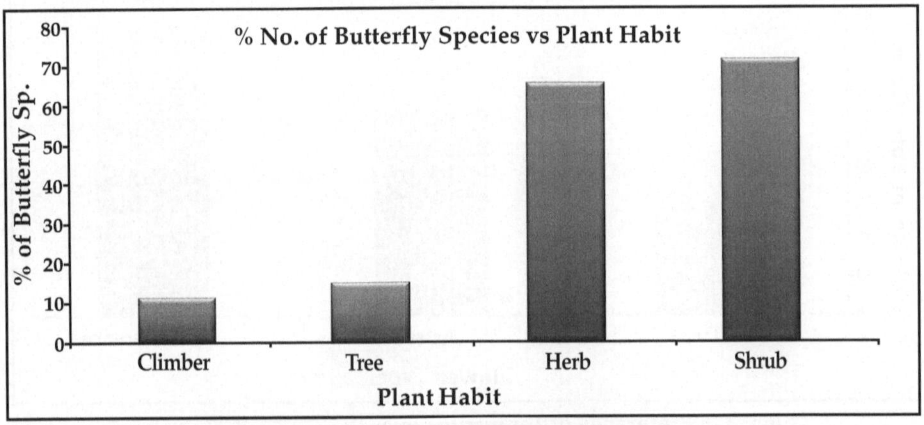


**Fig. 3.8: Graph Representing the Preference of Butterfly Species Over Host Plants of Specific Habits**

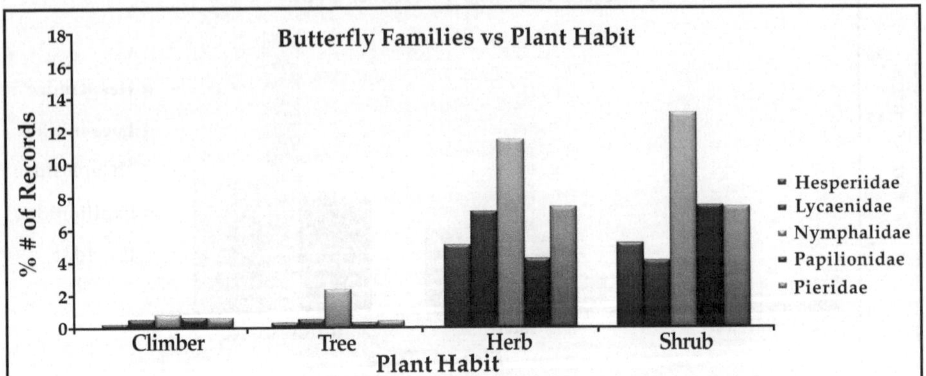


**Fig. 3.9: Host Plant-habit Preference of the different Butterfly Families in terms of Percent Number of Record/Observations**

### (e) *Most preferred plant host*

One hundred thirty three host plant species are recorded in the Western Ghats of India.Among them, ten most preferred plants are considered as important host plants for the butterflies of Western Ghats, India (Table 3.7 and Annexure II).Most of the butterfly species preferred to fed on the flowers of *Lantana camara* (Verbenaceae) withnearly 50% of the species of butterfly found feeding on this introduced and invasive species.This is followed by*Tridaxprocumbens* (25%) and *Chromoleanaodorata* (24.5%) both belonging to Asteraceae family. Interestingly, of the top ten most preferred plants, seven species are exotic and three are native to the Western Ghats. And two species are considered invasive (*Lantana camara*and *Chromoleanaodorata*) (Figure 3.10).

**Table 3.7: Most preferred host plants frequently visited by the butterfly species**

| Sl. No. | Plant Hosts | % Number of Butterfly Species | Status | Habit |
|---|---|---|---|---|
| 1. | *Catharanthusroseus* | 7.69 | Exotic | Shrub |
| 2. | *Celosia argentea* | 12.02 | Exotic | Herb |
| 3. | *Chromolaenaodorata* | 24.52 | Exotic, Invasive | Shrub |
| 4. | *Lantana camara* | 49.52 | Exotic, Invasive | Shrub |
| 5. | *Leeaindica* | 12.50 | Native | Shrub |
| 6. | *Stachytarphetaindica* | 17.31 | Native | Herb |
| 7. | *Tagetessp.* | 13.46 | Exotic | Herb |
| 8. | *Tridaxprocumbens* | 25.00 | Exotic, Weed | Herb |
| 9. | *Wendlandiatinctoria* | 11.54 | Native | Tree |
| 10. | *Zinnia eleganas* | 8.17 | Exotic | Herb |

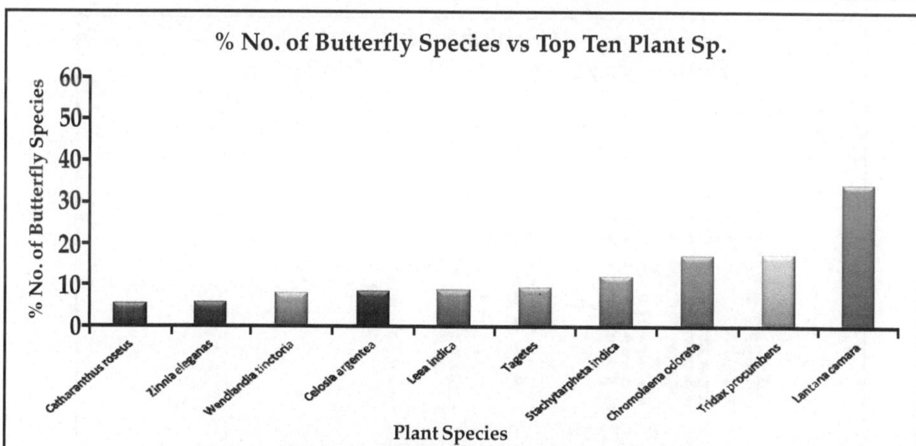


**Fig. 3.10: Top Ten Preferred Host Plants mostly Visited by Butterflies in the Western Ghats**

## Relationship between Plant and Butterfly Variables

### (a) *Proboscis Length and Flower Size*

The positive significant relationship was found between the proboscis length of butterfly species and the flower size of plants ($r$=0.189, $df$=651, $P$<0.05). This showed that butterfly species with longer proboscis preferred bigger flowers with long corolla tubes and those butterfly species with shorter proboscis prefer smaller flowers to some extent (Figure 3.11).

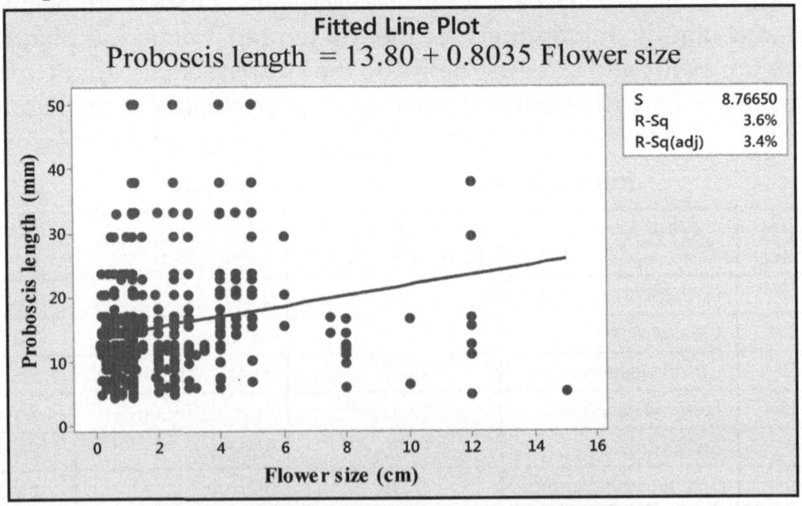


**Fig. 3.11: Correlation between the Proboscis Length of Butterfly species and the Flower Size**

### (b) *Butterfly Size and Flower size*

No significant relationship was found between the size of the butterfly and flower size ($r$=0.111, $df$=1044,$P$>0.05 and Figure 3.12).

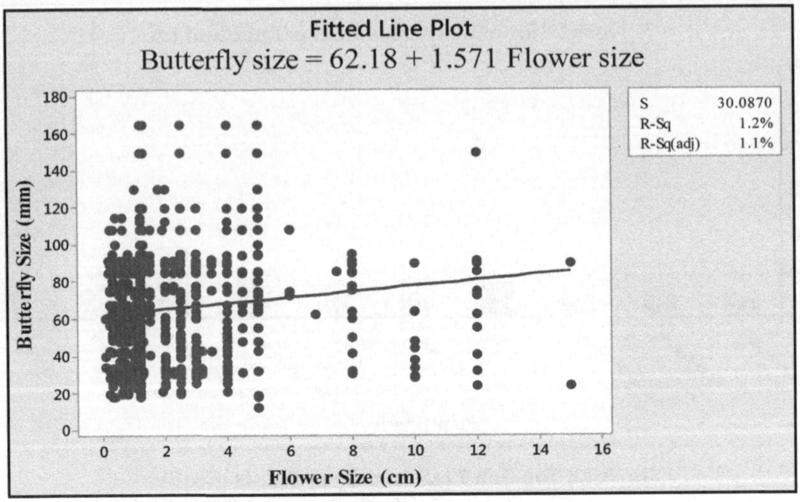


**Fig. 3.12: Relationship between the Size of the Butterfly and Flower Size**

**(c)** ***Butterfly size and Inflorescence size***

Similarly, no significant relationship was found between the size of the butterfly and inflorescence size (*r*=0.1008, *df*=918,*P*>*0.05* and Figure 3.13).

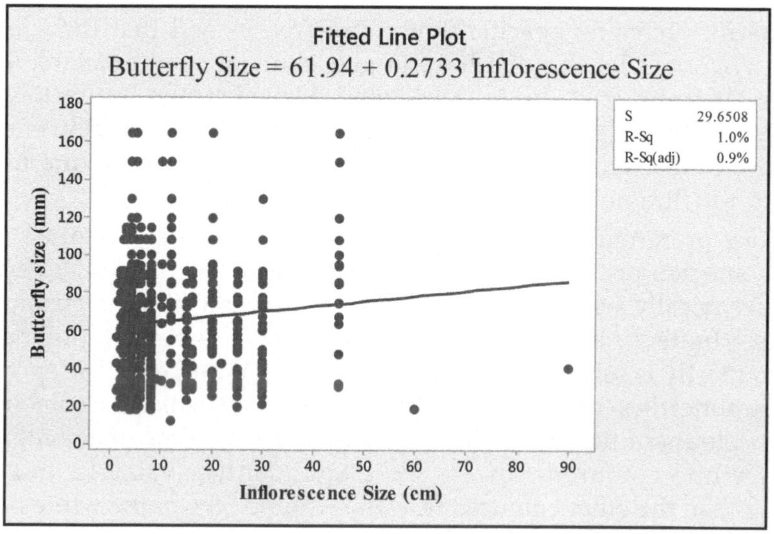


**Fig. 3.13: Relationship between Butterfly Size and Inflorescence Size**

**(d)** ***Butterfly size and number of florets in inflorescence***

Again, no significant relationship was found between the size of the butterfly and the number of florets in inflorescence (*r*=0.004, *df*=918,*P*>*0.05* and Figure 3.14).

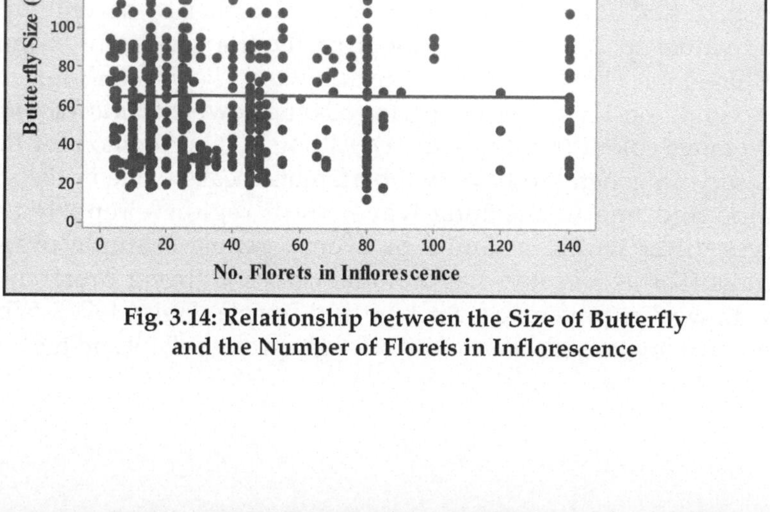


**Fig. 3.14: Relationship between the Size of Butterfly and the Number of Florets in Inflorescence**

## DISCUSSION

During the study analysis, we have analyzed the 1045 number of records belonging to 208 number of butterfly species belonging to five families of butterflies and 133 number of plant species.

Butterflies have no specific flower preferences and that their feeding behavior governed by the distribution and abundance of available nectar resources (Murphy *et al.* 1984; Dosa 1999). However, the butterflies were found to show flower preferences based on the two visual cues-flower colour and shape. Unlike humans, butterflies see colours differently due to their sensitivity to Ultraviolet sources.

Colour preference at community levelrevealed that the most of the butterfly species preferred white coloured flowers (57.69%) overother colours. Technically, when all wavelengths of the visible light spectrum strike the eye of a butterfly at the same time, white colour is perceived. Since, the eye of a butterfly is sensitive to both visible and UV ranges of the spectrum. Hence, the butterflies could easily identify white colour-which is a combination of all the colours of the visible light spectrum. At the time of photography, probably white coloured flowers were abundantly available and more rewarding than the other coloured flowers. Around 58% of the white flowers were found to be clustered flowers. Since the butterflies usually prefer to feed on clustered flowers, this trait added to the preference of white flowers. The butterflies were found to have little attractions to flowers in blue or green range. So it is requiredto see what kind of patterns is exhibited on white flowers under UV light. Also it is interesting to see if all white flowers irrespective of size and shape have same and different patterns which are used to attract butterflies.

Colour preference at family level revealed that different species of butterflies have different colour preferencesof flowers. Hence the members of the different families of the butterflies showed different colour preferences. Nymphalids prefer pink/yellow flowers, Hesperiids prefer pink flowers, Lycaenids and Pieridsprefer white flowers, and Papilionids prefer red flowers. This result showed the diversity in the colour preferences of flowersamong different species of butterflieshas been reported earlier by several workers that at individual species level, the colour preference varies. For example, a study by Freeman (1988) in Mocker Swallowtail (*Papiliodardanus*) under laboratory condition, the butterflies preferred blue flowers,*Phyciodescampestris* preferred orange colour (Pohl *et al.* 2011). Although it is common for flower-visiting insects in general to have two preference peaks – one in the violet–blue region and one in the long-wavelength region – reported color preferences differ within a family or even a genus; example pipe-vine swallowtails (*Battus philenor*, Papilionidae) have a strong preference for yellow, with weaker preferences for blue and purple (Weiss 1997). Whereas in Japanese swallowtails (*Papilioxuthus*) strongly prefer yellow and red colours when offered a choice of red, yellow, green and blue, and foraging citrus swallowtails (*Papiliodemoleus*) prefer purple and blue flower models from amongst a broad array of colors (Ilse and Vaidya 1955). The diversity of preferred flower colours is a function of a number of features, including the visual system of the butterfly, the choice of colors offered by the investigator, the background color and the nature of the ambient illumination.

From the data collected in the study, it was shown that most of the white, pink, pink/yellow flowers were smaller in size. Nymphalids, hesperiids, lycaenids and pierids are small butterflies hence it is convenient for them to feed on small sized flowers. The size of the flower is just an added criterion to the flower colour preference of these butterflies. Furthermore, most of the red coloured flowers were found to be larger in size. Hence, the Papilionids, which are large butterflies, preferred these flowers, because of both the colour-red and large size of the flowers.

In addition to flower colour, characteristics of flowers such as flower shape etc., also very important in determining the flower preferences of butterflies. The flower has to be able to support the weight of the butterfly (in case of large butterflies), and its legs have to be able to latch on to sit on the flower because butterflies don't hover while they feed. The shape of the flower or its florets arrangement may also be a factor in attracting butterflies for feeding.

Most of the butterflies preferred to feed on clustered or inflorescence type flowers. The inflorescence type flowers have many small flowers arranged in a group close to each other. These clustered flowers are a good choice because they offer a place for the butterflies to land and can support their weight. They also provide many sips of nectar close by to make feeding very efficient. Clustered flowers and flowers with spikes that have small, closely packed blooms may attract butterflies because they offer more sips of nectar in one visit.

Apart from inflorescence type of flowers, aster flowers are also preferred by many butterflies. This is because, these aster flowers offer landing space and flat platform for small and medium sized butterflies to sit and extract the resource.

Solitary large flowers will attract butterflies too, although they have a limited amount of nectar in one flower. Solitary flowers may offer less nectar to the butterflies and they will have look for other distant flowers to satisfy their hunger. But when the butterflies land on clustered flowers, they are offered more sips nectar at a shorter distance. From the past experience of butterflies in natural environment that has made them to select less preference to solitary flowers. The length of the corolla tube of the solitary flower is large and because the butterfly has to be able to reach its proboscis inside to drink the nectar and many species has small proboscis hence it might less favored.

All other families except Papilionid butterflies preferred solitary and inflorescence flowers over asters. Because of these large butterflies is that they are not offered a large landing space on asters as on other flower types. In order to avoid the loss of energy due to hovering, the Papilionids prefer to sit on flowers during feeding. Hence, they preferred large solitary flowers and clustered flowers over asters for feeding.

The feeding preferences of butterflies also depend on the habit of the host plant. Most of the species preferred to feed on the flowers of herbs and shrubs over trees and climbers. This could be due to most of the sampling artifact rather the true pattern in nature. Also, many butterfly species are understory species and hence prefer herbs and shrubs and have to spend lot of energy on flightto reach the flowers of the trees. Despite this the butterflies may also reach the canopy height to feed on the flowers of the trees, cost-benefit ratio is less.

Around half of the number of butterfly species preferred to visit the flowers of *Lantana camera* (Verbenaceae) to other plant species. This showed that there is a high preference for this exotic and invasive plant than the other plants as their hosts. *Lantana camara* is a perennial shrub in habit and they have clustered tubular flowers, which bloomed from January to November. Each inflorescence may vary in size from 4 to 5 cm and made up of 15-20 small sized florets. Flowers appears in many different colours including red, yellow, white, pink and orange which differ depending on location, age and maturity. After pollination,changes in occurrence of the coloured flowers (typically from yellow to red/pink/orange) believed to be a signal to pollinators that the pre-change colour contains a reward as well as being sexually viable, thus increasing pollination efficiency. Despite *L.camara*being a serious threat to the wildlife habitat, still it could be slightly excused to grow since most of the butterfly species prefer to feed on their flowers. In butterfly gardens, gardeners grow these plants in large numbers as they attract more butterflies to the garden. The butterflies prefer the flowers of *L.camara* because of their clustered nature. These flowers offer many sips of nectar to the butterflies close by; thus conserving their energy and time to search for new flowers in the locality. The flowers of *L.camara* provide a flat platform for the butterflies to land and feed. Moreover, these plants grow to around 2m in height; hence their flowers are at readily reachable height to the butterflies. The flowers of *L.camara* also have short tubes; hence the nectaries at the base of the tube are readily available to the butterflies.

There is an existenceof the relationship between the proboscis length of butterflies and the flower size. This indicates that butterflies with longer proboscis prefer to feed on large sized flowers and those with shorter proboscis prefer small sized flowers. This is self-explanatory that butterflies with long proboscis can reach the nectaries at the base of long corolla tubes of flowers, whereas butterflies with short proboscis can't reach the nectaries at all.

Larger butterflies usually prefer large flowers and smaller butterflies prefer small flowers. But no such relationship was found to exist between the variables Butterfly size and Flower size in the study. But there is an association between these variables to some extent in nature and this could not be made evident in this study.Likewise, no association was found between butterfly size and inflorescence size, and butterfly size and number of florets in inflorescence. But it is evident that butterflies prefer inflorescence flowers, which have larger number of florets in them.

Overall, the present study is first ever attempt to address the question "what coloured flowers do butterfly prefer?" and this is also a first attempt ever to use citizen science data, which is open access and free to do address this biological question. The present study has two fold uses, (1) a pure academic- which help us understand colour preference and factors associated with it and (2) conservation purpose. The results from this study can be used to design butterfly garden. We can certain that what plants are to be planted in order to attract maximum number of butterflies in the garden.

**Threats for Butterfly communities:** A global network of poachers and smugglers are wiping out threatened species of butterflies. Smugglers entice the locals and school children by paying them rupees fifty for every butterfly they catch. They are then killed, dried and used in greeting cards, wall plate hangings and for other ornamental and decorative purposes. In the international market some species of butterflies like the bird wing butterfly found on the Tiger hill of Jammu and Kashmir is sold at $2500. The yellow colour in the wings of some species is permanent and is used in gold ornaments. The most endangered species are the Giant Swallowtail (*Papilio homerus*), whose velvety black and gold wings are highly prized as decorative agents. In spite of butterflies being protected by international and national laws, butterfly smuggling is rampant in India, especially from the Western Ghats. Lack of expertise in the identification of butterflies (Endeared, rare, threatened species) helps smugglers get away. Such lacuna in the system needs to be corrected with immediate effect (Anand and Pereira 2008). Since the threats to the butterflies are rising at an alarming rate, it is highly essential to devise new strategies to conserve them. Some of the plans proposed for the protection of butterflies are (Anand and Pereira 2008):

- Habitat destruction of forest cover especially for species –specific host plants should be reviewed time to time.
- Increased vigilance on poaching of butterflies from the areas where they are found in abundance.
- Educate school children from primary level by introducing butterfly chapters in science books about their importance in various fields related to human life.
- Recognize and reward those experts who are already engaged in

butterfly conservation programmes and are working on their own as field guides in their area locally.

- Sponsored symposia and seminars in every academic institute for updating information on butterfly status in the country should be encouraged through government funding.
- Farmers in villages should be educated about butterfly's importance as a pollinator in agriculture.
- A data bank at national level should be created where information related to butterflies and their conservation is maintained with all details including regional nomenclature of all butterflies.
- Academic institutions should discourage students for submitting annual projects on butterfly collection and their albums.
- Discourage use of over dose of pesticides in crop fields and avoid overgrazing. They kill eggs and larvae of butterflies.
- Farmers should be made aware about crop rotation and monoculture plantation should be reduced. A study conducted in Assam Tea Estates shows that butterfly density was low in tea gardens because of monoculture as compared to other green forests.

## CONCLUSION

Butterflies have well developed colour vision. They can see colours that we cannot see, because of their sensitivity to the UV light. The adult butterflies mainly prefer to feed on nectar obtained from flowers. The flowers are detected by butterflies using their wide range of perception mechanisms. They use several cue or signals to recognize the flowers producing their favorite taste of nectar. The study is focused on two visual cues namely, flower colour and flower shape/morphology, used by butterflies to recognize their choice of flowers in a natural environment.

Different species of butterflies have different preferences of nectar, in colours, tastes and shapes. Each individual species of butterflies have preference for a particular flower colour since their birth, this flower colour preference is called innate color preference. But due to their experiences and challenges in nature, they may learn to associate with a new coloured flower, which is found to be adequately rewarding in the absence of the innately preferred flower colour. Thus, the flower colour choice by butterflies in the field is likely to reflect an interaction between innate and learned colour preferences.

Apart from the flower colour, the shape and structure of the flower also plays a major role in attracting the butterflies to the flowers. The main aim of the study is to determine the flower colors preferred by butterflies for feeding and the other floral attributes that influence the butterfly visitation.

The significance of the study can be divided into two categories, namely academic and applied. The Academic perspective included determining the flower colour preferences of butterflies as a part of education. The findings of the study add to a growing body of the current literature and form the basis for developing new strategies to conserve them. The out comings obtained from the former study can be used to set up butterfly gardens and this forms the applied perspective of the study.

It is important to conserve butterflies when possible since their habitat is constantly diminishing due to increasing needs and consequent development of roads and housing. As natural butterfly habitats are destroyed and agricultural interests continue to use insecticides that are harmful to the butterfly, gardeners have discovered they can provide new areas called Butterfly Gardens, where these delicate creatures can breed, find food, and lay eggs for future generations to enjoy. In providing for the needs of butterflies, the gardener has the pleasure of watching these colorful insects around them and the opportunity to keep in touch with nature. They also provide additional benefits in opportunities for education and photography and the pure enjoyment of their beauty. And most importantly these gardens can serve as sites of conservation for both endemic and endangered species of the locality.

Since, the butterflies are nearsighted; they are more attracted to large stands of a particular type of flower. For a garden to be most effective, it should contain large splashes of color. The solid masses of color make the flowers easier to locate, and each butterfly has to expend less energy flying from one location to another to acquire the fuel it needs to remain active and grow. The gardens should have a mixture of host plants producing all favorite coloured flowers of the butterflies. Many butterflies seem to navigate to white, pink, yellow and purple coloured flowers. Some species may also show preference to red and orange coloured flowers. Flowers in the blue-green or greenish-blue range are found to be less attractive to butterflies. Thus a butterfly garden should have plants bearing flowers in wide variety of colours, in order to attract more butterflies to the garden.

The study has gone some way towards enhancing our understanding of the colour and flower type preferences of butterflies. This information can be used to set up butterfly conservatories. Building butterfly conservatories are quite easier if one knows the feeding preferences of butterflies, which depend on the different cue signals as mentioned earlier.

This research has also thrown up many questions in need of further investigation. Firstly, to test whether there is any relationship between the sizes of butterflies and flowers. Do larger butterflies prefer larger flowers and vice-versa? Secondly, the environmental constraints which dictate the butterflies to show specific flower colour preferences.

**Future of faunal conservation:** Thus, butterflies are categorized as keystone species, which enable many smaller species of insects to thrive and reproduce in an ecosystem (Patrick 2012). In simple terms, it denotes that conservation of butterflies, also conserves, other species of insects. In fact, the basic health of our ecosystem is directly dependent on the number of butterfly species. Some of the beneficial roles of butterflies in the environment are (Anand and Pereira 2008):

- Act as indicators in monitoring environmental health
- Play an important role in food chains and food webs
- Excellent pollinators
- Bio-control of weeds

Sensitive to pollution and have been used as bio-indicators to detect the pollution levels.

## *REFERENCES*

Anand, T. and Pereira, G.N. (2008). Butterflies –the Flying Jewels of Western Ghats. Retrieved from: http://www.daijiworld.com/chan/exclusive_arch.asp?ex_id=1003. Accessed 2014 Feb 27.

Antram, C.B. (1924). Butterflies of India. Thacker, Spink & Co. Ltd., Calcutta & Simla.

Blair, R.B. (1999). Birds and Butterflies along an Urban Gradient: Surrogate Taxa for Assessing Biodiversity? *Ecological Applications*, 9: 164-170.

Briscoe, A.D. and Chittka, L. (2001). The Evolution of Color Vision in Insects. *Annual Review of Entomology*, 46: 471-510.

Corbet S.A. (2000). Butterfly Nectaring Flowers: Butterfly Morphology and Flower form. *Entomologia Experimentalis at Applicata*, 96: 289-298.

Crane, J. (1955). Imaginal Behavior of a Trinidad Butter-fly, *Heliconius erato hydara* Hewitson, with Special to the Social use of Colour. *Zoologica (N.Y.)*, 40: 167-196.

Devries, P.J. (1990). Enhancement of Symbioses between Butterfly Caterpillars and Ants by Vibrational Communication. *Science*, 248: 1104-1106.

Dosa G. (1999). Flower Visitation Patterns of Butterflies and Burnet Moths in the Aggtelek-Karst (Hungary). *Nota Lepidopterologica*, 22: 58-66.

Fleishman, E., Thomson, J.R., Mac Nally, R., Murphy, D.D. and Fay, J.P. (2005). Using Indicator Species to Predict Species Richness of Multiple Taxonomic Groups. *Conservation Biology*, 19: 1125-1137.

Gadgil, M. (2012). Report of the Western Ghats Ecology Expert Panel. Retrieved from: www.*westernghatindia.org* (Ministry of Environment and Forests, Government of India). Part 1: Summary XIX. Accessed 2014 May 4.

Ilse, D. and Vaidya, V. G. (1955). Spontaneous Feeding Response to Colours in *Papilio demoleus* L. *Proceedings of the Indian Academy of Sciences*, 43: 23-31.

Ilse, D. (1928). Über den Farbensinn der Tagfalter. *Z.f. vergl. Physiologie Bd.*, 8: 658-692.

Jennersten, O. (1984). Flower Visitation and Pollination Efficiency of some North European Butter-flies. *Oecologia* 63: 80-89.

Jolivet, P. (1986). Insects and Plants. Flora & Fauna Handbook, No. 2. E.J. Brill Flora & Fauna Publications, USA. *Journal of Comparative Physiology A*, 161: 891-898.

Kehimkar, I. (2001). Common Indian Wild Flowers. Bombay Natural History Society, Mumbai.

Kehimkar, I. (2008). The Book of Indian Butterflies. Bombay Natural History Society, Mumbai.

Kunte, K. (2000). Butterflies of Peninsular India. University Press (India) Pvt. Ltd., Hyderabad and Indian Academy of Sciences, Bangalore.

Mac Nally, R. and E. Fleishman. (2004). A Successful Predictive Model of Species Richness based on Indicator Species. *Conservation Biology*, 18: 646-634.

Mennechez, G., Schtickzelle, N. and Baguette, M. (2003). Metapopulation Dynamics of the Bog Fritillary Butterfly: Comparison of Demographic Taxonomic Groups. *Conservation Biology*, 19: 1125-1137.

Murphy D.D., Menninger M.S. and Ehrlich P.R. (1984). Nectar Source Distribution as a Determinant of Oviposition Host Species in *Euphydryas chalcedona*. *Oecologia*, 56: 269-271.

Padhye, A.D., Dahanukar, N., Paingaonkar, M., Deshpande, M. and Deshpande, D. (2006). Season and Landscape wise Distribution of Parameters and Dispersal between a Continuous and a Highly Fragmented Landscape. *Landscape Ecology*, 18: 279-291.

Pariset L. and Racheli T. (1998). Flower Preference, Colour Choice, and Voltinism in some Mediterranean Butterflies. *The Abstracts of XIth European Congress of Lepidopterology, (Malle) Belgium*: 81.

Patrick. B. (2012). Butterflies and Moths - Habitat and Ecological Roles. *Te Ara - the Encyclopedia of New Zealand*. 5-9.

Pohl, N., Van Wyk, J. and Campbell, D. (2011). Butterflies Show Flower Preferences but not Constancy. *Ecological Entomology*, 36: 290-300.

Pollard, E. (1991). Synchrony of Population Fluctuations: The Dominant Influence of Widespread Factors on Local Butterfly Populations. *Oikos*, 60: 7-10.

Porter K., Steel C.A. and Thomas J.A. (1992). Butterflies and Communities. In: *The Ecology of Butterflies in Britain*. (Dennis R.L.H., ed.), 139-177, University Press, Oxford, New York, Tokyo.

Proctor, M. and Yeo, P. (1975). The Pollination of Flowers. London: Collins Reference to the Social use of Colour. *Zoologica* (N.Y.), 40: 167-196.

Sharp M.A., Parks D.R. and Ehrlich P.R. (1974). Plant Resources and Habitat Selection. Ecology 55: 870-875.

Silberglied, R.E. (1984). Visual Communication and Sexual Selection among Butterflies. In The Biology of Butterflies (ed. R.I. Vane-Wright and P.R. Ackery). New Jersey: Princeton University Press. 207-223.

Weiss M.R. (1997). Innate Colour Preferences and Flexible Colour Learning in the Pipevine Swallow-tail. *Animal Behaviour*, 53: 1043-1052.

# ANNEXURE - I

## List of Butterfly Species Recorded

| Sl. No. | Family | Common Name | Scientific Name |
|---|---|---|---|
| (1) | (2) | (3) | (4) |
| 1. | Hesperiidae | Bevan's Swift | *Pseudoborbo bevani* |
| 2. | Hesperiidae | Bispot Banded Ace | *Halpe porus* |
| 3. | Hesperiidae | Branded Swift | *Pelopidas sp.* |
| 4. | Hesperiidae | Brown Awl | *Badamia exclamationis* |
| 5. | Hesperiidae | Bush Hopper | *Ampittia dioscorides* |
| 6. | Hesperiidae | Ceylon Palm Bob | *Suastus sp.* |
| 7. | Hesperiidae | Chestnut Bob | *Lambrix salsala* |
| 8. | Hesperiidae | Common Awl | *Hasora badra* |
| 9. | Hesperiidae | Common Banded Awl | *Hasora chromus* |
| 10. | Hesperiidae | Common Banded Demon | *Notocrypta paralysos* |
| 11. | Hesperiidae | Common Grass Dart | *Taractrocera maevius* |
| 12. | Hesperiidae | Common Small Flat | *Sarangesa dasahara* |
| 13. | Hesperiidae | Common Snow Flat | *Tagiades japetus* |
| 14. | Hesperiidae | Common Spotted Flat | *Celaenorrhinus leucocera* |
| 15. | Hesperiidae | Conjoined Swift | *Pelopidas conjuncta* |
| 16. | Hesperiidae | Dark Branded Swift | *Pelopidas agna* |
| 17. | Hesperiidae | Dark Palm Dart | *Telicota ancilla* |
| 18. | Hesperiidae | Dusky Spotted Flat | *Celaenorrhinus fusca* |
| 19. | Hesperiidae | Essex Skipper | *Thymelicus lineola* |
| 20. | Hesperiidae | Fulvous Pied Flat | *Pseudocoladenia dan* |
| 21. | Hesperiidae | Golden Tree Flitter | *Quedara basiflava* |
| 22. | Hesperiidae | Golden Angle | *Caprona ransonnetti* |
| 23. | Hesperiidae | Grass Demon | *Udaspes folus* |
| 24. | Hesperiidae | Indian Ace | *Halpe homolea* |
| 25. | Hesperiidae | Indian Awlking | *Choaspes benjaminii* |
| 26. | Hesperiidae | Indian Palm Bob | *Suastus gremius* |
| 27. | Hesperiidae | Indian Skipper | *Spialia galba* |
| 28. | Hesperiidae | Karwar Swift | *Caltoris canaraica* |
| 29. | Hesperiidae | Malabar Spotted Flat | *Celaenorrhinus ambareesa* |
| 30. | Hesperiidae | Paintbrush Swift | *Baoris farri* |
| 31. | Hesperiidae | Palm Bob | *Suastus minutus* |

(Contd...)

| (1) | (2) | (3) | (4) |
|---|---|---|---|
| 32. | Hesperiidae | Palm Dart | *Telicota ancilla* |
| 33. | Hesperiidae | Plain Banded Awl | *Hasora vita* |
| 34. | Hesperiidae | Restricted Demon | *Notocrypta curvifascia* |
| 35. | Hesperiidae | Rice Swift | *Borbo cinnara* |
| 36. | Hesperiidae | Sahyadri Banded Ace | *Halpe hindu* |
| 37. | Hesperiidae | Sahyadri Black Angle/flat | *Tapena twaithesi* |
| 38. | Hesperiidae | Small Branded Swift | *Pelopidas mathias* |
| 39. | Hesperiidae | Spotted Small Flat | *Sarangesa purendra* |
| 40. | Hesperiidae | Suffused Snow Flat | *Tagiades gana* |
| 41. | Hesperiidae | Tamil Dartlet | *Oriens concinna* |
| 42. | Hesperiidae | Tamil Grass Dart | *Taractrocera ceramas* |
| 43. | Hesperiidae | Tamil Spotted Flat | *Celaenorrhinus ruficornis* |
| 44. | Hesperiidae | Tawny Spotted Grass Dart | *Taractrocera ceramas nicevillei* |
| 45. | Hesperiidae | Tri-coloured Pied flat | *Coladenia indrani* |
| 46. | Hesperiidae | Vindhyan Bob | *Arnetta vindhiana* |
| 47. | Hesperiidae | Water Snow Flat | *Tagiades litigiosa* |
| 48. | Hesperiidae | White Banded Awl | *Hasora taminatus* |
| 49. | Hesperiidae | Yellow Spot Swift | *Polytremis eltola* |
| 50. | Lycaenidae | Angled Pierrot | *Caleta decidia* |
| 51. | Lycaenidae | Apefly | *Spalgis epius* |
| 52. | Lycaenidae | Balkan Pierrot | *Tarucus balkanicus* |
| 53. | Lycaenidae | Banded Blue Pierrot | *Discolampa ethion* |
| 54. | Lycaenidae | Blue bordered Plane | *Bindahara moorei* |
| 55. | Lycaenidae | Centaur Oakblue | *Arhopala centaurus* |
| 56. | Lycaenidae | Club SilverLine | *Spindasis syama* |
| 57. | Lycaenidae | Common Cerulean | *Jamides celeno* |
| 58. | Lycaenidae | Common Guava Blue | *Virachola Isocrates* |
| 59. | Lycaenidae | Common Hedge Blue | *Acytolepis puspa* |
| 60. | Lycaenidae | Common Pierrot | *Castalius rosimon* |
| 61. | Lycaenidae | Common Silverline | *Spindasis vulcanus* |
| 62. | Lycaenidae | Continental Green Flash | *Artipe eryx eryx* |
| 63. | Lycaenidae | Cornelian | *Deudorix epijarbas* |
| 64. | Lycaenidae | Dark Cerulean | *Jamides bochus* |
| 65. | Lycaenidae | Dark Grass Blue | *Zizeeria karsandra* |
| 66. | Lycaenidae | Eastern Large Hedge Blue | *Celastrina oreana* |

(Contd...)

| (1) | (2) | (3) | (4) |
|---|---|---|---|
| 67. | Lycaenidae | Forget Me Not | *Catochrysops Strabo* |
| 68. | Lycaenidae | Golden Sapphire | *Heliophorus brahma* |
| 69. | Lycaenidae | Gram Blue | *Euchrysops cnejus* |
| 70. | Lycaenidae | Grass Jewel | *Freyeria trochylus* |
| 71. | Lycaenidae | Indian Cupid | *Everes lacturnus* |
| 72. | Lycaenidae | Indian Plains Blue Royal | *Tajuria jehana* |
| 73. | Lycaenidae | Indian Red Flash | *Rapala airbus* |
| 74. | Lycaenidae | Indian Sunbeam | *Curetis thetis* |
| 75. | Lycaenidae | Indigo Flash | *Rapala varuna* |
| 76. | Lycaenidae | Large Oak Blue | *Arhopala amantes* |
| 77. | Lycaenidae | Lesser Grass Blue | *Zizina otis* |
| 78. | Lycaenidae | Lime Blue | *Chilades lajus lajus* |
| 79. | Lycaenidae | Long Banded Silverline | *Spindasis lohita* |
| 80. | Lycaenidae | Longtailed Pea Blue | *Lampides boeticus var.* |
| 81. | Lycaenidae | Malabar Flash | *Rapala lankana* |
| 82. | Lycaenidae | Malayan | *Megisba Malaya* |
| 83. | Lycaenidae | Metallic Cerulean | *Jamides alecto* |
| 84. | Lycaenidae | Pea Blue | *Lampides boeticus* |
| 85. | Lycaenidae | Peacock Royal | *Tajuria cippus* |
| 86. | Lycaenidae | Plain Hedge Blue | *Celastrina lavendularis* |
| 87. | Lycaenidae | Plains Cupid | *Chilades pandava pandava* |
| 88. | Lycaenidae | Plane | *Bindahara phocides* |
| 89. | Lycaenidae | Quaker | *Neopithecops zalmora* |
| 90. | Lycaenidae | Red Pierrot | *Talicada nyseus* |
| 91. | Lycaenidae | Rounded Pierrot | *Tarucus nara* |
| 92. | Lycaenidae | Slate Flash | *Rapala manea* |
| 93. | Lycaenidae | Small Cupid | *Chilades parrhasius* |
| 94. | Lycaenidae | Tail-less Line Blue | *Prosotas dubiosa indica* |
| 95. | Lycaenidae | Tiny Grass Blue | *Zizula hylax* |
| 96. | Lycaenidae | Tranparent 6-Lineblue | *Nacaduba kurava* |
| 97. | Lycaenidae | Zebra Blue | *Leptotes plinius* |
| 98. | Nymphalidae | Angled Castor | *Ariadne ariadne* |
| 99. | Nymphalidae | Autumn Leaf | *Doleschallia bisaltide* |
| 100. | Nymphalidae | Bengal Leopard Lacewing | *Cethosia cyane* |
| 101. | Nymphalidae | Black Rajah | *Charaxes solon* |

(Contd...)

| (1) | (2) | (3) | (4) |
|---|---|---|---|
| 102. | Nymphalidae | Blue Nawab | *Polyura schreiber wardii* |
| 103. | Nymphalidae | Blue Pansy | *Junonia orithya* |
| 104. | Nymphalidae | Blue Tiger | *Tirumala limniace* |
| 105. | Nymphalidae | Brown King Crow | *Euploea klugii kollari* |
| 106. | Nymphalidae | Ceylon Tiger | *Parantica taprobana* |
| 107. | Nymphalidae | Chestnut Streaked Sailer | *Neptis jumbah* |
| 108. | Nymphalidae | Chocolate Pansy | *Junonia iphita* |
| 109. | Nymphalidae | Clipper | *Parthenos sylvia* |
| 110. | Nymphalidae | Commander | *Moduza procris* |
| 111. | Nymphalidae | Common Baron | *Euthalia aconthea* |
| 112. | Nymphalidae | Common Bush Brown | *Mycalesis perseus* |
| 113. | Nymphalidae | Common Castor | *Ariadne merione* |
| 114. | Nymphalidae | Common Crow | *Euploea core* |
| 115. | Nymphalidae | Common Evening Brown | *Melanitis leda* |
| 116. | Nymphalidae | Common Five Ring | *Ypthima baldus* |
| 117. | Nymphalidae | Common Jester | *Symbrenthia lilaea* |
| 118. | Nymphalidae | Common Leopard | *Phalanta phalantha* |
| 119. | Nymphalidae | Common Nawab | *Polyura athamas* |
| 120. | Nymphalidae | Common Sailer | *Neptis hylas varmona* |
| 121. | Nymphalidae | Common Three Ring | *Ypthima asterope* |
| 122. | Nymphalidae | Cruiser | *Vindula erota* |
| 123. | Nymphalidae | Dakhan Common Caster | *Ariadne merione* |
| 124. | Nymphalidae | Danaid Eggfly | *Hypolimnas misippus* |
| 125. | Nymphalidae | Dark Blue Tiger | *Tirumala septentrionis* |
| 126. | Nymphalidae | Double Branded Crow | *Euploea sylvester* |
| 127. | Nymphalidae | Glassy Tiger | *Parantica aglea* |
| 128. | Nymphalidae | Grey Pansy | *Junonia atlites* |
| 129. | Nymphalidae | Indian Fritillary | *Argyreus hyperbius* |
| 130. | Nymphalidae | Indian Red Admiral | *Vanessa indica* |
| 131. | Nymphalidae | Indian Tortoise Shell | *Aglais cashmiriensis* |
| 132. | Nymphalidae | Lemon Pansy | *Junonia lemonias* |
| 133. | Nymphalidae | Leopard Lacewing | *Cethosia cyane* |
| 134. | Nymphalidae | Malabar Tree Nymph | *Idea malabarica* |
| 135. | Nymphalidae | Nilgiri Fritillary | *Argynnis hybrid* |
| 136. | Nymphalidae | Nilgiri Tiger | *Parantica melaneus* |

(Contd...)

| (1) | (2) | (3) | (4) |
|---|---|---|---|
| 137. | Nymphalidae | Painted Lady | *Vanessa cardui* |
| 138. | Nymphalidae | Peacock Pansy | *Junonia almanac* |
| 139. | Nymphalidae | Plain Tiger | *Danaus chrysippus* |
| 140. | Nymphalidae | Red disc Bushbrown | *Mycalesis oculus* |
| 141. | Nymphalidae | Red Lacewing | *Cethosia biblis* |
| 142. | Nymphalidae | Ringlet | *Aphantopus hyperantus* |
| 143. | Nymphalidae | Sahyadri Gaudy Baron | *Euthalia lubentina* |
| 144. | Nymphalidae | Southern Rustic | *Cupha erymanthis* |
| 145. | Nymphalidae | Striped Tiger | *Danaus genutia* |
| 146. | Nymphalidae | Tamil Lacewing | *Cethosia nietneri* |
| 147. | Nymphalidae | Tamil Yeoman | *Cirrochroa thais* |
| 148. | Nymphalidae | Tawny Coster | *Acraea terpsicore* |
| 149. | Nymphalidae | Vagrant | *Vagrans egista* |
| 150. | Nymphalidae | White Fourring | *Ypthima ceylonica* |
| 151. | Nymphalidae | Yellow Pansy | *Junonia hierta* |
| 152. | Papilionidae | Andaman Clubtail | *Atrophaneura rhodifer* |
| 153. | Papilionidae | Blue Mormon | *Papilio polymnestor* |
| 154. | Papilionidae | Common Banded Peacock | *Papilio crino* |
| 155. | Papilionidae | Common Bluebottle | *Graphium sarpedon* |
| 156. | Papilionidae | Common Jay | *Graphium doson* |
| 157. | Papilionidae | Common Mime | *Chilasa clytia* |
| 158. | Papilionidae | Common Mormon | *Papilio polytes* |
| 159. | Papilionidae | Common Rose | *Pachliopta aristolochiae* |
| 160. | Papilionidae | Crimson Rose | *Pachliopta hector* |
| 161. | Papilionidae | Fivebar Swordtail | *Graphium antiphates* |
| 162. | Papilionidae | Green Banded Peacock | *Papilio palinurus* |
| 163. | Papilionidae | Lime Butterfly | *Papilio demoleus* |
| 164. | Papilionidae | Malabar Banded Peacock | *Papilio buddha* |
| 165. | Papilionidae | Malabar Banded Swallowtail | *Papilio liomedon* |
| 166. | Papilionidae | Malabar Raven | *Papilio dravidarum* |
| 167. | Papilionidae | Paris Peacock | *Papilio paris* |
| 168. | Papilionidae | Red Helen | *Papilio helenus* |
| 169. | Papilionidae | Southern Birdwing | *Troides minos* |
| 170. | Papilionidae | Spot Swordtail | *Graphium nomius* |
| 171. | Papilionidae | Tailed Jay | *Graphium agamemnon* |

(Contd…)

| (1) | (2) | (3) | (4) |
|---|---|---|---|
| 172. | Pieridae | Chocolate Albatross | *Appias lyncida* |
| 173. | Pieridae | Cloudless Sulphur | *Phoebis sennae* |
| 174. | Pieridae | Common Albatross | *Appias albino* |
| 175. | Pieridae | Common Emigrant | *Catopsilia pomona* |
| 176. | Pieridae | Common Grass Yellow | *Eurema hecabe* |
| 177. | Pieridae | Common Gull | *Cepora nerissa* |
| 178. | Pieridae | Common Jezebel | *Delias eucharis* |
| 179. | Pieridae | Common Wanderer | *Pareronia valeria* |
| 180. | Pieridae | Crimson Tip | *Colotis danae* |
| 181. | Pieridae | Dark Clouded Yellow | *Colias fieldii* |
| 182. | Pieridae | Dark Wanderer | *Pareronia ceylanica* |
| 183. | Pieridae | Eastern Striped Albatross | *Appias olferna* |
| 184. | Pieridae | Great Orange Tip | *Hebomoia glaucippe* |
| 185. | Pieridae | Green Veined White | *Pieris napi* |
| 186. | Pieridae | Indian Cabbage White | *Pieris canidia* |
| 187. | Pieridae | Large Cabbage White | *Pieris brassicae* |
| 188. | Pieridae | Large Salmon Arab | *Colotis fausta* |
| 189. | Pieridae | Lesser Gull | *Cepora nadina* |
| 190. | Pieridae | Mottled Emigrant | *Catopsilia pyranthe* |
| 191. | Pieridae | Nilgiri Clouded Yellow | *Colias nilgiriensis* |
| 192. | Pieridae | One Spot Grass Yellow | *Eurema andersonii* |
| 193. | Pieridae | Painted Jezebel | *Delias hyparete* |
| 194. | Pieridae | Pioneer | *Belenois aurota* |
| 195. | Pieridae | Plain Orange Tip | *Colotis eucharis* |
| 196. | Pieridae | Plain Puffin | *Appias indra* |
| 197. | Pieridae | Psyche | *Leptosia nina* |
| 198. | Pieridae | Sahyadri Great Orange Tip | *Hebomoia glaucippe australis* |
| 199. | Pieridae | Small Grass Yellow | *Eurema brigitta* |
| 200. | Pieridae | Small Orange Tip | *Colotis etrida* |
| 201. | Pieridae | Small Salmon Arab | *Colotis amata* |
| 202. | Pieridae | Spot Puffin | *Appias lalage* |
| 203. | Pieridae | Spotless Grass Yellow | *Eurema laeta* |
| 204. | Pieridae | Striped Albatross | *Appias libythea* |
| 205. | Pieridae | Three Spot Grass Yellow | *Eurema blanda* |
| 206. | Pieridae | Tree Yellow | *Gandaca harina* |
| 207. | Pieridae | White Orange Tip | *Ixias Marianne* |
| 208. | Pieridae | Yellow Orange Tip | *Ixias pyrene* |

# ANNEXURE - II

## List of Host-Plant Species Recorded

| Sl. No. | Family | Plant Name (Scientific Name) |
|---|---|---|
| (1) | (2) | (3) |
| 1. | Acanthaceae | *Acanthus sp.* |
| 2. | Acanthaceae | *Asistacia gagetica* |
| 3. | Acanthaceae | *Diotacanthus grandis* |
| 4. | Acanthaceae | *Justicia procumbens* |
| 5. | Acanthaceae | *Justicia simplex* |
| 6. | Acanthaceae | *Strobilanthus* |
| 7. | Amaranthaceae | *Alternathera sessilis* |
| 8. | Amaranthaceae | *Amaranthus sp.* |
| 9. | Amaranthaceae | *Celosia argentea* |
| 10. | Amaranthaceae | *Gomphrena globosa* |
| 11. | Anacardiaceae | *Semecarpus kathalekanensis* |
| 12. | Apiaceae | *Daucus carota* |
| 13. | Apocynaceae | *Calotropis gigantea* |
| 14. | Apocynaceae | *Carissa congesta* |
| 15. | Apocynaceae | *Catharanthus roseus* |
| 16. | Apocynaceae | *Tabernaemontana* |
| 17. | Asclepediaceae | *Asclepias curassavica* |
| 18. | Asclepediaceae | *Asclepias tuberosa* |
| 19. | Asteraceae | *Ageratum conyzoides* |
| 20. | Asteraceae | *Anaphalis margaritacea* |
| 21. | Asteraceae | *Arnica angustifolia* |
| 22. | Asteraceae | *Aster sp.(creeper)* |
| 23. | Asteraceae | *Aster sp.(herb)* |
| 24. | Asteraceae | *Aster albescens* |
| 25. | Asteraceae | *Aster lanceolatus* |
| 26. | Asteraceae | *Aster linosyris* |
| 27. | Asteraceae | *Carduus nutans* |
| 28. | Asteraceae | *Centaurea orientalis* |
| 29. | Asteraceae | *Chromolaena odorata* |
| 30. | Asteraceae | *Chrysanthemum* |
| 31. | Asteraceae | *Cosmos bipinnatus* |
| 32. | Asteraceae | *Cosmos sulphureus* |
| 33. | Asteraceae | *Dahlia sp.* |

(Contd...)

| (1) | (2) | (3) |
|---|---|---|
| 34. | Asteraceae | *Grindelia squarrosa* |
| 35. | Asteraceae | *Helianthus annuus* |
| 36. | Asteraceae | *Matricaria maritima* |
| 37. | Asteraceae | *Mikania micrantha* |
| 38. | Asteraceae | *Parthenium sp.* |
| 39. | Asteraceae | *Pseudogynoxis chenopodioides* |
| 40. | Asteraceae | *Ratibida columnifera* |
| 41. | Asteraceae | *Rudbeckia subtomentosa* |
| 42. | Asteraceae | *Sencio bombayenesis* |
| 43. | Asteraceae | *Senecio confusus* |
| 44. | Asteraceae | *Senecio grahami* |
| 45. | Asteraceae | *Senecio triangularis* |
| 46. | Asteraceae | *Synedrella nodiflora* |
| 47. | Asteraceae | *Tagetes sp.* |
| 48. | Asteraceae | *Tagetes erecta* |
| 49. | Asteraceae | *Tagetes patula* |
| 50. | Asteraceae | *Tithonia rotundifolia* |
| 51. | Asteraceae | *Tridax procumbens* |
| 52. | Asteraceae | *Wedelia trilobata* |
| 53. | Asteraceae | *Wedelia uticaefolia* |
| 54. | Asteraceae | *Zinnia sp.* |
| 55. | Asteraceae | *Zinnia eleganas* |
| 56. | Balsaminaceae | *Impatiens balsamina* |
| 57. | Boraginaceae | *Heliotropium indicum* |
| 58. | Brassicaceae | *Lobularia maritima* |
| 59. | Combretaceae | *Terminalia crenulata* |
| 60. | Combretaceae | *Terminalia sp* |
| 61. | Commelinaceae | *Commelina communis* |
| 62. | Convolvulaceae | *Ipomoea sp.* |
| 63. | Cornaceae | *Cornus alternifolia* |
| 64. | Cornaceae | *Nyssa sp.* |
| 65. | Costaceae | *Costus sp.* |
| 66. | Crassulaceae | *Kalanchoe sp.* |
| 67. | Cucurbitaceae | *Momordica dioica* |
| 68. | Cucurbitaceae | *Solena heterophylla* |
| 69. | Euphorbiaceae | *Jatropha curcas* |
| 70. | Euphorbiaceae | *Jatropha gossypifolia* |

(Contd...)

| (1) | (2) | (3) |
|---|---|---|
| 71. | Euphorbiaceae | *Phyllanthus emblica* |
| 72. | Fabaceae | *Acacia caesia* |
| 73. | Fabaceae | *Bauhinia purpurea* |
| 74. | Fabaceae | *Caesalpinia pulcherrima* |
| 75. | Fabaceae | *Cassia auriculata* |
| 76. | Fabaceae | *Clitoria annua* |
| 77. | Fabaceae | *Crotalaria sp.* |
| 78. | Fabaceae | *Crotalaria juncea* |
| 79. | Fabaceae | *Dalbergia latifolia* |
| 80. | Fabaceae | *Tephrosia purpurea* |
| 81. | Gentianaceae | *Gentiana sp.* |
| 82. | Icacinaceae | *Mappia foetida* |
| 83. | Lamiaceae | *Hyptis suaveolens* |
| 84. | Lamiaceae | *Lucas aspera* |
| 85. | Lamiaceae | *Pogostemon deccanensis* |
| 86. | Lamiaceae | *Vitex negundo* |
| 87. | Lauraceae | *Litsea insignis* |
| 88. | Lauraceae | *Litsea wightiana* |
| 89. | Leeaceae | *Leea indica* |
| 90. | Liliaceae | *Gloriosa superba* |
| 91. | Liliaceae | *Lilium sp.* |
| 92. | Malvaceae | *Hibiscus rosa-sinensis* |
| 93. | Malvaceae | *Malvaceae Climber* |
| 94. | Malvaceae | *Sida acuta* |
| 95. | Malvaceae | *Urena lobata* |
| 96. | Mimosaceae | *Acacia pennata* |
| 97. | Mimosaceae | *Mimosa pudica* |
| 98. | Muntingiaceae | *Muntingia calabura* |
| 99. | Myrtaceae | *Callistemon citrinus* |
| 100. | Nyctaginaceae | *Bougainvillea sp.* |
| 101. | Oleaceae | *Jasminum grandiflorum* |
| 102. | Oleaceae | *Jasminum malabaricum* |
| 103. | Orchidaceae | *Dendrobium sp.* |
| 104. | Oxalidaceae | *Oxalis sp.* |
| 105. | Passifloraceae | *Passiflora sp.* |
| 106. | Polygonaceae | *Antigonon sp.* |
| 107. | Rhamnaceae | *Zizyphus oenoplia* |

(Contd...)

| (1) | (2) | (3) |
|---|---|---|
| 108. | Rubiaceae | *Borreria sp.* |
| 109. | Rubiaceae | *Borreria verticillata* |
| 110. | Rubiaceae | *Coffea arabica* |
| 111. | Rubiaceae | *Ixora sp.* |
| 112. | Rubiaceae | *Ixora sp.(exotic)* |
| 113. | Rubiaceae | *Ixora coccinea* |
| 114. | Rubiaceae | *Mussaenda galbrata* |
| 115. | Rubiaceae | *Oldenlandia corymbosa* |
| 116. | Rubiaceae | *Pentas sp.* |
| 117. | Rubiaceae | *Pentas lanceolata* |
| 118. | Rubiaceae | *Wendlandia tinctoria* |
| 119. | Rutaceae | *Murraya koenigii* |
| 120. | Solanaceae | *Datura sp.* |
| 121. | Thymeleaceae | *Gnidia glauca* |
| 122. | Tiliaceae | *Tilia sp.* |
| 123. | Verbenaceae | *Clerodendrum paniculatum* |
| 124. | Verbenaceae | *Clerodendrum serratum* |
| 125. | Verbenaceae | *Clerodendrum thomsonii* |
| 126. | Verbenaceae | *Clerodendrum viscosum* |
| 127. | Verbenaceae | *Duranta sp.* |
| 128. | Verbenaceae | *Duranta erecta* |
| 129. | Verbenaceae | *Lantana camara* |
| 130. | Verbenaceae | *Stachytarpheta indica* |
| 131. | Verbenaceae | *Verbena sp.* |
| 132. | Verbenaceae | *Verbena bonariensis* |
| 133. | Zingeberaceae | *Globba ophioglossa* |

Pages: 76-99

FOREST AND BIODIVERSITY CONSERVATION
*Edited by:* **Dr. Alka Chauhan** and **Dr. Pawan Kumar 'Bharti'**
**ISBN: 978-93-5056-873-6**
*Edition:* **2017**
*Published by:* **Discovery Publishing House Pvt. Ltd., New Delhi (India)**

# 4 Biodiversity Conservation in India

*Pulak Kumar Patra*


## *ABSTRACT*

Biodiversity refers to the variety and variability among the living organisms. It is generally expressed at three levels *i.e.* genetic diversity, species diversity and ecosystem diversity. To ensure region based conservation approach, India has developed a biogeographic classification for its land area which recognizes 10 zones, divided into 27 provinces. The benefits derived by humans from biodiversity is due its consumptive use, productive use, Ecosystem services, aesthetics & recreational use, Ethical & Moral value, Social value and Option value. About 1.8 million species (excluding bacteria) have been identified and named so far which represents a fraction of the total biodiversity. The distribution of biodiversity is also not uniform. Most macroscopic organisms have small, often cclustered geographical ranges. India's biological diversity is one of the most significant in the world. With only 2.4% of the world's land area, India harbours 7-8% of all recorded species. Of the 34 global biodiversity hotspots, India accommodates part of four hotspots *i.e.* the Himalayas, the Western Ghats, Indo- Burma and Sundaland.

The destruction of habitats is the primary reason for the loss of biodiversity. Habitat loss is mainly due to human population growth, industrialization and changes in the land use patterns. Other threats to biodiversity loss are over-exploitation of resource, poaching or illegal hunting, man- wild life conflicts and climate change. Conservation actions include activities associated with scientific resource management such as research, census, legislation, law enforcement, habitat maintenance and propagation of species. It includes both curative and preventive measures. The two basic strategies of biodiversity conservation are *in situ* (on site) and *ex situ* (off site) conservation.


Dept. of Environmental Studies, Visva-Bharati, Santiniketan - 731 235 (WB) (India)

The Convention on Biological Diversity (CBD) formed in 1993 works towards conservation and sustainable uses of biodiversity. India has shown her commitment to biodiversity conservation through the Biological Diversity Act, 2002.

## INTRODUCTION

Biodiversity refers to the variety and variability among the living organisms and the ecosystems they inhabit. It has been defined as "the variability among living organisms from all sources, including, *'inter alia'*, terrestrial, marine, and other aquatic ecosystems and the ecological complexes of which they are part: this includes diversity within species, between species and of ecosystems". A large variety of animals, plants and microorganisms live in air, water and on land in different parts of the earth. These organisms are interdependent and have their specific roles in maintaining the equilibrium in the biosphere. So loss of any single organism may affect the balance of the ecosystem, which is vital for the well being of humans. However, we are losing the biodiversity at an alarmingly fast rate, for which human intervention is the main cause. With increasing awareness of the value of biodiversity, many affirmative steps are being taken to protect the biodiversity. In this paper we discuss the important issues involving biodiversity and its conservation.

## LEVELS OF BIODIVERSITY

Biodiversity is generally expressed at three levels *i.e.* genetic diversity, species diversity and ecosystem diversity.

**Species Diversity:** Species is the fundamental unit of classification of the organisms and generally represents the group of individuals which can interbreed among themselves. Species diversity refers to the variety of species within a community or ecosystem. Simplest measure of species diversity is species richness, *i.e.* the number of species living in an area. Each species plays a specific role in an ecosystem and its loss has consequences for the ecosystem as a whole.

**Genetic Diversity:** Genetic diversity refers to the variation of genes among the individuals within a species. A gene is the part of a cell in a living organism which controls the characteristics such as colour, height etc. of that organism. Each species consists of many individual organisms and virtually no two individual are identical because of their unique genetic make-ups. Different genes are responsible for different traits. The number of genes ranges from about 1000 in bacteria to more than 400000 in many flowering plants. Genetic differentiation within species occurs as a result of sexual reproduction, in which different genes of parents are combined in their offspring to produce new a new set up of genes. Genetic diversity within a species often increases with environmental variability. This genetic variability is essential for a healthy breeding population of a species. It has a key role in the maintenance of diversity at species and community levels. If a species has more genetic diversity, it can adapt better to the changed environmental conditions. Lower genetic diversity within a species leads to uniformity which may result in reduced fertility and increased susceptibility to disease.

Genetic diversity is usually mentioned with reference to agriculture and maintaining food security. This is because genetic erosion of several crops has already occurred leading to the world's dependence for food on just a few High yielding varieties (HYV).

**Ecosystem Diversity:** Ecosystem diversity is a broad scale of biodiversity. It refers to the number of habitats or ecosystems present within a geographical area. It describes the differences among different habitats, ecological niches, trophic levels and various ecological processes than sustain energy flow, food webs and the recycling of nutrients. It has a focus on various biotic interactions and the role and function of some key species. Diverse communities are functionally more productive and stable, even under environmental stresses such as prolonged dry conditions. Ecosystem diversity has evolved with prevailing environmental conditions with well regulated ecological balance. Loss of any ecosystem will disrupt the ecological balance.

**Biodiversity Gradient:** Biodiversity is not evenly distributed; rather it varies greatly across the globe as well as within regions. Among other factors, the diversity of all living things depends on temperature, precipitation, altitude, soils, geography and the presence of other species. The study of the spatial distribution of organisms, species and ecosystems is the science of biogeography.

The latitudinal and altitudinal gradients of species diversity are two master gradients, although regional and taxa -related exceptions do occur. Favourable environmental conditions favour a larger number of species to occur and grow. Terrestrial biodiversity tends to be highest near the equator due to the warm climate and high primary productivity. It decreases as we move from low to high latitudes (*i.e.* from the equator to the poles). The climate conditions are favourable for growth of plants in tropical rainforests throughout the year whereas in the temperate region, it is severe with short growing period for plants. Similarly, we generally notice a decrease in species diversity from lower to higher altitudes on a mountain. Lower temperature and greater seasonal variability at higher altitudes causes reduction of biodiversity there.

It is also expected that the flora and fauna will be more diverse in complex and heterogeneous physical environments such as estuary ecosystem. Marine biodiversity tends to be highest along coasts in the Western Pacific, where sea surface temperature is highest and in mid-latitudinal band in all oceans.

## BIOGEOGRAPHIC CLASSIFICATION OF INDIA

As mentioned earlier, biogeography is the study of the spatial distribution of organisms, species, and ecosystems. Different parts of India are characterized by different geographical features such as climate, topography and soil types. These variations induce variability in flora and fauna at the landscape level. To study these variations and to ensure region based conservation approaches, India has developed a biogeographic classification for its land area. Within India, the biogeographic classification recognizes 10 zones, divided into 27 provinces. The zones are listed in Table 4.1 and shown in Fig. 4.1.

Among the biogeographic regions, Deccan peninsula has the most extensive coverage of the Indian landmass (42%). Western Ghats and North-east India are the most biodiversity-rich zones. Each of these zones has its own characteristic climate, soil, topography and biodiversity. Each biogeographic zone has several habitats, biotic communities and ecosystems.

## VALUE OF BIODIVERSITY

Biodiversity is important for many reasons. It underpins the form and function of ecosystems, which provide the life-supporting services to meet human needs, both material and non-material. The diversity of nature is the foundation of the world's material wealth. From biodiversity, we develop food crops and derive the raw inputs and genetic materials for industry, agriculture and medicine. Biodiversity also provides valuable indirect services through natural ecosystems. Sometimes we appreciate the value of an organism only after it is lost from earth. Moreover, biodiversity has non-use or existence value. The benefits or values we receive from the biodiversity can be categorized into following types:

**Consumptive Use Value:** The consumptive use of biodiversity refers to the direct utilization of the plant or animal products by the local community for their benefit. It includes the use of organism and their parts to meet the needs for food, fuel, fodder or timber. Of the several thousand species of edible plants, less than 20 plant species are cultivated to produce about 85 per cent of the world's food. Wheat, corn and rice, the three major carbohydrate crops, yield nearly two third of the food sustaining the human population. Fats, oils, fibres, etc. are other uses for which more and more new species need to be investigated.

**Productive Use Value:** Productive use value refers to the use of biological materials for producing marketable goods. These include the values of natural products for developing pharmaceuticals, for developing and maintaining the genetic basis for agriculture and for supporting biological product based industries.

**Table 4.1: Biogeographic zones of India**

| Biogeographic Zones | Biotic Provinces | Major Conservation Issues |
|---|---|---|
| **Trans-Himalayan** | One biotic Province in the snow covered, cold mountainous region of Ladakh. | Livestock pressure, tourism, exotic plantations, extraction of medicinal plants and NTFPs, poaching, human-animal conflict, climate change. |
| **Himalayan** | Four Provinces; Northwest, West, Central and East Himalayas | Climate change, deforestation, invasive species, extraction of medicinal plants and NTFPs, fire, land use change, development and urbanization, mining, tourism. |
| **Gangetic Plains** | Two provinces; Upper and Lower Gangetic Plain. | Deforestation, invasive species, grassland degradation, land use change, mining, urbanisation, livestock pressure, pollution and eutrophication. |
| **Deccan Penninsula** | Five provinces; Deccan Plateau, South-central Plateau, Eastern Plateau, Chhota Nagpur and Central Highlands. | Deforestation, grassland degradation, invasive species, development and urbanisation, mining, pathogens and disease transmission. |
| **Desert** | Three provinces; -Thar in Rajastan, Kutch in Gujarat and Ladakh in J&K | Invasive species, land use change, livestock pressure, grassland degradation, mining. |
| **Semi-arid** | Two Provinces- Central India and Gujarat-Rajwara | Land use change, mining, livestock pressure, grassland degradation, poaching. |
| **North-East India** | Two provinces; Brahmaputra valley and North-Eastern hills in North-Eastern States. | Deforestation, shifting cultivation, mining, hydropower development, poaching, climate change. |
| **Western Ghats** | Two provinces; Western Ghat Mountains and Malabar coast | Invasive species, exotic plantations, encroachment, mining, extraction of medicinal plants & NTFPs, livestock pressure, fire, poaching, pathogens and disease transmission, climate change. |
| **Islands** | Three provinces; Andaman Islands, Nicobar Islands and Lakshadweep islands | Climate change, invasive species, development and urbanization. |
| **Coasts** | Two provinces; West and East coast | Climate change, pollution, development and urbanization, mining, tourism, aquaculture, invasive species. |

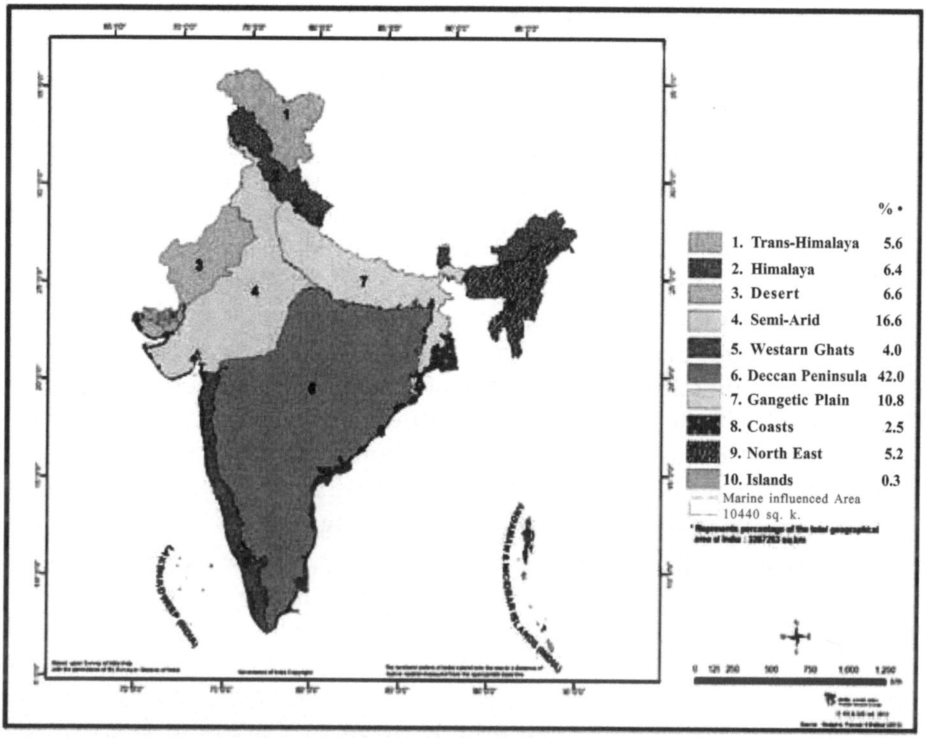


**Fig. 4.1: Biogeographic Zones of India**

Biodiversity is a rich source of substances with medicinal properties. Biological diversity provides the raw material from which new drugs can be identified. Examples of plant derived substances developed into valuable drugs are: Quinine (*Chinchona ledgeriana* ) used for treatment of malaria and Taxol, an anticancer drug obtained from the bark of the yew tree (*Taxus brevifolia, T. baccata* ). Currently, 25 per cent of the drugs in the pharmacy are derived from a mere 120 species of plants. But, throughout the world, traditional medicines make use of thousands of plant species.

The biotechnologist uses genetic properties in plants or animals to develop better varieties of crops that are used in farming and plantation programs or to develop better livestock. Diversity is the basis of selection and further more it is the raw genetic material for continuous improvement in domesticated plant species. Diversity of wild species provides a good source of genes for imparting tolerance/resistance to many stresses. The commercial, domesticated species are crossbred with their wild relatives to improve their traits. Genes of wild species are used to confer new properties, such as disease resistance or improved yield in domesticated species. For example, genes received from a single wild rice species (*Oryza nivara*) from India have been used to develop resistance against four main diseases in cultivated paddy varieties. To industrialists, biodiversity is a rich store-house from which to develop new products. Paper, textile, silk, leather industries are dependent on the biodiversity products.

**Ecosystem Service Value:** Ecosystem services are the conditions and processes through which natural ecosystems and the species that constitute them sustain and fulfill human life. Biodiversity is essential for the maintenance and sustainable utilization of goods and services from ecological systems as well as from the individual species. Biological diversity provides many benefits to humans, supporting the systems that store and cycle nutrients essential for life, absorbing and breaking down pollutants, recharging groundwater, producing soil and protecting it from excessive erosion. Many aspects of the stability, functioning, and sustainability of ecosystems depend on biodiversity. These services include maintenance of gaseous composition of the atmosphere, climate control by forests and oceanic systems, natural pest control and pollination of plants by insects and birds. In more general terms, the variation in life provides the basis for adapting to changing conditions.

**Recreation and aesthetic Value:** Biodiversity is a wonderful aspect of nature. The appreciation of biodiversity for its inherent value and beauty contributes to our aesthetics and creativity. Examples of aesthetic rewards include nature-based activities such as ecotourism, bird watching, hiking, fishing, and photography. The recreational use of natural areas and their significance for aesthetics and cultural heritage are important factors.

**Ethical and Moral Value:** The ethical values value of biodiversity includes feelings of ethical obligation to protect other species from extinction, religious values associated with cherishing the Earth and its inhabitants and the desire to leave for future generations that which we are able to enjoy. In some ways, these concerns are the core motives for protecting biodiversity. It is related to biodiversity conservation based on the feeling that all forms of life have the right to exist beyond human needs or economic returns.

**Social Value:** Social values are associated with the social life, customs, religion and spiritual aspects of people. Throughout human history, people have related biodiversity to the very existence of human race through cultural and religious beliefs. Biodiversity and ecosystem diversity are reflected in the cultural and religious diversity of India through the varied values attached to biodiversity components and landscapes. India's many traditional knowledge systems and ethno-medicinal practices are based on a close understanding of and dependence on biodiversity. The cultural or religious importance of species and designation of sacred areas are well-known in India. In a majority of Indian villages and towns, plants like *Ocimum sanctum* (Tulsi), *Ficus religiosa* (Pipal), and *Prosopis cineraria* (Khejri) and various other trees are planted, which are considered sacred and worshipped by the people. Several birds, and even snake, have been considered sacred.

**Option Value:** Option value of biodiversity refers to the possibilities of their use in future. It is impossible to predict which species or varieties of plants and animals will be of great use in the future or which type of bio-molecules will be needed for human welfare and which genes will fortify our crop plants and domesticated animals against diseases or enhance their productivity. To continue to improve cultivars and domestic livestock, we need to return to wild relatives of crop plants and animals.

Because each organism has its specific roles in the ecosystems, the loss of even a single species can cause much larger, often unforeseen changes to the ecosystem. The value of biodiversity and the ecosystem services they provide are not fully captured by the contemporary accounting system. The Gross Domestic Product (GDP) of a country incorporates mainly market-based commodities such as timber and some Non Timber Forest (NTFPs) from forestry. The other values of biodiversity including their ecosystem services are challenging to assess monetarily and include in national accounting.

## BIODIVERSITY AT GLOBAL, NATIONAL AND LOCAL LEVELS

Due to the importance of biodiversity to human society, it is pertinent that we know the richness of the global biodiversity. At first we have to identify and scientifically name the huge number of species that live in different parts of the world. However, our knowledge of the diversity of life is meagre. Biodiversity can be measured in many ways. The simplest method is the species richness i.e. number of existing species. The estimated value for the total number of species varies greatly from 5-100 millions. The most acceptable value is 8 million out of which only 1.8 million species (excluding bacteria) have been identified and named.

**Global Biodiversity:** The salient features of global biodiversity are:

1. Our knowledge and documentation of the large organisms such as vertebrates (mammals, birds etc) are better than the smaller insects, micro-organisms. While 90% of the vertebrates are identified, less than 5% of the world's microorganisms have been described.
2. The distribution of biodiversity is not uniform. Most macroscopic organisms have small, often clustered geographical ranges, leading to centers of both high diversity and endemism, frequently concentrated in isolated or topographically variable regions (islands, mountains, peninsulas).
3. A large proportion of the world's terrestrial biodiversity at the species level is concentrated in a small part of the world, mostly in the tropics. About 50 to 80% of global biodiversity lives in tropical rainforests. Temperate forests have less biodiversity, but it is better documented.
4. Marine diversity may be much higher than terrestrial biodiversity. But they are less known and described.

5. The disparity in the distribution and endemism of flora and fauna is a complex issue. Many economically poor countries in tropics possess richer biodiversity than the developed countries in the temperate region. However, the value of biodiversity is reaped more by the developed countries. Also the developing countries are losing their biodiversity in pursuit of development.
6. The biodiversity cannot be considered as a 'common property resource'. At the same time nobody can have the right to exploit the biodiversity (even if it is in his territory) due to its value to others. Thus biodiversity and economic issues need to be integrated.

**Temporal Distribution of Global Biodiversity:** The present biodiversity is a result of organic evolution of millions of years. Life on earth is believed to have started 3.5 billion years ago *i.e.* 1 billion years after the earth's existence. Again for the next 3 billion years the life forms were mostly single celled organisms like bacteria. The diversification of multi-cellular organisms occurred 550 million ago, popularly known as *Cambrian explosion*. The different taxonomic groups of plants, animals and other microorganisms are being evolved since then. New species are evolved from the existing ones. Man appeared on earth 2 million years ago. Many species has also disappeared from the earth which is called *extinction*. However, the overall tendency is to increase the diversification of organisms (Fig. 4.2). Though there are short periods of *mass extinction* during which a large percentage of species got extinct together, new species always replace the old ones. Five such mass extinctions are known. We are now heading for the sixth mass extinction, which is purely man made.

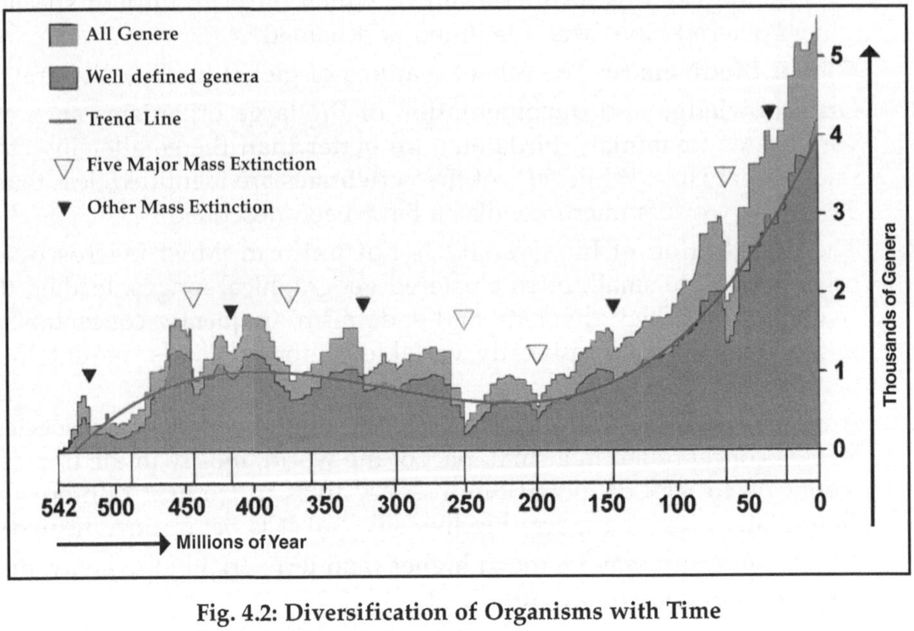


Fig. 4.2: Diversification of Organisms with Time

**Biodiversity at National and Local Level:** Every country is characterized by its own biodiversity depending mainly on its climate. Some countries and areas are richer in biodiversity than others. The areas with a higher density of different species are not necessarily where the environment is best protected. Tropical rainforests are the top biodiversity-rich ecosystems. The Amazon rainforest harbours one out of every ten known species of our planet. The World Conservation Monitoring Centre of the UN Environment Programme (UNEP-WCMC) has identified 17 mega diverse countries (Table 4.2). These countries have the highest number of endemic species (*i.e.* species found only in that country) and have a major responsibility to protect their diversity.

**Table 4.2: Mega diversity Countries of the World**

| Continents | Countries |
|---|---|
| South America | Brazil, Colombia, Ecuador, Peru and Venezuela |
| Asia<br>Africa | The Philippines, India, Indonesia, Malaysia, China<br>Madagascar, Democratic Republic of the Congo, Republic of South Africa |
| North America | Unites States and Mexico |
| Oceania | Australia and Papua New Guinea |
| Europe | — |

The earth's biodiversity is distributed in specific ecological regions. Many species have specialised ecological niches that make them vulnerable to extinction when their natural habitat or niche is destroyed. So there is an urgent need to map the biodiversity in different locality for their conservation and practical utilization. There are over a thousand major eco-regions in the world. Of these, 200 are said to be the richest, rarest and most distinctive natural areas. These areas are referred to as the Global 200 and most crucial to the conservation of global biodiversity. The Global 200 list actually contains 238 eco-regions, made up of 142 terrestrial, 53 freshwater, and 43 marine eco-regions.

## INDIA: A MEGA DIVERSITY NATION

India's biological diversity is one of the most significant in the world. With only 2.4% of the world's land area, India harbours 7-8% of all recorded species. As many as 29,000 species of plants and over 96,000 species of wild animals have so far been recorded from India. Many of these organisms are endemic to India and are found nowhere else in the world.

India is amongst the few countries that have developed a bio-geographic classification for conservation planning, and has mapped biodiversity-rich areas in the country. The major controls of highly varied patterns of ecosystems in the India are geographical, topographical, hydrological and climatic factors. Variation in moisture levels, because of the amount of precipitation and the length of the monsoon in different regions, plays a major role in the pattern of regional species diversity. The great physical variations from the lofty mountains regions, to low lying plains are responsible for local variations in species diversity. The highest concentrations of species are found in the North-East of India, the Western Ghats and the Andaman and Nicobar Islands. In these areas, both plant and animal species are abounding.

**Animal Diversity:** India has 96,000 species of animals including 63,000 insects (Table 4.3).

**Table 4.3: Animal diversity in world and India**

| Animal Groups | No. of Species in World | No. of Species in India | % of Species in India |
|---|---|---|---|
| (1) | (2) | (3) | (4) |
| Kingdom Protista, Phylum Protozoa | 31,259 | 3509 | 11.23 |
| Phylum Mesozoa | 71 | 10 | 14.08 |
| Phylum Porifera | 5000 | 500 | 10.0 |
| Phylum Cnidaria | 10,107 | 1052 | 10.41 |
| Phylum Ctenophora | 100 | 12 | 12.00 |
| Phylum Platyhelminthes | 17,513 | 1653 | 9.43 |
| Phylum Rotifera | 2,044 | 370 | 18.10 |
| Phylum Gastrotricha | 3,000 | 100 | 3.33 |
| Phylum Kinorhyncha | 100 | 10 | 10 |
| Phylum Nematoda | 30,034 | 2,911 | 9.69 |
| Phylum Acanthocephala | 800 | 229 | 28.63 |
| Phylum Sipuncula | 145 | 35 | 24.14 |
| Phylum Echiura | 127 | 43 | 33.86 |
| Phylum Mollusca | 66,535 | 5,178 | 7.78 |
| Phylum Annelida | 17,002 | 1002 | 5.89 |
| Phylum Onychophora | 100 | 1 | 1.00 |
| **Phylum Arthropoda** | | | |
| Class Crustacea | 60,003 | 3,565 | 5.94 |
| Class Insecta | 10,20,169 | 63,706 | 6.24 |
| Class Arachnida | 73,470 | 5882 | 8.01 |
| Class Pycnogonida | 600 | 17 | 2.83 |
| Class Chilopoda | 8000 | 101 | 1.26 |
| Class Diplopoda | 7500 | 162 | 2.16 |
| Class Symphyla | 120 | 4 | 3.33 |
| Class Merostomata | 4 | 2 | 50.00 |
| Phylum Phoronida | 11 | 3 | 27.27 |

(Table Contd...)

| (1) | (2) | (3) | (4) |
|---|---|---|---|
| Phylum Bryozoa | 4000 | 200 | 5.00 |
| Phylum Entoprocta | 60 | 10 | 16.67 |
| Phylum Brachiopoda | 300 | 4 | 1.33 |
| Phylum Chaetognatha | 111 | 30 | 27.03 |
| Phylum Tardigrada | 514 | 30 | 5.84 |
| Phylum Echinodermata | 6600 | 779 | 11.80 |
| Phylum Hemichordata | 120 | 12 | 10.00 |
| Phylum Protochordata | 2106 | 119 | 5.65 |
| **Phylum Chordata** | | | |
| Class Pisces | 32156 | 3092 | 9.62 |
| Class Amphibia | 6776 | 371 | 5.48 |
| Class Reptilia | 9232 | 530 | 5.74 |
| Class Aves | 9,026 | 1,234 | 13.67 |
| Class Mammalia | 5416 | 423 | 7.81 |
| Total (Animalia) | 13,98,972 | 93,382 | 6.68 |
| Grand total (Protista + Animalia) | 14,30,231 | 96,891 | 6.77 |

*Source:* ZSI (Venkataraman, et.al.) 2015

It is estimated that the number of unknown species could be several times higher. The main features of animal diversity are:

- India's avifauna is remarkably rich and its 1200 bird species cover 14% of world avifauna.
- India has 350 species of wild mammals, living in different ecosystems. Out of 135 genera of land mammals in India, 85 (63%) are found in the North East.
- A major proportion of amphibian and reptiles, especially snakes, are concentrated in the Western Ghats.
- In terms of endemism of vertebrate groups, India's global ranking is 10th in birds, with 69 species, fifth in reptiles, with 156 species, and seventh in amphibians, with 110 species. Out of the recorded vertebrates, 53% freshwater fish, 62% amphibians, 36% reptiles and 10% mammalian fauna are endemic. The endemic are concentrated mainly in northeast, Western Ghats, northwest Himalaya and Andaman and Nicobar Islands.
- High endemism has also been recorded for various groups of insects. Several marine worms, centipedes, mayflies and fresh water sponges are also known to be endemic.

**Plant Diversity:** With an estimated 29,105 species of algae, bryophytes, pteridophytes, gymnosperms and angiosperms, India holds 9.13% of the world's known floral diversity in these groups. Andaman and Nicobar Islands alone have as many as 2200 species of flowering plants and 120 species of ferns. The richness of Indian plant species as compared with the world is shown in Table 4.4.

**Table 4.4: Plant species in World and India**

| Plant Groups | No. of Species in World | No. of Species in India | % of Species in India | No. of Endemic Species in India | % of Endemic Species |
|---|---|---|---|---|---|
| Algae | 40,800 | 7,244 | 17.75 | 1,949 | 26.91 |
| Bryophytes | 14,500 | 2,504 | 17.27 | 642 | 25.64 |
| Pteridophytes | 12,000 | 1,267 | 10.56 | 196 | 15.47 |
| Gymnosperms | 650 | 74 | 11.38 | 8 | 10.81 |
| Angiosperms | 250,000 | 17,926 | 7.17 | 4,045 | 22.57 |
| Total | 317,950 | 29,015 | 9.13 | 6850 | 23.57 |

*Source:* BSI ( Singh and Dash), 2014

**Marine Biodiversity:** India's coastal and marine areas hold many biological treasures. Dense mangrove forest of Sunderbans, the world's largest congregations of nesting turtles in Odisha, beautiful sea grass beds in Palk Bay, dolphins and dugongs in the Gulf of Mannar, majestic whale sharks in the Gulf of Kachchh and some of the world's most beautiful coral reefs are just a few examples of the treasures of India's coastal and marine biodiversity. The marine floral and faunal biodiversity of India is remarkable, with over 200 diatom species, 90 dinoflagellates, 844 marine algae, 560 species of corals and 39 mangrove species, more than 10,000 invertebrate species and 2,500 vertebrate species.

**Domesticated Biodiversity:** More than 800 cultivated plants and 900 of their wild relatives have been documented. India also has a vast and rich repository of farm animals, represented by a broad spectrum of native breeds of cattle (34), buffaloes (12), goat (21), sheep (39) and chicken (15). Many indigenous breeds of animals are showing declining trends in the country.

**Microbes Diversity:** India is home to billions of diverse microbes, many of which are found nowhere else in the world. The country is also endowed with enormous variability in agriculturally important microorganisms. The variability in fungi, bacteria, actinomycetes, viruses, cyanobacteria etc. appears to have evolved with their hosts *vis-à-vis* the environment and forms invaluable gene pool resources. India harbours large number of lichen species with at least 2300 species belonging to 305 genera and 74 families having been reported. Due to intensification of agricultural practices and population pressure, the microbial variability is eroding.

The biological diversity of many ecosystems still remains poorly explored in India. These ecosystems include the deep oceans, wetlands and lakes, and habitats such as the tree canopy and soil of tropical rain forests. India's explosive population and the related need for land and natural resources, is rapidly eroding this great source of potential wealth. Short - term gains are being made, leading to long -term ecological and economic losses. The rate at which the extinction of species is occurring throughout the country remains obscure. It is likely to be extremely high as our wilderness areas are shrinking rapidly.

## HOTSPOTS OF BIODIVERSITY

The idea of hotspots was first given by ecologist Norman Myers, who defined a hotspot as an area of exceptional plant, animal and microbe wealth that is under threat. The two key criteria for determining a hotspot are endemism (the presence of species found nowhere else on earth) and degree of threat. To qualify as hotspots an area must contain at least 0.5 per cent or 1500 of the worlds 3,00,000 plants species as endemics. Endemic life forms are the most vulnerable to become extinct due to their restricted geographical distributions. Myers *et al.* (2000) demarcated 25 global biodiversity hotspots in the world to which another 9 hotspots based on the criteria of exceptional concentration of endemic plants and higher degree of anthropogenic pressure were added in 2009. These hotspots harbour many rare and endangered species. It has been estimated that 60,000 endemic plants which comprise 20% of global plant life occur in these hot spots. The biodiversity hotspots situated in densely populated tropical countries are experiencing dynamics due to urbanization, agricultural expansion and rapid economic development.

Of the 34 global biodiversity hotspots, India accommodates part of four hotspots: the Himalayas, the Western Ghats, Indo- Burma and Sundaland. The major part of the Himalayas and the Western Ghats are in India. Indo-Burma and Sundaland hot spots are represented in the North-east region and the Nicobar Islands respectively. The four biodiversity hotspots in India are under undue pressure due to anthropogenic disturbance and climate change.

The Himalayas were included on global biodiversity hot spot in 2009. It comprises of Western and Eastern Himalayas. Many endemic medicinal plants and trees found here.

Western Ghats are part of the Western Ghats-Sri Lanka global hotspot, running roughly in a North-south direction for about 1500 km parallel to the coast bordering the Arabian Sea. It is home to a number of endemic plants, animals, birds, amphibian and reptilian species. The Western Ghats is considered as one of the top ten global biodiversity hot-spots. It has over 7300 species of flowering plants, over 450 species of birds (35% endemic), 140 mammal species (around 20% endemic) and 260 reptile species (over 60% endemic), a number of fresh water fishes and invertebrates most of which are endemic to the region. Considering the outstanding universal values and exceptionally high levels of endemism in the Western Ghats, 39 sites in the States of Kerala, Karnataka, Tamil Nadu and Maharashtra have been inscribed on the United Nations Education Scientific and Cultural Organization (UNESCO) World Heritage List in 2012.

Some parts of the North-eastern region of India, excluding the Himalayan region, are contiguous with the Indo-Burma biodiversity hotspot. The topography of the hotspot is complex and is characterized by a series of North-south mountain ranges that descend from the Himalayan chain and its South-eastern extensions.

The Nicobar Islands are part of the Sundaland hotspot, which includes Malaysia, Singapore, and Indonesia. They belong to the Andaman and Nicobar group of islands and consist of some of the most pristine island ecosystems in the world. These islands are fringed by one of the most spectacular and globally significant reefs of the Indian Ocean region. Mangrove forests are found in most of these islands.

## THREATS TO BIODIVERSITY

As mentioned earlier, extinction of species is a natural outcome of organic evolution. During evolution process, lots of species belonging to various taxonomic divisions has permanently disappeared from earth in the geologically past. Their place has been taken over a new set of organisms. The most spectacular example is the extinction of dinosaurs some 65million years ago which paved the way for diversification of mammals. The rate of loss of species in geologic past has been a slow process, though scientists have identified 5 periods of short span called *mass extinction*. However, the rate of extinction of species and ecosystems has been fast in recent years, mostly due to human activities. About 60% of world's plant, bird, animals, reptiles and amphibian species (many of them being endemic ones) are under tremendous threat, having lost more than 70% of their primary habitat. Human actions are expected to exterminate 25% of world's species in next 20-30 years. The mega extinction spasm is related to human interventions. This manmade mass extinction represents a very severe depletion of biodiversity, particularly because it is occurring within a short period of time. According to WWF, 2014 report, Earth has lost half of its wildlife in the past 40 years. The primary threats to biodiversity are discussed below.

**Habitat Destruction and Fragmentation:** The destruction of habitats is the primary reason for the loss of biodiversity. When people cut down trees, fill a wetland, plough grassland or burn a forest, the natural habitat of a species is changed or destroyed. These changes can kill or force out many plants, animals, and microorganisms, as well as disrupt complex interactions among the species. A forest patch surrounded by croplands, orchards, plantations, or urban areas is an example of fragmented habitats. With the fragmentation of a large forest tract, species occupying deeper parts of forests are the first to disappear.

Habitat loss is mainly due to human population growth, industrialization and changes in the land use patterns. Activities such as logging of wood, increased agriculture, increased human habitation has led to destruction of forests and pollution of rivers. Mining, construction of large dams, highway construction has also caused significant destruction of habitats. Few years ago, most of the biodiversity rich forests were inaccessible and remote. Now, due to better infrastructure, contact of these areas with humans has increased. These factors are causing extinction of species that cannot survive in the changed environment. The common process of land cover/land use changes are:

- Forests and grasslands are converted to agricultural land.
- Natural wetlands are drained to establish crop lands.
- Mangroves are cleared for fuel wood and prawn farming,
- Grasslands are changed to other forms, degraded by overgrazing.
- Natural forests are deforested for timber and replanted for teak, sal *etc.*
- Introductions of exotic weeds *eg.* lantana bushes, *Eupatorium* shrubs and congress grass are invading at the expense of indigenous undergrowth species.
- Traditional farming techniques like slash and burn in Himalayas.

**Overexploitation of Resource:** Man has begun to overuse or misuse most of the natural ecosystems. Due to unsustainable resource-use, many productive forests and grasslands have been turned into deserts and wastelands. Excess collection of fire wood by lopping of branches of trees opens up the canopy and alters the local biodiversity. Over harvesting of fish by large trawling boats is leading to depletion of fish stocks. A variety of wild plants with real or sometimes, dubious medicinal values are being overharvested. Overexploitation of a particular species reduces the size of its population to an extent that it becomes vulnerable to extinction.

**Poaching:** Poaching or illegal hunting is prevalent for many specific animals, mainly for large economic benefits. The skin and bones from tigers, ivory from elephants, horns from rhinos and perfume from the musk deer are extensively used abroad. Large mammals such as the tiger, rhinoceros and the elephant face the possibility of complete extinction due to rampant hunting and poaching. Though poaching is in decline due to efforts by conservationists, the trade in tiger hide, elephant tusks, tiger teeth, rhinoceros horn remains profitable and rampant. Corals and shells are also collected for selling. Tortoises, exotic birds and other small animals are packed into tiny containers and smuggled for the pet trade.

**Man Wild Life Conflicts:** Shrinking forest cover, human encroachment, lack of food etc. sometimes forces the wild-animals enter the nearby human settlements. The conflicting situations with wild life cause immense damage and danger to man. Villagers try to protect themselves by killing (i.e. putting electric fence etc.) the wild animals. Many incidents with elephants, tigers, leopards *etc.* are in news.

**Climate Change:** Due to global warming and climate change, the temperatures, rainfall patterns of many ecosystems are being affected. The vulnerable plant and animal species are most affected by these changes. Many plant species in the biodiversity hotspots like Western Ghats are getting extinct due to climate change.

## ENDANGERED AND ENDEMIC SPECIES IN INDIA

The species whose existence is in danger and that face a significant risk of extinction in the near future are called *endangered species*. Endangered species which are on verge of extinction are called *threatened species* International Union for Conservation of Nature and Natural Resources (IUCN) publishes the "Red Data Book" which included the list of endangered species of plants and animals. The red data symbolizes the warning signal – if not protected the species are likely to become extinct in near future. By the end of 2014, India had 988 threatened species on the list, which included critically endangered, endangered and vulnerable species. It is 15 more species than the listed 973 species in 2013. With 659 species in 2008, the increase over seven years is 50 per cent, in part due to better research identifying more threatened species and deforestation. Most of the endangered species are found today only in protected areas (PAs). At least 10 per cent of India's recorded wild flora, and possibly more its wild fauna, are on the list of threatened species, many on the verge of extinction. The exploitation of land and forest resources by humans along with hunting and trapping for food and sport has led to the extinction of many species in India in recent times. These species include mammals such as the Indian/Asiatic Cheetah, Javan Rhinoceros and Sumatran Rhinoceros. While some of these large mammal species are confirmed extinct, there have been many smaller animal and plant species whose status is harder to determine.

The species which are unique to a locality/region are called *endemic species*. Some species are found only in India and are thus endemic (restricted to our country). Some have very localized distribution and are considered highly endemic. Some species of this category are Indian wild ass, kashmiri stag, golden langur, pigmy hog.

**Table 4.5: A list of endangered animals in India**

| |
|---|
| *Bengal Tiger:* The Bengal Tiger is the national animal of both, India and Bangladesh. The tiger's coat is yellow to light orange, with stripes ranging from dark brown to black. The number of tigers has reduced dramatically in the past few years, due to poaching and human-tiger conflict. Can be spotted at: Tadoba National Park, Ranthambore National Park, Sundarbans National Park, Sariska Tiger Reserve, Jim Corbett National Park, Bandhavgarh National Park. |
| *Asiatic Lion:* Asiatic Lion or the Indian Lion or Persian Lion is a lion subspecies which is endangered. It differs from the African lion by less inflated auditory bullae, a larger tail tuft and a less developed mane. Can be spotted at: Gir Forest National Park, Gujarat. |
| *Snow Leopard:* The snow leopard is a large cat native to the mountain ranges in Central and South Asia. Snow leopards have long, thick fur, and their base color varies from smoky gray to yellowish tan, with whitish under parts. Can be spotted at: Hemis National Park, Ladakh, Nanda Devi National Park, Uttarakhand, Dibang Wildlife Sanctuary, Arunachal Pradesh, Kibber Wildlife Sanctuary, Lahaul Spiti, Himachal Pradesh, Pin Valley National Park, Lahaul Spiti, Himachal Pradesh, Great Himalayan National Park, Kullu, Himachal Pradesh. |
| *Blackbuck:* The Blackbuck is an ungulate species of antelope and it is near threatened. The main threat to this species is poaching, predation, habitat destruction, overgrazing, inbreeding and sanctuary visitors. Can be spotted at: Guindy National park, Tamil Nadu, Rollapadu, Andhra Pradesh, Chilka, Orissa. |
| *Red Panda:* Red Panda is also known as lesser panda or red cat-bear. It is an arboreal mammal native to the eastern Himalayas. Red Panda's population is on a decrease given to habitat loss and fragmentation, poaching, and inbreeding depression. Can be spotted at: Sikkim, Arunachal Pradesh and West Bengal's Khangchendzonga and Namdapha National Park. |
| *One Horned Rhinoceros:* The One-horned rhino is a large mammal, found in Assam. Excessive hunting has reduced the number of this species. These rhinos are killed to saw off their horn, which are sold at a very high value. Can be spotted at: Kaziranga National Park, Dudhwa Tiger Reserve, Pobitora Wildlife Sanctuary. |
| *The Nilgiri Tahr:* The Nilgiri Tahr is an ungulate, endemic to the Nilgiri Hills. Nilgiri tahrs are stocky goats with short, coarse fur and a bristly mane. Can be spotted at: Eravikulam National Park, Nilgiri Hills, Anaimalai Hills, Periyar National Park, Palni Hills. |
| *Kashmir Red Stag (Hangul):* The Kashmir stag also known as Hangul is a critically endangered species. This deer has a light rump patch without the tail. Each of its antlers consists of 5 tines. Can be spotted at: Dachigam National Park, Rajparian Wildlife Sanctuary, Overa Aru, Sind Valley, and in the forests of Kishtwar and Bhaderwah, all of which are a part of Jammu and Kashmir. |
| *Lion Tailed Macaque:* The Lion-tailed macaque is an Old World Monkey, endemic to the Western Ghats of South India. Its outstanding characteristic is the silver-white mane which surrounds the head from the cheeks down to chin. Can be spotted at: Silent Valley National Park, Kerala, Papanasam part of the Kalakkad Mundanthurai Tiger Reserve, Tamil Nadu and Sirsi-Honnavara rainforests of North-Western Ghats in Karnataka. |
| *Indian Bison (Gaur):* Indian Bison is the largest extant bovine, native to South Asia and South-East Asia. The bisons are highly threatened by poaching for trade to supply international markets. Can be spotted at: Arignar Anna Zoological Park, Chennai and Chinnar Wildlife Sanctuary, Kerala. |

*Source:* http://travel.india.com/articles/10-endangered-animals-india-see-vanish/

**Table 4.6: A list of endangered plants in India**

| |
|---|
| *Polygala irregularis:* Gujarat commonly known as Milkwort is an annual or perennial herb. Blooms during July and August. The plants are found at an altitude of 1000 meters. The flowers are found in blue, near white,pink and white in color. The plants are destroyed due to human habitation and land for agriculture. |
| *Lotus corniculatus:* Gujarat this plant belongs to pea family. The plant bear pretty little yellow flowers grow in a circle, at the end of a stem. They are very bright and easily spotted along the roadside. It is used in agriculture as a forage plant, grown for pasture, hay and silage. Plants are perennial, herbaceous similar to some clover. |
| *Amentotaxus assamica:* Arunachal Pradesh otherwise called Assam catkin yew. They are shrubs or small trees found in moist deciduous forest of Assam. It belongs to a species of coniferous trees found only in India. They are found in Turoo hills, Delei Valley Dafla hills of Arunachal Pradesh. |
| *Diospyros celibica:* Karnataka Ebony tree -It is a flowering tree and considered highly by woodworkers as they are widely used for making high quality furniture. The trees can grow up to 20 metres height under favourable conditions. But in the past two centuries it has become a very scarce and hardly found in India. |
| *Actinodaphne lawsonii:* Kerala It belongs to lauraceae family. It is endemic and is threatened by habitat loss. It is found in high elevation evergreen forest between 1200 to 2400 meters. The leaves are aromatic and has medicinal use. |
| *Acacia planifrons:* Tamilnadu (umbrella thorn) They grow as a shrub or a short tree. In Tamil they are called kudai ve., The tree is used as a fuel and fodder for sheep and goats. When the tree is fully grown it appears as a spreaded umbrella. |
| *Chlorophytum malabaricum:* Tamilnadu. Known as malabar lily, it is a small herb with stem closely attached with leaves. Flowers are star shaped and highly fragrant. They are found in Western Ghats. |
| *Ceropegia odorata:* It can be found in Pavagah in Gujarat and Mount Abu in Rajasthan, only in high altitude at about 3000mts. It is the only species of the genus whose flowers have very strong fragrance hence the name odorata. They bloom for few days and they are called Jeemikanda in Gujarat. These plants have medicinal values and are chewed to cure stomach pain and juice from the tubers is used in treating eye medicine. |

*Source:* http://hubpages.com/education/Rare-and-Endangered-plants-of-India

## CONSERVATION OF BIODIVERSITY

Conservation of biodiversity refers to all activities that can bring any endangered species to the point at which it is no longer endangered or threatened to extinction. Conservation actions include activities associated with scientific resource management such as research, census, legislation, law enforcement, habitat maintenance and propagation of species. It includes both curative and preventive measures. There are two basic strategies of biodiversity conservation, *in situ* (on site) and *ex situ* (off site).

### *In Situ* Conservation

*In-situ* conservation involves conservation of species in its natural environment or habitat. The natural surroundings or the ecosystems are protected and maintained so that all the constituent species are conserved and benefitted. It emphasizes protection of total ecosystems. The method involves promotion of natural systems to take care of its own self. Biodiversity at all levels can be best preserved *in situ* by setting aside wildness as protected areas with distinctive ecosystem included in the network. Such networks preserve the total diversity of life of the region.

Protected areas are those areas in which human occupation or at least the exploitation of resources is limited. It also includes Marine Protected Areas, the boundaries of which include some area of ocean, and trans-boundary Protected Areas that overlap multiple countries which remove the borders inside the area for conservation and economic purposes. There are several kinds of protected areas, which vary by level of protection depending on the enabling laws of each country or the regulations of the international organizations involved. The protected areas in India include national parks, wildlife sanctuaries, conservation areas, community areas and biosphere reserves.

**National parks and wildlife sanctuaries:** These are areas of land and/or sea, especially dedicated to the protection and maintenance of biological diversity, and of natural and associated cultural resources. These are managed through legal or other effective means. While forestry activities are prohibited in national parks, they are permitted in wildlife sanctuaries to an extent that they do not affect the wildlife adversely. The Jim Corbett National Park was the first National Park established in India.

**Conservation reserves and community reserves:** These are protected areas which typically act as buffer zones to or connectors and migration corridors between established national parks and wildlife sanctuaries. The conservation areas are uninhabited and completely owned by the Government of India but used for subsistence by communities. Community reserves are private land being accorded protection under the Indian legislature. It provides a flexible system to achieve wildlife conservation without compromising community needs. Community Reserves have been established in India from 2007 onwards and Conservation Reserves from 2005 onwards.

**National biosphere reserves:** The term 'Biosphere Reserve' denote an area which is, set aside for the conservation of the resources of the biosphere and for the improvement of the relationship between man and the environment They are areas of terrestrial and coastal ecosystems promoting solutions to reconcile the conservation of biodiversity with its sustainable use. Each Biosphere Reserve is intended to fulfil three basic functions,

- A conservation function - to contribute to the conservation of landscapes, ecosystems, species and genetic variation.
- A development function - to foster economic and human development which is socio-culturally and ecologically sustainable;
- A logistic function - to provide support for research, monitoring, education and information exchange related to local, national and global issues of conservation and development.

There are fourteen biosphere reserves in India that cover all its major bio-geographic regions. They have been identified based on their rich genetic diversity, floristic uniqueness, endemic wealth of flora/fauna, and that they are the representative ecosystems occurring in different bio-geographic regions.

Total Protected Areas constitutes 4.88% of the total 32,87,590 km$^2$ geographical area of India. Over 100 PAs are created in Andaman and Nicobar to preserve the special island ecosystem. Dachigam, J&K sanctuary for hangul or kashmiri stag; Kaziranga and Manas national park in Assam for one horned rhinoceros and pigmy hog respectively are some of the examples worth mentioning under *in situ* conservation.

**Table 4.7: Protected Areas of India from 2000- 2015 (as on 06 October, 2015)**

| Year | National Parks | | Wild Life Sanctuaries | | Conservation Reserves | | Community Reserves | | Total Protected Areas | |
|---|---|---|---|---|---|---|---|---|---|---|
| | No. | Area | No. | Area in km$^2$ | No. | Area km$^2$ | No. | Area km$^2$ | No. | Area km$^2$ |
| 2000 | 89 | 37594 | 489 | 117882 | – | – | – | – | 578 | 155476 |
| 2010 | 102 | 40074 | 516 | 122585 | 4 | 21 | 47 | 1382 | 669 | 164063 |
| 2014 | 103 | 40333 | 525 | 116254 | 4 | 21 | 60 | 2037 | 692 | 158654 |
| 2015 | 103 | 40500 | 531 | 117607 | 26 | 47 | 66 | 2344 | 726 | 160500 |

*Source:* http://www.wiienvis.nic.in/Database/Protected_Area_854.aspx

**Table 4.8: List of Biosphere Reserves in India**

| Sl. No. | Name | Area of Biosphere (sq km) | Date of Establishment | State |
|---|---|---|---|---|
| 1. | Achanakmar-Amarkantak | 3835 | 2005 | Madhya Pradesh and Chhattishgarh |
| 2. | Agasthyamalai | 1701 | 2001 | Kerala |
| 3. | Dehang-Debang | 5111 | 1998 | Arunachal Pradesh |
| 4. | Dibru-Saikhowa | 765 | 1997 | Assam |
| 5. | Great Nicobar | 885 | 1989 | Andaman and Nicobar |
| 6. | Gulf of Mannar | 10,500 | 1989 | Tamil Nadu (TN) |
| 7. | Khangchenjunga | 2619 | 2000 | Sikkim |
| 8. | Manas | 2837 | 1989 | Assam |
| 9. | Nanda Devi | 5860 | 1988 | Uttaranchal |
| 10. | Nilgiri | 5520 | 1986 | TN, Kerala, Karnataka |
| 11. | Nokrek | 80 | 1988 | Meghalaya |
| 12. | Pachmarhi | 4926 | 1999 | Madhya Pradesh |
| 13. | Simlipal | 4374 | 1994 | Orissa |
| 14. | Sunderbans | 9630 | 1989 | West Bengal |

### *Ex situ* Conservation

Ex situ conservation refers to conservation of an endangered species outside its natural habitat in a carefully controlled situation. It becomes necessary when the survival of the species in its natural habitat is doubted. The *ex situ* conservation strategies include botanical gardens and zoological parks. Breeding programmes in zoos provide animal needs including enclosures that simulate their wild habitat. Conservation of biological diversity in botanical gardens is already in practice. There are more than 1500 botanical gardens and arboreta in India. Successful examples of ex situ conservations in India include breeding of crocodiles in Madras crocodile zoo, pigmy hog in Guchali zoo and Manipur brow antlered deer in Delhi zoo. The successful breeding programme also aims at reintroduction of the species into wild habitat, with simultaneous removal of problems like poaching and other human influences.

The plant and animal genetic resources are conserved essentially through *ex situ* conservation strategies. Germplasms of endangered/extinct animals and plants are preserved in a *gene or seed bank* for future needs. Seed gene banks are the easiest way to store germplasm of wild and cultivated plants at low temperature either though cryopreservation in liquid nitrogen. Preservation of genetic resources is also carried out in field gene banks under normal growing condition.

Fifty years ago nearly 30,000 rice varieties were grown in India. Few high yielding varieties (HYV), developed using the germplasms of these original types, have now replaced the traditional varieties. However, if all these traditional types vanish, it would be difficult to develop new disease resistant varieties for future. Though the germplasms of these varieties can be/are preserved in gene banks, their use is expensive and risky. Hence, farming of traditional breeds/varieties needs to be encouraged for preserving the genetic variability.

**National Bureaus of Genetic Resources:** To conserve India's rich domesticated biodiversity and promote underutilized crops and animal breeds, the Ministry of Agriculture has set up six national bureaus namely, plant genetic resources, animal genetic resources, fish genetic resources, agriculturally important insects, agriculturally important microorganisms and soil sciences. These bureaus serve as the nodal organizations for characterization, evaluation, cataloguing and establishing of national databases of living organisms corresponding to their mandates. The gene bank at NBPGR (Plant genetic resources) has seen a significant increase in its holdings/accessions over the years.

The National Bureau of Animal Genetic Resources (NBAGR) has taken steps to characterize the indigenous farm animals. Presently 90% of the indigenous farm animal breeds registered at the NBAGR have been characterized phenotypically and genetically. It has a total holding of more than 1.2 lakh frozen semen doses from breeding males representing breeds of cattle, buffalo, sheep, goat, camel, yak and horse for *ex situ* conservation. National Bureau of Agriculturally Important Microorganisms (NBAIM) is a microbial bioresource centre for conserving and preserving microorganisms. NBAIM has a repository of 4668 cultures, which includes 4644 indigenous and 24 exotic accessions. The diversity of fungi, as well as bacteria, in the collection is very wide. There are more than 700 species belonging to 250 genera of fungi and more than 100 species belonging to 35 genera of bacteria. National Bureau of Fish Genetic Resources (NBFGR) is mandated to carry out research related to cataloguing, characterization and conservation of country's fish germplasm resources.

## GLOBAL AND NATIONAL EFFORTS FOR BIODIVERSITY CONSERVATION

Following the United Nations' Conference on Environment and Development, 1992, The Convention on Biological Diversity (CBD) was formed in 1993 with the following 3 main objectives:

1. The conservation of biological diversity
2. The sustainable use of the components of biological diversity
3. The fair and equitable sharing of the benefits arising out of the utilization of genetic resources

Though efforts are continuing, the rate of biodiversity loss is still in rise. After the failure of meeting the earlier targets, in 2010 at *Aichi*, Japan, CBD fixed another set of 20 targets to slow the destruction of species, habitats, cut pollution and stop overfishing by the end of the decade. The Global Biodiversity Strategy document calls for a decade (2010-20) of action to conserve the world's biodiversity for the benefit of present and future generations. The action plans for meeting the biodiversity targets includes:

- Establishing a national policy framework for biodiversity conservation.
- Creating an international policy environment that supports national biodiversity conservation.
- Creating conditions and incentives for local biodiversity conservation.
- Managing biodiversity through the human environment.
- Strengthening protected areas.
- Conserving species, populations and genetic diversity.
- Expanding human capacity to conserve biodiversity.

A mid-term assessment in 2014 showed that the situation has not improved so far. Though the progress toward a target of gaining protected status for 17% of ecosystems on land is on track, the situation of the planet's most threatened species, which include 90% of all lemurs and species such as the blue-tongued forest giraffe and spoon-billed sandpiper, is getting worse rather than better. The average risk of extinction for birds, mammals, amphibians and corals shows no sign of decreasing.

India is taking significant steps towards achieving the Aichi Biodiversity Targets. An implementation of action plan for conservation of Biodiversity requires knowledge of resources, documentation, legal framework and above all will for implementation. India has taken significant steps in inventorizing her vast and diverse biological heritage. India has enacted the *Biological Diversity Act, 2002* for preservation of its biological diversity and to provide mechanism for equitable sharing of benefits arising out use of traditional biological resources and knowledge. To implement the provisions under the Act, The National Biodiversity Authority (NBA) headquartered in Chennai was established in 2003. State Biodiversity Boards (SBB) has been created in 28 States along with 31,574 Biological Management Committees (BMC) for each local body across India. The NBA performs facilitative, regulatory and advisory functions for the Govt. of India on issues of conservation, sustainable use of biological resources and fair and equitable sharing of benefits of use. The NBA works with SBBs at the provincial level and BMCs at the local level to implement biodiversity strategies *inter alia* through development of People's Biodiversity Registers (PBRs)

## *REFERENCES*

Myers N, Mittermeier R.A., Mittermeier C.G., Fonseca G.A., Kent J. (2000) Biodiversity Hotspots for Conservation Priorities. *Nature*, 403: 853-858.

Singh, P. & Dash, S.S. (2014) *Plant Discoveries 2013–New Genera, Species and New Records.* Kolkata: Botanical Survey of India.

Venkataraman K., Sheela S., Kumar P.G. (2015) *Animal Discoveries 2014- New Species and New Records*. Kolkata: Zoological Survey of India.

http://www.wiienvis.nic.in/Database/Protected_Area_854.aspx

http://hubpages.com/education/Rare-and-Endangered-plants-of-India

http://travel.india.com/articles/10-endangered-animals-india-see-vanish/

Pages: 100-113

**FOREST AND BIODIVERSITY CONSERVATION**
*Edited by:* **Dr. Alka Chauhan** and **Dr. Pawan Kumar 'Bharti'**
**ISBN: 978-93-5056-873-6**
***Edition:* 2017**
***Published by:* Discovery Publishing House Pvt. Ltd., New Delhi (India)**

# 5 Diversity of Ant Species (Hymenoptera: Formicidae) in the Campus of Maharani's Science College for Women Mysuru City, Karnataka, India

*Mahalakshmi, B.R.,* and *Sachidanandamurthy, K.L.*

## *ABSTRACT*

The study examined the diversity of ants in the Campus of Maharani's Science College, Mysuru city, Karnataka, as there is no adequate information pertaining on ant diversity of this region. The present study was carried out during January to June 2015. We have sampled ants by employing intensive all out search method. This result showed that a total of 978 individuals were captured in the study area. The sampled specimens representing 20 species belonged to 12 genera and four subfamilies. The most diverse subfamily was Myrmicinae (5 genera with 7 species), followed by *Formicinae* (3 genera with 7 species) and Ponerinae (3 genera with 4 species). The smallest number of species belonged to the Pseudomyrmicinae (1 genus with 2 species). Among the sampled genera, one which showed the highest number of species representation was *Camponotus* with 4 species. *Few ant genera as Crematogaster and Pheidole of Myrmicinae, Camponotus and Polyrhachis of Formicinae and Leptogenys of Ponerinae are mostly found everywhere. Some* genera viz; *Oecophylla, Meranoplus, Myrmicaria, Solenopsis, Anochetus* and *Diacamma* are represented by lone species each. The present study has yielded valuable information of ant *availability in this region and also* revealed that the campus of *Maharani's science college, Mysuru has a rich diversity of ants, which has to be studied.*

**Key words:** Diversity, Ant, Study area, Formicidae, Mysuru.

Postgraduate Department of Applied Zoology, Maharani's Science College for Women, Mysuru - 570 005 (Karnataka) (India)

## INTRODUCTION

Ants are most dominant components of terrestrial ecosystem because they constitute greater part of biomass. These ants contribute a conspicuous component of terrestrial biodiversity and are the most divergent group among all social insects. They act as ecosystem engineers. They play very important role in the ecosystem by improving the soil and assisting in the decomposition process. (Watanasit, S., *et al*, 2000) and are considered as good biological indicators due to mutualistic behavior with both flora and fauna. They are eusocial insects, lead high level interactive lives assisting each other to survive. These are highly evolved hymenopteran showing polymorphism. They belong to the family Formicidae, included in superfamily Vesoidea of order Hymenoptera placed under class Insecta of phylum Arthropoda.

Ants are ubiquitous in distribution and occupy almost all terrestrial ecosystems. There are about 15000 species of ants (T.Andrade, 2007); only 11,769 species have been described. (Agosti, 2004). The family Formicidae contains 21 subfamilies, 283 genera and about 15000 living ant species of which 633 ant species belonging to 82 genera, 13 subfamilies are reported from India. About 226 species of ants belonging to 63 genera and 11 subfamilies are estimated from Karnataka state (Varghese, 2009). The main aim of the present study was to conduct survey, to document the ant species diversity in the campus of *Maharani's science college, Mysuru* and prepare a partial checklist of ants in the study area.

## MATERIALS AND METHODS

### Study Area

The field work was conducted in the campus of *Maharani's Science College, Mysuru* City, Karnataka. (Figure 5.1)

The Maharani's Science College Campus, Mysuru is situated at the heart of the Mysuru city (12° 33′ N and 80° 11′ E) covering four and half hectare of land area encompasses Mysuru city (JLB Road) on the east, District Collectors office on to the west. Maharaja pre university college campus on the north and Hotel Regalis on to the south. The unique interaction throws biological consortia peculiar to this ecosystem. It spreads through the biologically diverse and productive habitat of native flora aesthetically blended with introduced heritage buildings all around the campus.

## HABITAT CHARACTERIZATION

The main type of vegetation in Maharani's College campus is dry evergreen and scrub comprising of members predominantly belonging to the families: *Poaceae, Fabaceae, Cyperaceae, Asteraceae, Euphorbiaceae, Verbenaceae, Solanaceae, Rubiaceae, Convolvulaceae Amaranthaceae and Asteraceae* plants.

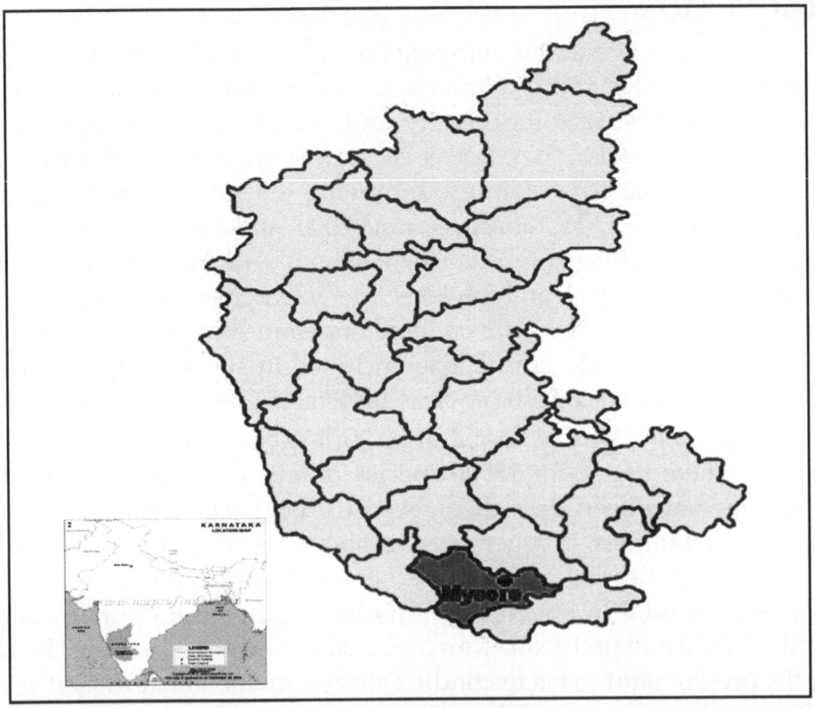


**Study Site: Mysore**

**Fig. 5.1: Study Area – Maharani's Science College Campus, Mysuru**

## SAMPLING DESIGN

**Selection of study site**

⇓

**All out search method- Manual collection by using brush and forceps**

⇓

**Sorting**

⇓

**Ants' identification-Stereo microscope**

⇓

**Labelling**

⇓

**Mounting**

⇓

**Preservation**
**(Dry and Wet preservation)**

⇓

**Documentation of the species**

## ANT SAMPLING METHOD

Field work was carried out in and around Maharani's Science College campus, Mysuru. Ant field sampling was done during January to June 2015. We employed intensive all out search method. i.e. Manual collection by using a brush and forceps during daytime from 9 AM to 6 PM every day. Generally, mornings and evenings gave best results for all out search method. (Gadagkar *et al.*, 1993). The information about Date and time of collection, habitat, locality, was also recorded at the time of collection. The collected specimens were then transferred into vials containing 70% ethyl alcohol. Then ants were brought to the laboratory of Department of Zoology, Maharani's Science College for identification, labeling and preservation.

## ANT CLEANING AND SORTING

Any dirt or adhered material to the body of the ant is cleaned with the help of brush dipped in water.

Sorting is most basic thing, which needs to be done carefully. Samples should be segregated from debris and washing in alcohol before preserving them. Immediately after collection all specimens should be sorted out first into similar groups and each group can be named as group 1, group 2 etc. more than one species are not put into the same vial. Use separate vials for different species. It should be kept in separate vials with appropriate labels in order to avoid confusion (Varghese, T. 2003).

## IDENTIFICATION

The collected ant specimens were brought back to the department of Zoology, Maharani's Science College, for further identification. Ant specimens were tentatively identified up to the genus level by using stereo microscope based on taxonomic keys prepared by Balton (1994). In cases where identification of species was not possible, specimens were then sent to experts for identification. Species level identification was confirmed by Thresiamma Varghese, Myrmicologist, Centre for Ecological Sciences, Indian Institute of Science, Bangalore.

## LABELLING

The permanently preserved specimens were provided with identification and data labels. They are written on good quality paper with India ink. Data label should contain the information about date and time of collection, name of collector, the habitat and locality whereas identification label should contain the species common name and scientific name with author, genus, family and order.

| | |
|---|---|
| Species name............ (Author name & year) | Date............ |
| Common name............ | Time............ |
| Genus............ | Locality............ |
| Family............ | Habitat............ |
| Order............ | Name of collector............ |

## PRESERVATION

The collected ants were preserved for a long time by both wet preservation and dry preservation.

## WET PRESERVATION/LIQUID PRESERVATION

In this method ants can be directly put into separate vials containing 70% ethyl alcohol. All vials should invariably contain small labels showing details of the locality, date of collection, name of the collector, habitat (whether it is arboreal or ground dwelling) and all other possible information about the species. More than one species are not put into the same vial. Use separate vials for different species.

## DRY PRESERVATION

It is the most advisable method of preservation for ants. In this method ants can be glued down to the apex of a small triangular strip of paper or card, in the region between the fore and middle coxae. Finally push one insect pin through the base of the card. The labels are attached to this insect pin. Pinned specimens should be stored in standard insect boxes. Insect pins of various sizes and insect boxes are available in various scientific supply houses. (King and porter, 2004)

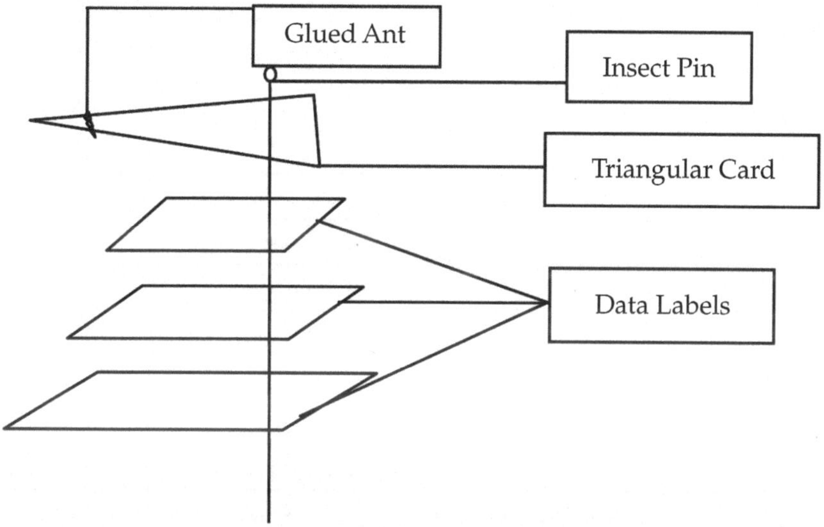


**Mounting (Pinning) of Ants**

## RESULT

Ant diversity in the campus of Maharani's Science College, Mysuru has been analyzed in this study. During this study a total of 978 sampled specimens were captured in the study area. The 20 ant species are belonging to 12 genera and four subfamilies. They are as follows, the Myrmicinae were represented by 7 species and 5 genera. The Formicinae were represented by 7 species and 3 genera. The Ponerinae represented by 4 species and 3 genera. The Pseudomyrmicinae represented by 2 species and 1 genus. The most speciose genus of these 4 subfamilies was *Camponotus* with 4 species.

Among these species *Camponotus compressus* was high compare to other species and noticeably found in everywhere in study site. The species of *Oecophylla* and *Crematogaster* were dominant on tree trunk which nested on trees.

*Few ant genera as Crematogaster and Pheidole of Myrmicinae, Camponotus and Polyrhachis of Formicinae and Leptogenys of Ponerinae are mostly found everywhere. Some* genera such as *Oecophylla, Meranoplus, Myrmicaria, Solenopsis, Anochetus* and *Diacamma* were represented by lone species each.

The table 5.1 & 5.2 (Figs. 5.2 & 5.3) shows detailed distribution of diversity of ants. A number of factors seem to be involved in the increased diversity. It includes food resources, nesting habit etc. The environs of the study area are rich in ant species deserve. To date, no research has been conducted on the diversity of ants. The above information will be useful for the preparation of a management plan for myrmecologists.

**Table 5.1: Checklist of Ants in the Maharani's Science College Campus, Mysuru city**

| Sl. No. | Scientific Name | Common Name | Ecological Status |
|---|---|---|---|
| 1. | *Camponotus compressus* (Fabricius, 1787) | Carpenter ant | Common |
| 2. | *Camponotus* sp.2 | | Common |
| 3. | *Camponotus* sp.3 | | Common |
| 4. | *Camponotus sericeus* (Fabricius, 1798) | | Common |
| 5. | *Oecophylla smaragdina* (Fabricius, 1775) | Weaver ant | Common |
| 6. | *Polyrhachis* sp.1 | Spiny ant | Common |
| 7. | *Polyrhachis* sp.2 | | Rare |
| 8. | *Crematogaster* sp.1 | | Rare |
| 9. | *Crematogaster* sp.2 | | Common |
| 10. | *Meranoplus bicolor* (Guerin-Meneville, 1844) | Shield ant | Common |
| 11. | *Myrmicaria brunnea* (Saunders, 1842) | Harvester ant | Rare |
| 12. | *Pheidole* sp. | Big headed ant | Rare |
| 13. | *Pheidole watsoni* (Forel, 1902) | | Rare |
| 14. | *Solenopsis geminate* (Fabricius, 1804) | Fire ant/thief ant | Common |
| 15. | *Anochetus* sp. | Trap jaw ant | Common |
| 16. | *Diacamma ceylonense* (Emery, 1897) | Queenless ant | Common |
| 17. | *Leptogenys* sp.3 | Long legged ant | Rare |
| 18. | *Leptogenys processionalis* (Jerdon, 1851) | | Common |
| 19. | *Tetraponera* sp.2 | Arboreal ant | Rare |
| 20. | *Tetraponera rufonigra* (Jerdon, 1851) | | Common |

Total 20 ant species were recorded in the study area during this study. Among them *Polyrhachis* sp.2, *Crematogaster* sp.1, *Myrmicaria brunnea* (Saunders, 1842), *Pheidole* sp., *Pheidole watsoni* (Forel, 1902), *Leptogenys* sp.3 and *Tetraponera* sp.2 are rarely found the study area are represented in the (Fig. 5.4) and listed in table 5.1.

**Table 5.2: Summary of ant species collected from sampling site.**

| Sub Families | Genera | Species Found |
|---|---|---|
| Formicinae | *Camponotus* | 4 |
| | *Oecophylla* | 1 |
| | *Polyrhachis* | 2 |
| Myrmicinae | *Meranoplus* | 1 |
| | *Myrmicaria* | 1 |
| | *Pheidole* | 2 |
| | *Crematogaster* | 2 |
| | *Solenopsis* | 1 |
| Ponerinae | *Anochetus* | 1 |
| | *Leptogenys* | 2 |
| | *Diacamma* | 1 |
| Pseudomyrmicinae | *Tetraponera* | 2 |
| **Total** | **12** | **20** |

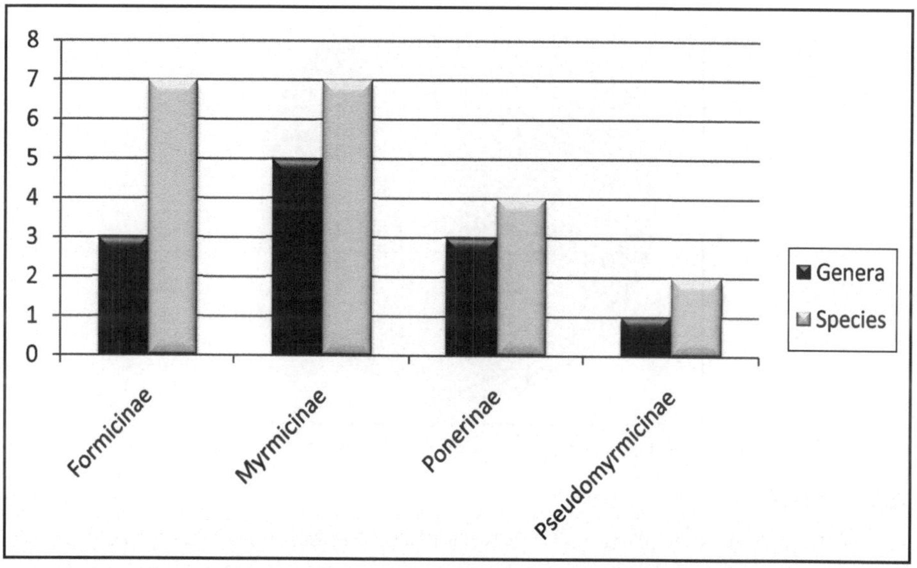


**Fig. 5.2: Diversity of Ants Representing Subfamily, Genera with Species**

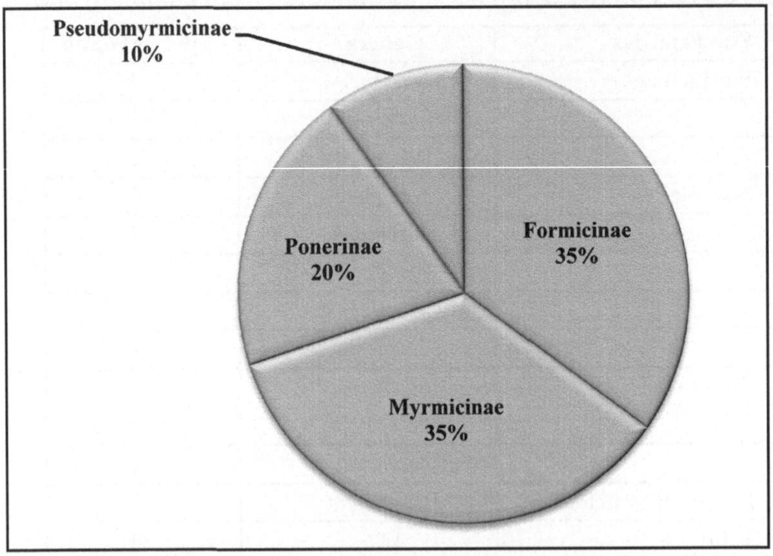


**Fig. 5.3: Subfamily wise Distribution of Ants found at Study Area**

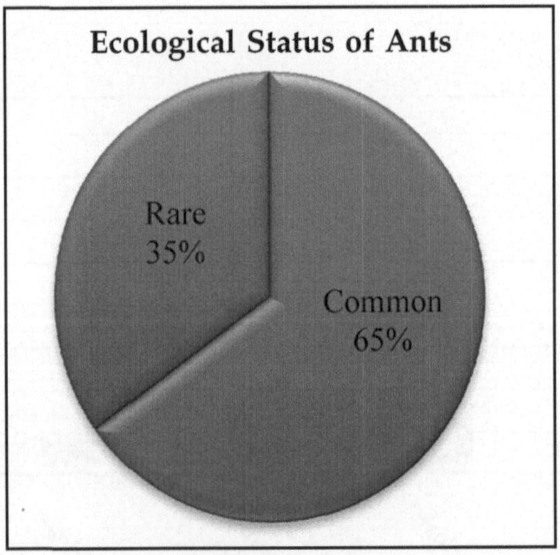


**Fig. 5.4: Ecological Status of Ant Fauna of Study Area**

## DISCUSSION

A total of 4 subfamilies, 12 genera and 20 species of ants were recorded from the campus of Maharani's Science College, Mysuru. The majority of species were in the Myrmicinae (35%) and Formicinae (35%) followed by Ponerinae (20%). At the genus level, *Camponotus, Polyrhachis, Pheidole* and *Crematogaster* were the most speciose genera in this study with 4, 2, 2 and 2 respectively.

The rich diversity of the ants documented during this study may be because of adequate nesting sites and availability of food as well foraging. The high diversity of ants in this area is showed that this area is good habitat for ants.

## SUBFAMILY MYRMICINAE

Myrmicinae were the most abundant in numbers of ants and the most diverse group (7 Species) in this study area. This family showed a significant difference between seasons (Watanasit.S *et al*, 2000). The number of individuals was higher in the wet season. They nested in soil humus, in hollow twigs, under bark, inside galls or in nuts of woody plants. It is therefore not surprising that we collected them in greater numbers. These ants were more specific due to availability of food and nesting sites. These are also the exclusively arboreal and terrestrial taxa. *Pheidole* nested in soil, *Crematogaster* nested in dead wood on trees, *Myrrmicaria* nested at tree base, *Meranoplus* had nests in open canopy areas and *Solenopsis* nested under rocks and rotten logs.

## SUBFAMILY FORMICINAE

The Formicinae were the most abundant in the study area. The extreme dominance exhibited by Formicinae sub family with seven species in this study. Formicinae did not show a significant difference between seasons. Humidity may influence nest building. The genus *Camponotus* were record of four species. *Camponotus* was a frequently occurring species in everywhere. The *Camponotus* had the greatest individual numbers. These ants are called as carpenter ants because of their "Nesting behaviours"(Chavhan.A *et al*, 2011). Food sources may have been important (Watanasit.S *et al*, 2000). The most common among them were *Oecophylla smaragdina*, a truly arboreal species. These ants nested in shady places and require broad leaves to stitch their nest. All the recorded species of *Polyrhachis* were arboreal and found in undisturbed areas. These ants nested on the ground.

## PHOTO PLATES

### 1. Sub-family: Formicinae

|  | 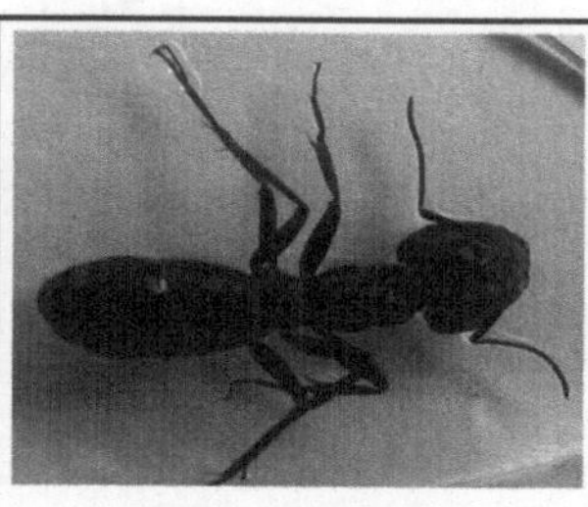 | 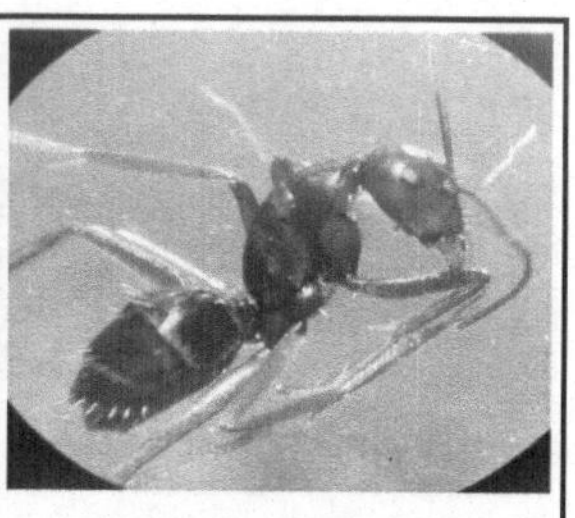 |
|---|---|---|
| *Camponotus compressus* | *Camponotus sp. 2* | *Camponotus sp. 3* |

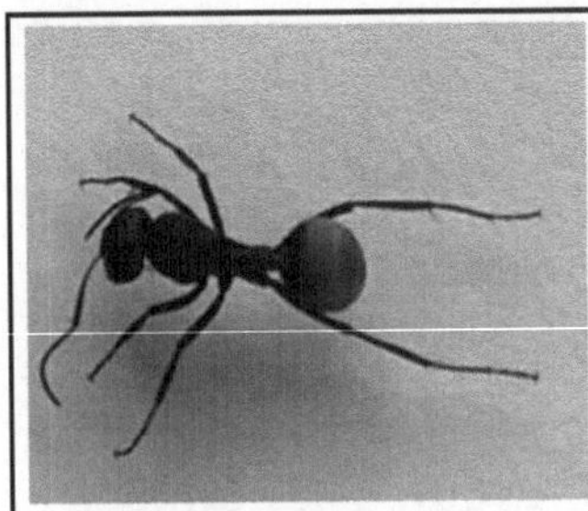

*Camponotus sericeus*

*Oecophylla smaragdina*

*Polyrhachis Sp. 1*

*Polyrhachis sp. 2*

## 2. Sub-family: Myrmicinae

*Meranoplus bicolor*

*Myrmicaria brunnea*

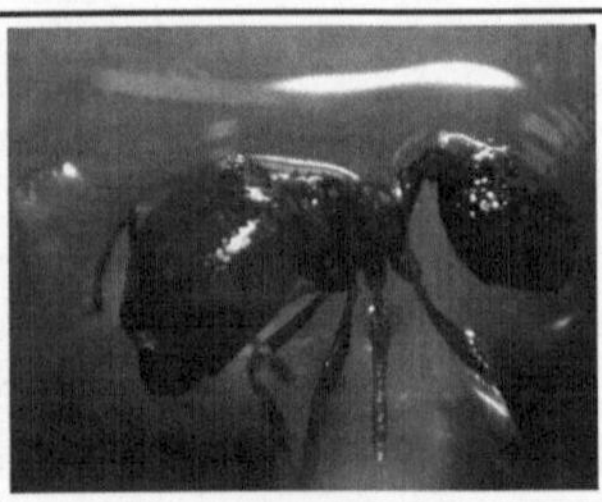

*Pheidole sp.*

*Crematogaster sp. 1*

*Crematogaster sp. 2*

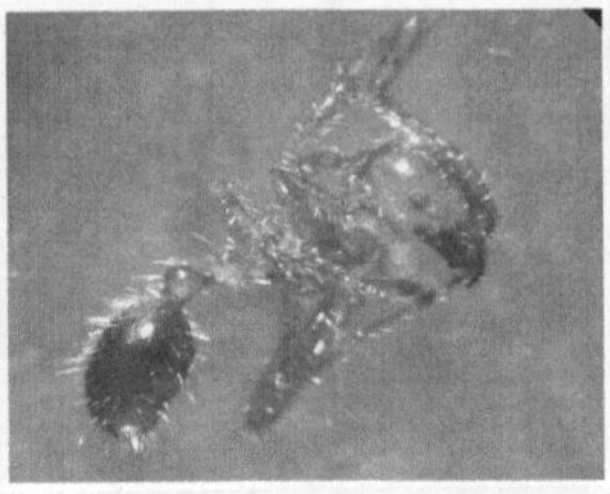

*Solenopsis geminate*

*Pheidole watsoni*

## 3. Sub-family: Ponerinae

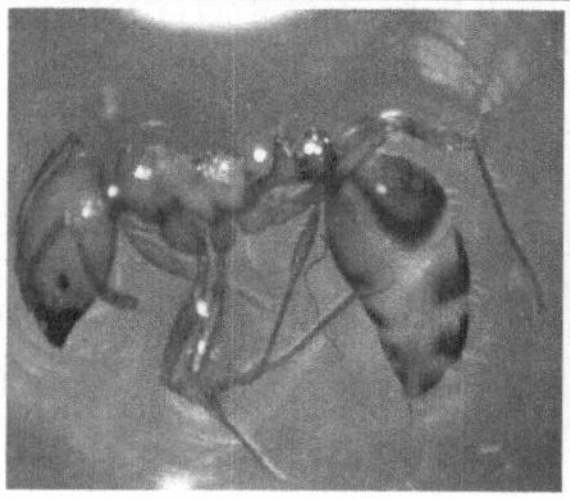

*Anochetus sp*

*Leptogenys sp. 3*

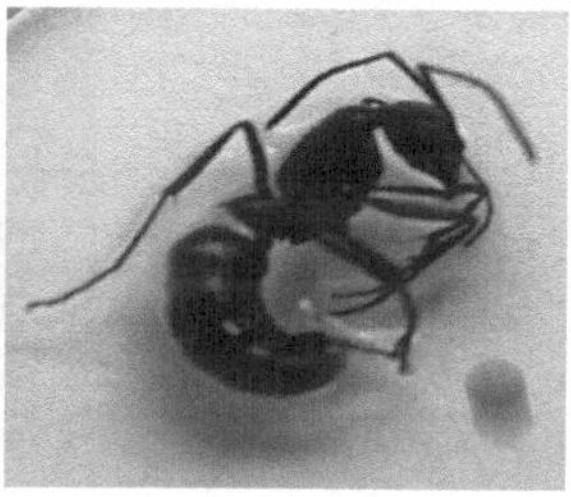

*Leptogenys processionalis*

*Diacamma ceylonense*

## 4. Sub-family: Pseudomyrmecinae

*Tetraponera rufonigra*

*Tetraponera sp. 2*

## SUBFAMILY PONERINAE

Ponerinae sub family was more specific about its niche and food habits ( Ramachandra.T.V., *et al*, 2012). They feed on a wide range of food. Food resources may have played an important role influencing numbers of Ponerinae (Watanasit.S *et al*, 2000). *Anochetus* and *Diacamma* were nested in soil or even in rotten logs. *Leptogenys* prefer cavities in logs or large branches to construct their nests.

## SUBFAMILY PSEUDOMYRMICINAE

Only one genus *Tetraponera* representing Pseudomyrmicinae has been recorded. Neither seasonal change nor did physical factors influence the numbers of this group. These are solitary foragers and make their nests in fallen dead wood and rotten logs. *Tetraponera rufonigra* was dominant compared to *Tetraponera* sp.2 in the study area.

## CONCLUSION

The present investigation on diversity of ants in the Maharani's Science College Campus, Mysuru clearly shows the richness of ants fauna in the city. We have recorded 20 species of ants belonging to 4 sub families. The campus of Maharani's Science College, Mysuru city embodies ant diversity. Our results support the prediction that ant diversity is greater in this campus. The present study will yield valuable information of ant *availability in the region.*

## *REFERENCES*

Agosti, *et al*. *"Litter Ant Communities of the Brazilian Atlantic Rain forest region"*.

Andrade, T.(2007): "Diversity of Ground Dwelling Ants in Cerrado: An Analysis of Temporal Variations and Distinctive Physiognomies of Vegetation (Formicidae: Hymenoptera), Vol. 50.

Bolton, B. (1994): *"Identification Guide to the Ant Genera of the World"*. Harvard University Press, Cambridge, Massachusetts, USA. 222 pp.

Chavhan, A. and Pawar, S.S. (2011): "Distribution and Diversity of Ant Species in and Around Amravati City of Maharashtra, India". pp: 395-400.

Gadagkar, *et al*. (1993):"Ant Species Richness and Diversity in some Selected Localities of Western Ghats, India". pp: 79-94.

Guruprasad, B.R. and Tiwari, A.K. (2011): *"Ant: Handbook of Insect Biology"*. pp: 38-59.

King, J.R. and Porter, S.D. (2004): "Recommendations on the use of Alcohols for Preservation of Ant Specimens". pp: 197-202.

Ramachandra, T.V., *et al*. (2012): "Ant Species Composition and Diversity in the Sharavathi River Basin-Central Western Ghats". pp: 1-51.

Staffan, B., and Maclsaac, A.M. (2002): "A Preliminary Study of Ant Diversity and of Ant Dependence on Dead Wood in Central Interior British Columbia". pp: 111-119.

Sunil Kumar, M., *et al*. (1997): *"Ant Species Richness at Selected Localities of Bangalore"*. pp: 3-5.

Varghese, T., *et al*. (1997): "Ant Species Richness at Selected Localities of Bangalore". pp: 3-5.

Varghese, T. (2003): *"Ants of the Indian Institute of Science Campus. Technical Report No. 98., Centre for Ecological Sciences, Indian Institute of Science, Bangalore"*.

Varghese, T. (2009): *"A Review of Extant Subfamilies, Tribes and Ant Genera in India"*. pp: 81-89.

Watanasit, S., *et al.* (2000): *"Diversity of Ants from Ton Nga Chang Wildlife Sanctuary, Songkhla,Thailand"* pp: 187-194.

Pages: 114-130

FOREST AND BIODIVERSITY CONSERVATION
*Edited by:* Dr. Alka Chauhan and Dr. Pawan Kumar 'Bharti'
ISBN: 978-93-5056-873-6
*Edition:* 2017
*Published by:* Discovery Publishing House Pvt. Ltd., New Delhi (India)

# 6 Ecosystem Management for Sustainable Development

*Dr. Babita Agrawal*

## INTRODUCTION

Ecosystem management is widely proposed in the popular and professional literature as the modern and preferred way of managing natural resources and ecosystems. Ecosystem management as an approach that will protect the environment, maintain healthy ecosystems, preserve biological diversity, and ensure sustainable development. Ecosystem management defines a paradigm that weaves biophysical and social threads into a tapestry of beauty, health, and sustainability. It embraces both social and ecological dynamics in a flexible and adaptive process and celebrates the wisdom of both our minds and hearts, and lights our path to the future (Cornett, 1994). Ecosystem management is a response to today's deepening crises. Utmany ecologists have advocated many important determinants of the contemporary ecosystem discussion. The first book length treatment on ecosystem management appeared in 1988. Jim Agee and Darryll Johnson (1988) presented a theoretical framework that included both general goals and processes for achieving goals and processes for achieving goals. These authors embedded ecosystem management within a dynamic pattern and process view of nature. Accordingly to them ecologically defined boundaries, clearly stated management goals, interagency cooperation, monitoring of management results, and leadership at the policy level were essential elements.

It is recognized that human behaviour is linked to ecosystem wellbeing and humans are considered integral parts of ecosystems, as opposed to being considered separate entities. Thus, environmental and human community assessments, in conjunction with one another, are required to effectively manage regions, whether ecologically and/or socially defined. Ecosystem

Ex-Associate Professor, SVIM, Indore, M.P (India)

management, one of several approaches to achieving sustainability, emphasizes mostly in ecologically driven regions and is employed by ecologists and natural resource managers and agents. Other different approaches may include: the natural capital approach, popular with ecological economists; sustainable urban design, which is typically used by land use planners, architects, and local officials; and, metropolitan governance, employed by those who seek a regional policy approach.

An ecosystem serves a purpose of a job of nurturing community, sharing the everyday jobs for and the power of executive and for developing collaborative land management. The inclusion of people and their economic needs is a fundamental part of the approach. Decisions are not only more likely to be implemented if they come from the community, they also will be better as they will strike a more appropriate balance for that place in that time. Unlike traditional pattern in management, ecosystem management does not begin with enumerating outputs; in ecosystem management objectives are related first and foremost to the condition of the ecosystem, Ecosystem management makes ecological sustainability long-term maintenance of ecosystem productivity and resilience a primary goal. Protection and estoration of ecosystem structures and processes, particularly biodiversity, is paramount. Ecosystem management further recognizes a critical interdependence between social and ecological vitality and includes humans and human societies in resource management to an unprecedented extent. It breaks new ground by insisting that the social and political basis of natural resource management goals be made explicit and by encouraging their development through an inclusive and collaborative decision making process. Ecosystem management is based on an ecosystem science that integrates many disciplinary approaches. The various complexities and dynamic nature of ecological and social systems, ecosystem management embraces the concept of adaptive management, which requires constant reassessment and revision as new information becomes available. Principally ecosystem management basically falls into two categories, viz; (i) addressing scientific issues, and; (ii) addressing policy, planning and management. With this notion, ecosystem management should be guided by ecological principles of biodiversity, ecosystem complexity, scales of analysis, hierarchies of components, ecosystem boundaries, baselines and monitoring, stability and resiliency, carrying capacity, and most importantly, holistic analysis. Planning and management should be guided by the principles of interdisciplinary and intergenerational planning, integration of economic/environmental/social value system, information transfer, public participation, human ecosystems, equitability, adaptive management, and recognition of constraints and limitations.

The increasing exercise of ecosystem management to attain sustainable natural resource management is based on a acknowledgment of management approaches which generally resulted in a loss of biodiversity and degradation of the environment. The basic and common approach is conserving ecosystem functions and integrity is vital because possible ecosystems are the basic life support system for individual. The approach is therefore seen as a constructive tool for maintaining a particular region's natural resources and for promoting sustainable development. A fundamental principle of the ecosystem management realm is that natural resource development should occur at multiple scales, within ecosystem boundaries, not administrative boundaries. This approach recognizes that ecosystems are both biophysical and socio-cultural systems that is, ecosystems include social and cultural uses, not just the more generally recognized physical and biological properties.

Several factors contribute to this disparity between goals and practices, including: (1) gross under sampling of nearly all environments and consequent poverty of information on their biological diversity; (2) widespread ignorance of the function and dynamics of ecosystems; (3) the openness and interconnectedness of ecosystems on scales that exceed greatly the bounds of any management authority; (4) a prevailing public perception that exploitation of supposedly renewable resources has immediate economic and social value sufficient to outweigh the risks of damage to future ecosystem services or any alternative management goals of ecosystem integrity.

Ecosystem Management Includes the Following Elements:

1. **Sustainability:** Sustainability is developing the needs of the present without compromising the ability of future generations to meet their own needs.
2. **Goals:** Goals must be unambiguously stated in provisions of detailed "desired upcoming trajectories" and "desired future behaviours" for the ecosystem components and processes necessary for sustainability. Furthermore, these goals should be stated in terms that can be measured and monitored.
3. **Sound ecological models and understanding:** Ecosystem Management depends on examination performed at all levels of organization, from exploration of the morphology, physiology and behaviour of individual organisms, through studies dynamics of populations and communities, to examine of patterns and processes at the level of ecosystems and landscapes.
4. **Complexity and connectedness:** Biological diversity and structural complexity of ecosystems are central to key ecosystem functions such as primary production and nutrient cycling. They also impart resistance to and resilience from disturbance, and the genetic resources necessary to adapt to long term change. The dynamic character of ecosystems.
5. **Adaptability and accountability:** Ecosystem agents must be aware of that the knowledge base is incomplete and subject to change.

Management goals and strategies must be viewed as hypotheses to be tested by research and monitoring programs that compare specific expectations against objective measures of results.

**Ecosystem Management in India**

There is a strong connection between the environment and disasters. Surprisingly the ecosystem management approach is not integrated yet with implementation practices of sustainable livelihood and other disaster risk reduction options. Specific subject based initiatives on living and ecosystem management focusing on wide-ranging risk reduction through budding frameworks are predestined. This would further strengthen vertical and horizontal integration by engaging related sectors and concerned organizations. Environmental deprivation is a major problem in dry lands, where forests and foliage contribute significantly to rural livelihoods. About 69% of country's total geographical area is under dry lands. These areas ironically are highly populated which makes the people exposed to environmental stress and impacts livelihoods directly. Government is directly engaged in these issues, 22 programmes have been implemented by Government of India (GOI), including, the 'Mission for Green India' one of the Missions under the National Action Plan on Climate Change. The objective of initiating these programme are to address dry land forests, in addition to other ecosystems. Through the various mechanisms, approaches and methods, government is combining native and scientific knowledge of restoring and sustaining the natural resource base, including its biodiversity, while taking into the consideration of climate impact. Various running awareness programs have improved the potential of the local communities in sustainable utilizing their natural capital. In 75 villages of Thar Desert ecosystem in western India, the rural communities have been empowered by some government practices in reviving and promoting the traditional incorporated water and land management systems. About 62 micro projects have been implemented. Grass varieties like Moda Dhaman (Cenchrus sp.) with high caloric value are being grown. Revival of long-established plants/trees and planting methods with the procedural support of government institutions is on the rise. The project has given natives to discuss their inconvenience with government institutions and collectively find a way out. The project has ensured active participation of women in 'jal sabhas' (water committees) which manage the water resources. The marine fishers in the state of Maharashtra were facing problems due to distribution shift of pelagic fishes, submergence of their low lying fish drying platforms, unseasonal and extreme rains. Madhya Pradesh Forest Department is using practice for the fire alert messaging, forest offence management and wildlife alert messaging system at a very nominal cost.

**Stakeholders' Contribution in Ecosystem Management**

An important factor in the success of many ecosystem management projects has been involving stakeholders from the beginning, especially those stakeholders who are most resistant to the idea. Managers of ecosystem based projects need to focus on acquiring the knowledge and skills to work effectively with stakeholders. Government the requisite skills and to support outreach work. Participants, particularly community members and First Nations, may need training and resources to build capacity and participate effectively in these processes. Various stakeholders may contribute in the development of ecosystem management of any country. Charter of commitments towards stakeholders:

- Employees
- Members/shareholders, financial community
- Clients/customers
- Suppliers
- Financial partners (banks, insurance companies and financial services)
- State, local authorities and public administration
- Community

Cultural and spiritual ideals are vital driving forces in nature preservation and ecosystem management. The cultural importance of natural ecosystems not only consists of tangible goods and services, but also includes many often intangible, nonmaterial or information services. People perceive nature is basically depends on ethnically defined value and belief systems that form an important, often source of information. Ecosystems is basically influenced by physical attributes and cultural perceptions as well. Therefore, it importantly examines those sacred values that are shared or group values and, to a lesser end, individual values. More precisely, it is concerned with those nonmaterial values, including spiritual values that are shared by cultural groups and may thus be regarded as culturally defined.

**Economic Valuation of Cultural Importance**

One way of approximating the value of expressions of intrinsic and extrinsic values may be the use of economic approaches. It is clear that economic valuation approaches, such as measuring 'willingness to pay' or the 'increased market price' for property in a natural setting, may function as a tool to put a price tag on the aesthetic functions of the landscape. Hence such methods may assist in addressing some of the human ecosystem relations, such as leisure or aesthetics, but do not work when reciprocity dominates value systems. Often the monetary value is merely a poor reflection or an approximation of the 'full value' of the human ecosystem relationship that does not do justice to the cultural and spiritual values attached to the ecosystem as a whole. Moreover, these values are often based on perceptions that did not consider local and/or indigenous people to whom ecosystem values might include special cultural and spiritual dimensions. Legally binding multilateral agreements depend upon the quality and enforcement of national legislation and political commitment of its signatories. In absence of political commitment to establish any legal basis or resolution, which contents the sharing and possible rearrangement of benefits derived from nature, is in some cases induced through the pressure of private stakeholders with vested power interests. CBD and WIPRO are committed to apply mechanisms that have their roots in right based society rather than a responsibility based society.

***Increasing the Companies' Sustainability***

The economic activities exert a strong pressure on the natural environment for the whole chain of transformations of the raw materials in products and services for consumption. For this reason transposing in practice of the sustainable principles requires preoccupies of firms for evidencing and control the impact of their activities 12 on the nature and society, and transition to business sustainability model. It signifies a modality of firms' functioning in which all efforts concerning product design, manufacturing, delivery, distribution and disposal throughout the product life cycle are oriented to the reduction of impact on the life and ecosystems (Hogevold and Svenson, 2012). Various companies are adopting a responsible attitude concerning the impact produced on the external environment constituting a directed transition towards an economic growth of sustainable type, the economic advantages through upgrading of effectiveness and escalating of the competitiveness on market. Within the social benefits, it appears as many benefits for employees related to extend of the corporate social responsibility, and at the entire economy level will be produced an improvement in the quality of life through a better protection of the people's natural frame. It has also been seen at the same time the commercial and cooperation relationships between companies will create the favourable conditions for transmission the sustainable practices in various sectors of economy. It is considered that changes of the production systems in order to obtain sustainable products and services, represents an important modality to restructure the firms' economy and to orient them toward the sustainable practices. The production systems of sustainable type generate greater positive or reduced negative social, environmental and economic impacts along the value chain from producer to end" and offer comparative advantages in the competitive environment (Borregaard and Dufey, 2005). Development of the concept of clean products (Shaltegger, 2008) means stimulating of some investments projects for achieving the ecologic production and develop some practices for measure and accounting of the environment performance (Burritt, 2000). Also, the quality of working life of various adapting of their functions for having a better connexion with complexity of economic, social and environmental demands. Movement of the economic organisms should have to be appreciated through consumers' satisfaction for the products and services, and economic performance.

**Five Documents resulted from the Earth Summit held in Rio in 1992**

The *Rio Declaration on Environment and Development* includes principles defining the right and the responsibilities of nations as they pursue human development and well being. The following principles are especially important for management as well as for research: People are at the centre of concerns for sustainable development. They are entitled to a healthy and productive life in harmony with nature (Principle 1).

The right to development must be fulfilled so as to equitably meet development and environmental needs of present and future generations (Principle 3).

In order to achieve sustainable development, environmental protection shall constitute an integral part of the development process and cannot be considered in isolation from it (Principle 4).

States shall cooperate in a spirit of global partnership to conserve, protect and restore the health and integrity of the Earth's ecosystem (Principle 7). States should cooperate to strengthen endogenous capacity building for sustainable development by improving scientific understanding through exchanges of scientific and technological knowledge, and by enhancing the development, adaptation, diffusion and transfer of technologies, including new and innovative technologies (Principle 9). In order to protect the environment, the precautionary approach shall be widely applied by the States according to their capabilities (Principle 15). Environmental impact assessment, as a national instrument, shall be undertaken for proposed activities that are likely to have a significant adverse impact on the environment and are subject to a decision of a competent national authority (Principle 17).

*Agenda 21*

Agenda 21 reflects a global consensus and commitment at the highest political level on how to make development socially, economically, and environmentally sustainable. Among other options it includes protecting the atmosphere, an integrated approach to planning for and managing land resources, combating deforestation, 16 managing fragile ecosystems: combating desertification and drought and sustainable mountain development, promoting sustainable agriculture and rural development, conservation of biological diversity, managing biotechnology, protecting and managing the oceans, protecting and managing fresh waters, and supporting science for sustainable development.

**The Inputs for Sustainable Development (Ecosystem Management)**

1. **Public engagement:** Stating in its key principles that environmental issues are at best handled with the participation of all concerned citizens and that each individual shall have appropriate access to information and the opportunity to participate in decision making processes. Management institution must be open to change induced by recommendations from outside and within the organization. Therefore, the institution must be flexible enough to question itself. If an institution were to fulfil this premise, it could formulate objectives of how the ecosystem might function, decide what management steps should be tried and include the results in the formulation of further management strategies
2. **Leadership:** Leaders play a critical role in leading change and transforming governance into ecosystem management system. The transformation involves coordination information and ongoing activities, building knowledge and understanding of ecosystem dynamics. Providing leadership in the form of visions and goals, and developing a social network for ecosystem management. The transformation of the previous management system into a trajectory of ecosystem management required seizing a window of opportunity and linking organizations and institutions across scales. Management theorists have assumed that if humans aren't rational in a logical way, then they ought to be. Economists, who played such a outstanding role in the development of the management field, described this version of rationality best. Managers are seen as "imaginative, evaluative, and maximizing" to use a more topical formulation. Initially, this view of messengers, leaders as rational agents serve the business schools, organizations and their clients well.
3. **Communication:** Facilitating communication among scientists, planners, regulators, policy makers and managers is a key ingredient of ecosystem management. These dialogues develop the shared vision a desired future outcomes that guide the practice of ecosystem management. Collaborative dialogues create bridges connecting diverse areas of expertise and knowledge. The resulting network of connections, the kaleidoscope of expertise, can be cultivated and maintained as a resource for ecosystem management.
4. **Incentives:** Three levels of government of the country (Central, state and local) and private companies increasingly use economic tools that create incentives for preservation and sustainable management of biodiversity and ecosystems. Due to the enormous pressure on ecosystem services, the regulatory instruments alone are not enough to

conserve or ensure the sustainable use of biodiversity. There is a need to design, test and execute economic instruments that harmonize and strengthen effective regulatory instruments. These methods must also set economic incentives ensure agricultural production, while conserving and sustainable using biodiversity and ecosystem services.

5. **Monitoring:** Monitoring refers here to data gathering and analysis focused on management expectations and designed to test the success and efficacy of management actions. Within the framework of ecosystem management, monitoring programs should be designed to determine whether management actions &e moving the ecosystem toward desired future conditions and trajectories, i.e., toward goals and expectations. It aims at recovering ecosystem functioning and flexibility by addressing the drivers of change and ensuring impartial access to ecosystem services. The process of monitoring involves: Determine which services have priority, Develop effective intervention strategies, and Ensure equitable access and use of ecosystem services by all stakeholders.
6. **Interactions between Sectors:** The only way to deal with the cumulative effects of human influences on marine ecosystems is for various contributing sectors to set common goals for the protection or management of ecosystems (Leslie *et al.* 2008). While some policies may only affect a single sector, others may affect multiple sectors. A policy for the protection of endangered marine species, for example, could affect recreational and commercial fisheries, mining, shipping and tourism sectors to name a few (Leslie *et al.* 2008). More effective ecosystem management would result from the collective adoption of policies by all sectors, rather than each sector creating their own isolated policies.
7. **Adaptive management:** In managing biological resources we are confronted with the complexity of ecosystems, with long term processes, with unpredictable natural disturbances as well as with human influences. Even with the best available science complete answers to all management questions will not be attainable. Stankey and Shindler (1996), in a study of the FEMAT adaptive management areas, identified several barriers confronting effective implementation of the adaptive management. They presented a set of four propositions that address these potential barriers: (1) area boundaries must possess social meaning for stakeholders; (2) a focus on adaptive management areas will highlight limitations in scientific knowledge; (3) management of the adaptive management areas will highlight differences in how the world is perceived; and (4) effective management of the adaptive management areas will challenge existing institutional arrangements.
8. **Sustainability:** If managed properly, ecosystems can provide a cost efficient and effective way to reduce the impacts of climate change while

meeting development objectives. Various organizations consult with ministries of environment, planning and finance to promote the incorporation of the ecosystem approach into national development planning and investment strategies. Ecosystem management is not only having science based ecological elements but also contains socio-economic and political aspects of the system. Understanding the entire ecosystem was seen as important to maintaining ecological integrity in a sustainable manner. Healthy ecosystems perform a diverse array of functions that provide both goods and services to humanity.

## REVIEW OF LITERATURE

Loring *et. al.* (2013) analyzed an ongoing planning process in Greenlandic fisheries governance aiming to reform the coastal Greenland halibut fishery. It examined the way certain truths about this fishery and the need for reform are produced up to and in the final policy document 'regulation concerning the coastal fishery for Greenland halibut'. Findings highlighted the way the small scale Greenland halibut fishery system became a particular governance problem with respect to particular contextual meanings of sustainability and long term planning. The article then examined whether this governance problem could also be understood as primarily a problem to a certain 'governmentality' mode of governance. Whereas some fishery studies document how governmentality modes of governance in fisheries succeeded in transforming subjectivities, this study offered a view into the process that might go before successful governmentality:

The study of Broch *et. al.* (2013) followed the development of such a framework for the Barents Sea Lofoten area in Norway, which to a large extent builds upon existing practices, but also suggests additional monitoring programs. It described how the construction of governance instrumentation for ecosystem based management takes place. In doing so, it focuses on pollution monitoring. The study shaded light on the ways in which the ecosystem is made readable and measurable. In addition, it offered insight into the scientific and institutional challenges in the practices towards making ecosystem based management instrumental and operational. They suggested here that both the formal and informal types of cooperation are the only factors at work in promoting small scale aquaculture's survival, but by using an ethnographic approach it is nonetheless possible to make a strong case for their critical importance in the Killary site.

Ito *et. al.* (2013) studied a process by which a large set of quantitative biological, physical, chemical and social indicators may be transformed into a simple, but informative, numerical index that represents the overall ecosystem health, while also identifying the likely source and scale of pressure for remedial management action. The flexibility of the proposed approach means that it can be readily adapted to other lake systems and environments, or even to include or exclude different indicators.

Dubey (2013) emphasized on the use of management practices in preference to the use of off farm inputs, taking into account that regional conditions require locally adapted systems. Organic farming emerged as a potential alternative for meeting food demand, maintaining soil fertility and increasing soil carbon pool. Organic production systems have been particularly suitable to smallholder farmers as these systems depend on the sustainable use of local resources and on farmers' traditional knowledge and social networks.

Angelstam *et. al.* (2013) reviewed the landscape concepts' biophysical, anthropogenic, and intangible dimensions. Second, we exemplify how the different landscape concepts can be used to derive measurable variables for different sustainability indicators. Third, they reviewed gradients in the three dimensions of the term landscape on the European continent, and propose to use them for the stratification of multiple case studies of social ecological systems. They stressed the benefits of the landscape concepts to measure sustainability, and how this can improve collaborative learning about development toward sustainability in social – ecological systems.

Winn & Pogutz (2013) aimed to encourage research into how organizations can manage their relationship with the natural environment so as not to destroy the very life supporting foundations provided by nature. Bridging knowledge domains, the article introduced key concepts from ecology and social ecology to organization and management studies—*ecosystems, biodiversity, ecosystem services,* and *ecological resilience.* They illustrated these concepts with advances in ecosystems management and conclude with suggestions for future research in sustainability management, organization theory, and strategic management.

Ewa Bojar (2012) in study Eco Management in Polish Companies revealed that the economic activity has an enormous influence on the environment. Enterprises contribute to the progressing degradation of existing ecosystems, cause serious threats to the biological diversity of our planet, emit hazardous pollutants and use available natural resources excessively, which can lead to their premature exhaustion. Therefore, for the world's nations to grow and develop in a sustainable manner there is an urgent need to minimize the adverse impact of business activities, households and whole societies on the environment. The main purpose of the study was to analyze the environmental activities and initiatives undertaken by enterprises operating in the region, directions of pro environmental investments, implemented environmental management systems, as well as motivations of business managers to pay more attention to environmental issues.

Shikui Dong (2010) in study 'Implication of Coupled Natural and Human Systems in Sustainable Rangeland Ecosystem Management', focused on the sustainable development of rangeland ecosystems, the vital ecosystems providing many important ecosystem services for millions of people in the Hindu Kush Himalaya region is presently confronted with a number of challenges. It was concluded although the research sites and objectives were very different, that these three case studies had many commonalities that addressed the complex interactions and feedbacks between natural and human systems, and highlighted the integration of various tools and techniques from the ecological and social sciences, as well as other disciplines, in sustainable rangeland management. These case studies have offered unique interdisciplinary insights into complexities that cannot be gained from ecological o social research alone. The results from these case studies can be applied to many other coupled systems at local, national, and global levels.

## RESEARCH METHODOLOGY

### The Nature of the Present Research Design

The research design of the present study is based on the understanding that because of the paucity of research on this particular topic it is an explanatory study utilising a combination of quantitative and qualitative techniques.

### Objectives of the Study

1. To estimate the requirement of various inputs for development and to enrich the ecosystem to provide those inputs on sustainable basis.
2. To examine the relationship between Economic Factors and Eco Management for Sustainable Development.
3. To examine the relationship between Social Factors and Eco Management for Sustainable Development.

### Survey Research

In this study, survey research design is adopted. Survey research design was chosen because the sampled elements and the variables that are being studied are simply being observed as they are without making any attempt to control and manipulate them. The theoretical population of the study consists of the Companies, Manufacturing Units, Stakeholders, NGOs and Academicians in Indore district.

### Sampling Techniques

A stratified sampling technique was used to select a total of 400 respondents that constituted our sample size. It should be pointed out that limited financial resources at the researcher's disposal could not permit or allow for a greater sample size.

### Sample Size

Due to time constraints, a sampling procedure was used. The total sample size for the study is 400 respondents. The samples were collected from each organization:

Companies = 50 Educational Institutions = 50 Manufacturing Units = 50

Policy Makers = 50 Stakeholders = 50 Hospitals = 50 NGOs = 50 Customers = 50

### Data Collection Instrument

The data for this study was mainly collected from primary sources i.e. companies, academicians, manufacturers, suppliers, contractors, customers etc. in Indore. A well structured and close ended questionnaire was designed and utilized to measure the cultural, social, economic and environmental factors and its association with the ecosystem management for sustainable development. The respondents were asked to respond on 'Likert Scale' (Five Point Scale) ranging from "Strongly Disagree" to "Strongly Agree". The additional data needed to support the study was also be collected from secondary sources like: online publications, journals, magazines, newspapers, books etc.

**Data Instrument:** Self Structured Questionnaire on 5point Likert Scale.

### Tools for Data Analysis

Correlation & Regression were applied through SPSS 20.0 version.

## RESULTS AND DISCUSSIONS

### Hypotheses Tested

$H_{01:}$ There is no significant relationship between various inputs and outputs of Ecosystem Management.

$H_{11:}$ There is a significant relationship between various inputs and outputs of Ecosystem Management.

**Table 6.1: Model summary on various inputs and outputs of ecosystem management**

| Model | R | R Square | Adjusted R Square | Std. Error of the Estimate | F Value |
|---|---|---|---|---|---|
| 1. | .854[a] | .729 | .728 | 13.79087 | 802.629 |
| a. | Predictors: (Constant), Inputs b. | | | | Sig. .000 |
| b. | Dependent Variable: Outputs | | | | |

### Regression Analysis

Outputs are taken as a dependent variable and Inputs considered as independent variable.

Model summary shows that coefficient of determination $R^2$ is 0.729 with standard error of estimate equal to 13.79, which not very large. We can interpret this as about 73% of the variation in outputs is explained by inputs. This value of coefficient of determination ($R^2$) is significant and therefore the association can be considered as significant. Since p value is less than 0.05

the hypothesis that the slope of the regression line is zero is rejected. The model is considered to be statistically acceptable. Hence, null hypothesis is rejected and an alternate hypothesis is accepted.

**$H_{02}$**: Economic Factors do not positively correlated with Ecosystem Management for Sustaining the Development.

**$H_{12}$**: Economic Factors are positively correlated with Ecosystem Management for Sustaining the Development.

**Table 6.2: Model summary on economic factors and ecosystem management for sustaining the development**

| R | R Square Change | F Change | df1 | df2 | Sig. F Change |
|---|---|---|---|---|---|
| .632 | .399 | 197.868 | 1 | 398 | .000 |

b. Dependent Variable: Ecosystem Management.

From the model summary it can be observed that multiple correlation coefficient R=0.632 and Adjusted $R^2$=0.399, $R^2$ change is also 0.399 and these values are significant because p value is zero which is less than 0.05, which indicates that the strength of association is significant. The value of coefficient of determination $R^2$ is 0.399; therefore, approximately 40% of the variation in ecosystem management is explained by economic factors. Hence, null hypothesis is rejected and an alternate hypothesis is accepted.

**$H_{03}$**: Social Factors do not positively correlated with Ecosystem Management for Sustaining the Development.

**$H_{13}$**: Social Factors are positively correlated with Ecosystem Management for Sustaining the Development.

**Table 6.3: Model summary on social factors and ecosystem management for sustaining the development**

| Model | R | R Square | Adjusted R Square | Std. Error of the Estimate | F-Value |
|---|---|---|---|---|---|
| 1 | .916[a] | .839 | .839 | 10.61872 | 1558.435 |
| a. Predictors: (Constant), Social Factors<br>b. Dependent Variable: Ecosystem Management | | | | | Sig.000 |

Ecosystem management is taken as a dependent variable and social factors are taken as independent variable. Model summary shows the values of $R^2$, adjusted $R^2$ and $R^2$ change, which are all same in this case. Here $R^2$ is 0.839 with standard error of estimate equal to 10.618. We can interpret this as 83.9% of the variation in ecosystem management is explained by social factors. This value of coefficient of determination ($R^2$) is significant and therefore the association can be considered as significant. Hence, null hypothesis is rejected and an alternate hypothesis is accepted.

## FINDINGS

Sustaining the biosphere with adequate provisions for maximizing future options includes providing for human economic and social improvement for current and future human generations within a framework of cultural diversity while: (a) making adequate provisions for the maintenance of biological diversity; and (b) maintaining the biogeochemical integrity of the biosphere by conservation and proper use of its air, water, and land resources. Achieving these goals requires planning and action at local, regional and global scales and specifying short and long term objectives that allow for the transition to sustainability.

The concept recognizes that economic, environmental, and social issues are interdependent and integrated. These three factors are essential for managing the ecosystem as strong economy includes: higher wages, job security, to keep pace with the changing environment through IT enabled services for the economic development of one's country. As far as social issues are concerned these can be described in terms of corporate social responsibility towards Nation, Community, Society and stakeholders. Every business has a code of conduct so that economic growth will translate to sustainable development and it will be achieved only when environmental capital is enriched. The corporates are expected to uphold ethical stamina which can be taken as foundation for formulating policies, vision and mission statements in the organization. This can be made practical only through human efforts. Globally there is a growing interest in broadening the concept of social responsibility towards customers, government, employees and society at large through business ethics have become a challenge to the organizations.

The responsibility of the environmentalist is to preserve habitat, eliminate pollution, awareness about the solar plant, wildlife and bio-diversity by taking various measures, formulating policies etc. On the other hand society is also responsible. Every person has to contribute in managing ecosystem. Various social issues must be resolved through community efforts such as dissemination of education among weaker sections of society, crime, equity, community building, spirituality, environmental justice, etc. Since this report is focusing on P2 activities, the social issues are not emphasized. However, social issues are considered an important leg of the sustainability stool. Stakeholders include the general public, academia, industry, government, environmental groups, and community groups. Such a process frequently is very time consuming and may take years to develop. Often many public community meetings are held as part of this process as the different groups learn to trust, communicate with, and listen to one another. To summarize, a sustainable community effort consists of a long term integrated and systems approach to developing and achieving a healthy community by addressing economic, environmental, and social issues. Fostering a strong sense of community is also an important part of such efforts.

## CONCLUSION

People, worldwide, are becoming aware of the need to use our natural resources with the life quality of current and future generations in mind. Policy makers, managers, scientists, governments, private industry, and nongovernmental organizations are developing, sometimes together, new visions for their management. These new visions require a shift from mainly commodity production oriented management towards a management addressing simultaneously ecological, economic, and social issues. This change of paradigm is not without contradiction, controversy, and tension. For example, the concept of ecosystem management developed in the United States is still defined and interpreted in too many different ways. However, the concept also includes enough useful principles that, if applied in practice, it can allow society to take some steps in the direction of sustainable development.

## SUGGESTIONS AND RECOMMENDATIONS

The following measures can be taken to preserve the ecosystem management:

- Managing natural resources for sustainable development should tend towards sustainable use of ecosystem resources.
- Managing natural resources for sustainable development should be holistic.
- Managing natural resources for sustainable development should be Ecosystemic.
- Managing natural resources for sustainable development should be done with a landscape perspective.
- Managing natural resources for sustainable development should have intersectoral multiple objectives.

## *REFERENCES*

Ewa Bojar (2012) Eco-management in Polish Companies: Problems of Sustainable Development, Lublin University of Technology, Vol. 7, No. 2, 107-113.

Berkes F. Colding J. and Folke C. (2000). Rediscovery of Traditional Ecological Knowledge as Adaptive Management, Ecological Application, 10(5), 2000, pp. 1251-1262.

Bousquet F.& Page C. L. (2004). Multi-agent Simulations and Ecosystem Management: A Review, Ecological Modelling 176 (2004) 313-332.

Burritt R., (2006). Implementing Environmental Management Accounting: Status and Challenges, Publisher Springer Netherlands.

Borregard N., Dufey A., (2005). Challenging Preconception about Trade in Sustainable Products, Sustainable Markets Discussion Paper Number 1, p. 1-33.

Dubey R.K. (2013). Organic Farming Beneficial to Biodiversity, Indian Journal of Applied Research, Vol. 3, No. 11.

Edward Maltby (2010) Ecosystem Approach: From Principle to Practice, IUCN, Commission on Ecosystem Management, The Royal Holloway Institute for Environmental Research, Royal Holloway, University of London, Surrey GU25 4LN, UK, pp. 205.

Harald Beyer Broch, Peter Cush, Maaike Knol, Tony Varley,Maritime Studies (2013). Vol. 12, No. 1, pp. 1-17.

Høgevold N.M., Svensson G., (2012). A Business Sustainability Model: A European Case Study, Journal of Business and Industrial Marketing, Vol. 27(2), pp. 142-151.

Howitt, R. (2001) 'Frontiers, Borders, Edges: Luminal Challenges to the Hegemony of Exclusion,' Australian Geographical Studies, 39(2): 233-245.

Ito M., Wiegand A.N., Ochieng G.M., Walker C., Azam S., Ojo O. I., Duncan P.F., Otieno F. A., Roiko A., Mwaka B., Tindale N. (2013). Environmental Systems Research, Vol. 2, No. 2, pp. 1-12.

Loring P.A., Jacobsen R.B. and Harrison H.L. (2013). That's what Opening Day is For: Social and Cultural Dimensions of (not) Fishing for Salmon in Cook Inlet, Alaska, Maritime Studies, Vol. 12, No. 1, Dec, pp. 1-19.

Mayer, A.; Rietkerk, M.G. (2004). The Dynamic Regime Concept for Ecosystem Management and Restoration, Bio-Science, Volume 54, Issue: 11, pp. 1013-1020.

Monika I, Winn, Pogutz S. (2013). Business, Ecosystems, and Biodiversity New Horizons for Management Research, Published online before Print May 26, 2013, doi:10.1177/1086026613490173

Per Angelstam, Michael Grodzynskyi, Kjell Andersson, Robert Axelsson, Marine Elbakidze, Alexander Khoroshev, Ivan Kruhlov, Vladimir Naumov (2013) Measurement, Collaborative Learning and Research for Sustainable Use of Ecosystem Services: Landscape Concepts and Europe as Laboratory, Springer, AMBIO 2013, 42: 129-145.

Plummer R. (2005). A Review of Sustainable Development Implementation through Local Action from an Ecosystem Management Perspective, Journal of Rural and Tropical Public Health 4: 33-40.

Richter B.D., Mathews R., Harrison D.L., Wigington R. (2003). Ecological Sustainable Water Management: Managing River Flows for Ecological Integrity, Ecological Applications, 13(1), 2003, pp. 206-224.

Schaltegger S., Bennett M., Burritt, R., Jasch C., (2008): Environmental Management Accounting As a Support for Cleaner Production, in: Schaltegger, S.; Bennett, M.; Burritt, R. & Jasch, C. (Eds): Environmental Management Accounting for Cleaner Production, Dordrecht: Springer, 15-46.

Shikui Dong (2010) in Study 'Implication of Coupled Natural and Human Systems in Sustainable Rangeland Ecosystem Management', Front. Earth Sci. China 2010, 4(1): 42-50.

Pages: 131-166

**FOREST AND BIODIVERSITY CONSERVATION**

*Edited by:* **Dr. Alka Chauhan** and **Dr. Pawan Kumar 'Bharti'**

**ISBN: 978-93-5056-873-6**

*Edition:* **2017**

*Published by:* **Discovery Publishing House Pvt. Ltd., New Delhi (India)**

# 7

# Microbial Biodiversity
## *Types, Utility and its Conservation*

*Balwinder Singh Sooch*[1*]
*Yogita Lugani*[1]

## INTRODUCTION

Microbial diversity means the variability among all the microorganisms that exist on earth. Microorganisms have been evolved on earth about 3.8 Ga ($10^9$ yrs) ago and provided suitable conditions on the planet, which have made it habitat for all other species (Das *et al.*, 2006). Unlike animal or plant diversity, microbial diversity is one of the most difficult area of biodiversity research (Watve *et al.*, 1999).Microbial diversity is mainly found at three levels: within species (genetic), species number (species) and community (ecological) diversity (Harpole, 2010). Microbes are the smallest living creature that found on earth, which play an important role in the functioning of ecosystem like cycling of many essential elements like carbon (C), nitrogen (N), sulphur (S), potassium (K), phosphorous (P) in addition tobioremediation and bioleaching. These small creatures are found to be most abundant living ones found on the entire biosphere (Pold and DeAngelis, 2013). Microorganisms are of microscopic size (nm orμm) with ubiquitous natureand possess a very high degree of adaptability in diverse environment like soil, water, air, sea, thermal vents, glaciers, ocean depths, artic ice and with the bodies of living plants and animals (Pelczar *et al.*, 1993; Willey *et al.*, 2008). The life cycle of each microbe passes through four different phases of growth(lag phase, log phase, stationary phase and death phase). Microorganisms include both prokaryotic (bacteria) and eukaryotic (protozoa, fungi, algae) organisms.

Historically for the first time, microorganism was reported by Antony van Leeuwenhoek after observing these small creatures in a single lens

[1] Enzyme Biotechnology Laboratory, Department of Biotechnology, Punjabi University, Patiala-147 002, (Punjab) (India)

microscope and he is called as father of bacteriology and protozoology. The first living cell was found on earth about 4,000 million years ago and it was unicellular in nature. The first microorganism was reported after the discovery of microscope in the mid of 16th century by Italian astronomer Galileo. Robert Hooke published the first original drawings of fruiting bodies of fungi and published them by entitling as *Micrographia* or *some physiological discriptions of minute bodies made by magnifying glasses with observations and inquirirs thereupon*. The extraordinary transformations of microbiology were observed during the period from 1930-1950, just prior to the publication on the structure of DNA by Watson and Crick in 1953. From 1898 onwards Beijerinck worked on enrichment culture for the isolation of both nitrifying and cellulolytic bacteria. A brief history of taxonomic concepts is given in Table 7.1. The term *Bacterium* was originated from a Greek word which means staff. Louis Pasteur is called as Father of microbiology. The production of useful industrial products with the help of microorganisms by fermentation technique was also started by Louis Pasteur. Germ theory of disease is the other great contributions of Pasteur in microbiology. The first introduction of vaccination for the prevention of smallpox, via the introduction of scraping from cowpox pustule was given by English physician, Edward Jenner in 1798. The beginning of antibiotics was with the discovery of penicillin by Fleming in 1928 by accidental introduction of spores of mold on agar plates seeded with staphylococci. Luria (1953) defined viruses as submicroscopic entities capable of being introduced into specific living cells and of reproducing inside such cells only. Viruses are obligate intracellular parasites, whichare highly infectious agents and they are found at the borderline of life (Willey *et al*., 2008).

**Table 7.1: History of taxonomic concepts**

| Name | Number of Kingdoms | Name of Kingdom |
|---|---|---|
| Carlous Linnaeus (1758) | 2 | Animalia, Vegetabilia |
| Ernst Haeckel (1866) | 3 | Protista, Plantae, Animalia |
| Herbert Copeland (1956) | 4 | Monera (Prokaryotes), Protoctista, Plantae, Animali A |
| Robert H.Whittaker (1969) | 5 | Monera, Protista, Fungi, Plantae, Animalia |
| Carl Richard Woese (1977) | 6 | Eubacteria, Archeabacteria, Protista, Fungi, Plantae, Animalia |
| Thomas Cavalier-Smith (1998) | Revised 6 | Bacteria, Protozoa, Animalia, Fungi, Plantae, Chromista |

The microorganisms are classified on the basis of their morphology (shape, size), taxonomy (classification, identification and nomenclature), habitat (aquatic, marine, terrestrial) and biology (growth, metabolism and reproduction). In order to understand the phylogenetic perspective, mechanism of degradation and development of novel strategies of treatement, the study of microbial diversity at the genetic level is necessary. *Haemophilus influenzae* and *Mycoplasma genitalium* were the first two microbes whose complete genome was sequenced. Till date, only 10% of the microbial diversity have been discovered because most of the microorganisms that exist in nature can't be isolatedunder laboratory conditions using traditional techniques (Lal, 2007).For the investigation of diversity (culturable as well as non-culturable)and structure of microbial communities, molecular methods are promising tools. The study of total microbial community from a particular niche can be possible by using molecular tools like TRFLP (Terminal Restriction Fragment Length Polymorphism), DGGE (Denaturing Gradient Gel Electrophoresis), ARDRA (Amplified Ribosomal DNA Restriction Analysis) and LH-PCR (Length Heterogeneity- Polymerase Chain Reaction).The fundamental reasons for studying the microbial diversity include increase the knowledge of the genetic resources and understanding the distribution of organisms, understand the regulation and consequences of biodiversity and identify differences in diversity associated with management distribution (Fakruddin *et al.*, 2013).

In addition tomany beneficial roles of different microbes, some of the deleterious effects on humans are also associated with some pathogenic microbes.The microorganisms which have harmful affects on human life includes bacteria (*Bacillus anthracis, Brucella abortus. Burkhloderia mallei, Clostridium botulinum, Yersinia pestis, Francissella turlarensis, Ricketsia rickettsii, R. prownzekii and Coxialla burnetii*), fungi (*Aspegillus niger, A fumigates, Candida albicans, Trichoderma viridae, Monilla, Penicillium* and *Mucor*) and viruses (Ebola virus, H1N1 virus, Crimean congo hemorrhagic fever virus, South America hemorrhagic fever virus, Venezuelan equine encephalitis virus, Lassa fever virus, Variola (small pox), Yellow fever virus) (Willey *et al.*, 2008).Some microbes are also involved in bioterrorism during World war II, the existence of *Bacillus anthracis* (causing anthrax) spore in the environment was reported in Scotland.Some other microbes like *Yersinia pestis, Clostridium botulinum, Brucella suis, Coxiella burnetii,* Varila virus and Ebola virus were also reported to be suitable biological agents for bioterrorism (Bhargava *et al.*, 2011; Amura and Marneedi, 2015).

The climate change showed significant changes on the biodiversity by direct or indirect effects (Meynecke, 2004). Major threats in microbial biodiversity include alteration in reproduction timing (Winkler *et al.*, 2002), changes in habitat resources (Visser and Both, 2005), differing habitat use or soil niche site selection (Telemeco *et al.*, 2009) and alterations in mortality rates (Chamaille-James *et al.*, 2009). With the increase in threat to microbial diversity due to adverse environmental conditions, there is a need to preserve microbes through different modes.

## CLASSIFICATION OF MICROORGANISMS

Microorganisms are classified on different basis like cell structure, nutritional requirement, ecological niche and environmental adaptations etc. The detailed classification is presented in Figure 7.1.

### Classification on the basis of Cell Structures

The broad classification of microorganisms is on the basis of their cell structure like whether true nucleus is absent (prokaryote) or present(eukaryote) (Sarethy *et al.*, 2014). The universal phylogenetic tree based on comparative ribosomal RNA sequences, whichclassifies the prokaryotes into eubacteria and archaeabacteria. Therefore, there are three domains of microorganisms from the universal ancestor i.e. eubacteria, archaea and eukarya (Woese, 1998). Eubacteria and Archaebacteriacomes under the kingdom monera and the other microorganisms are classified under kingdom protista and fungi.

#### *Kingdom Monera*

Members of Eubacteria and Archaebacteria comes under the kingdom monera.The members of this Kingdom are found everywhere in large numbers. The most primitive (3.5 billion years old) and successful groups of organisms on earth are gram negative cyanobacteria/oxyphotobacteria/blue green algae. Cyanobacteria are photosynthetic prokaryotes which capture sunlight for energy using photosynthetic pigment (chlorophyll a) and various accessory pigments (chlorophyll b, c, d, phycocyanin, phycoerythrin etc.). They are common in lakes, ponds, springs, wetlands, streams and rivers. Cyanobacteria occur in individual cell, as small clusters or colonies or as long as filamentous chains. Cyanobacteria can show locomotion by means of rotator motion or by gliding over the gelatinous layer secreted through cell surface. Inside the cytoplasm of cyanobacteria, a large variety of inclusion bodies (carboxysomes, cyanophycin granules, myxophycean starch and polyglucon granules) are found. On the basis of classic botanical taxonomic scheme, five orders of cyanobacteria have been recognized (Chroococcales, Pleurocapsales, Oscillatoriales, Nostocales, Stigonematales). Cyanobacteria showsenzymatic defences against reactive oxygen species, such as superoxide dismutase with a variety of damage repair mechanisms to identify and repair UV-damaged proteins. They play a major role in nutrient cycling (nitrogen, carbon, and oxygen dynamics) of many aquatic environments. Nitrogen fixation can be shown by some species of cyanobacteria (e.g. *Anabaena, Nostoc, Mastigocladus*) in the special type of cells called heterocysts (Shapiro, 1988; Vincent, 2009).

Among all the microbes of microbial biodiversity, bacteria are adapted to almost all the different environments that exist on the earth and they are able to decompose all the chemical components made by living organisms (Fakruddin and Mannan, 2013). Bacterial cells can possess different cell shapes

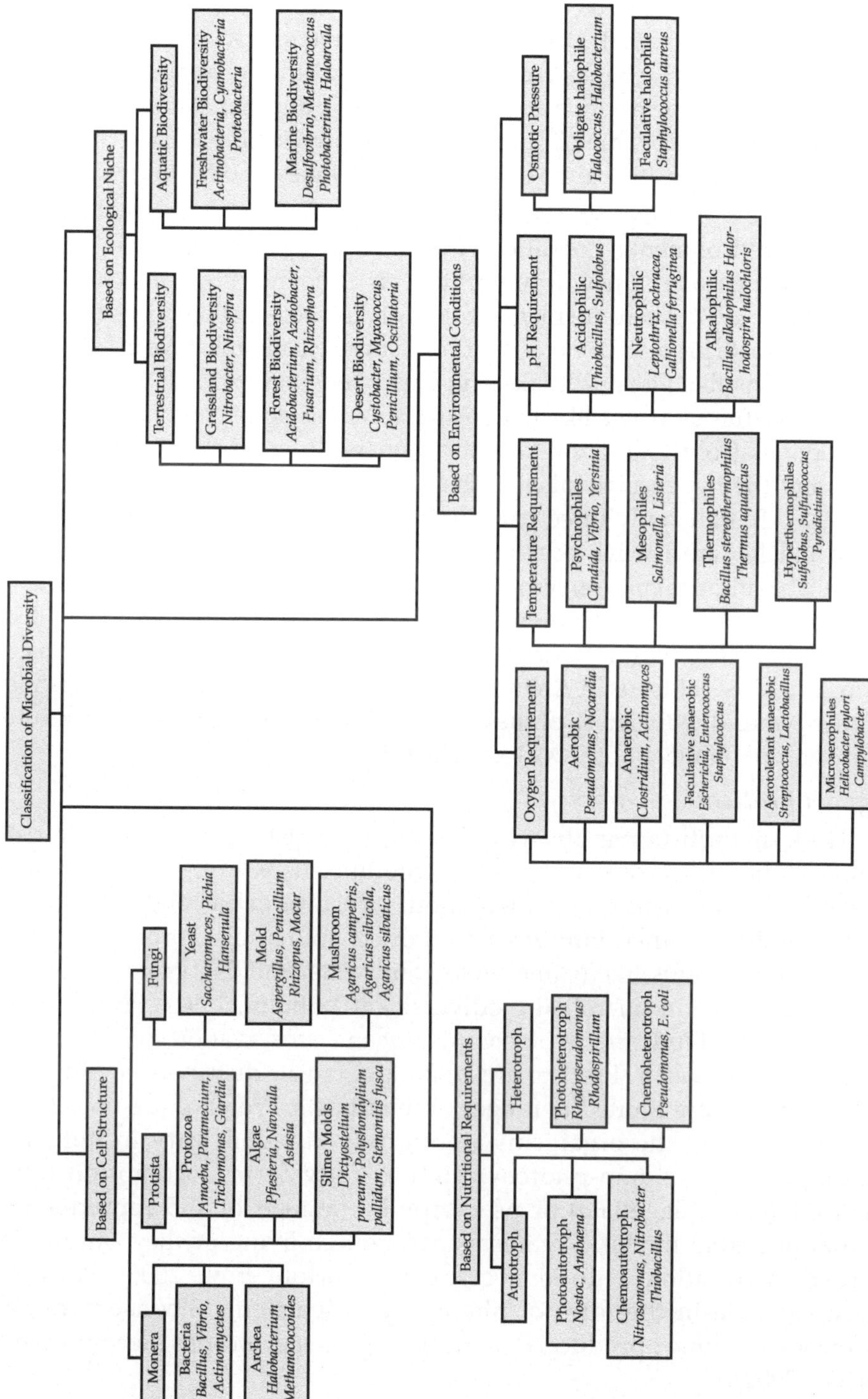


**Fig. 7.1: Classification of Microbial Diversity**

like bacillus (rod like), coccus (spherical or ovoid), spiral (corkscrew or curved) and square or star shaped. Bacterial cells can live singly, but clustering of bacterial cells in pairs, chains, clusters or in some other groupings are found in some genus or species of bacteria. On the basis of gram staining, cell wall composition, cell shape, metabolism and toxin production eubacteria can be classified as Gram positive and Gram negative (Dubey and Maheswari, 2005).

The second member of kingdom monera is Archaebacteria, which live in extreme environmental conditions like hot springs, deserts, snow etc. The discovery of archea as 'a new form of life' was announced by Carl Woese and his colleagues (1977).There are many groups of Archaea- methanogens (produce methane as waste product from respiration), extreme halophile (live in extremely dark conditions like Great salt lake and Dead Sea) and extreme thermophiles (livein hot sulfurous water like hot spring at Yellowstone National Park) and psuchrophiles (cold loving, prokaryotic biomass in coastal Antarctic surface waters, and the hypersaline lakes of the Vestfold Hills lake system in Eastern Antarctica). To date, only three psychrophilic archaeal strains were originally isolated and they are free living with members of the subdomain Eukaryarchaeota (are available in pure culture). From the bottom of Ace Lake, Antarctica, where the methane saturated waters remain between 1 and 2°C, psychrophiles like *Methanococcoides burtonii* (-2.5°C) and *Methanogenium frigidum* (-10°C) were isolated. The major industrial focus in Archea is for the production of biotechnologically useful enzymes due to ability of these microbes to function at the temperature, salinity and pH limits of life. (McLain, 2004; Littlechild, 2015).

***Kingdom Protista***

The term Protista was given by German zoologist Ernst Haeckel. Protists are unicellular eukaryotes and possess true nucleus with membrane bound organelles. On the basis of nutrition, mode of reproduction and locomotion, protists can be classified into three categories: animal like (protozoa), plant like (algae) or fungus like (slime molds and water molds). Protozoans play an important role in microbial biodiversity (Clarholm, 1994). Protists play important role in biodiversity, biocomplexity and conservation considerations of life on planet earth. Protists are cosmopolitan in distribution, although symbiotic forms are limited to ranges of their hosts. Protozoa are unicellular eukaryotes andall the organisms among this kingdom vary in nutrition (photosysnthetic or non-photosynthetic), body form, locomotion (cilia (ciliate), flagella (flagellate) or pseudopodia (amoebae) and reproduction (asexual or sexual mode). Organisms can be free living or they can live in symbiotic association with other organisms(Tortora *et al.*, 2006). Protozoa play many rolesin the form of phagotrophs (particulate consumers), as phototrophs (primary producers) or most fungi as saprotrophs (decomposers) (Corliss, 2002).

The second member of kingdom protista are algae, which possess cell wall made up of either cellulose or mixture of pectin and silica. They are unicellular in nature and possess photosynthetic pigments like chlorophyll a, c, carotene and xanthophylls. The storage material can be in the form of oil or starch and they generally reproduce by both sexual and asexual reproduction. The third member of kingdom protista are slime molds, which possess both fungal and amoebal characteristics. They are highly conspicuous organisms which can magically appear overnight on mulch, plants, and turf and there are 700 different species of known slime molds. There are two phyla of slime molds i.e. cellular slime molds and plasmodial sime molds. Cool, moist and shady conditions promote the development of slime molds.

***Kingdom Fungi***

Organisms of this kingdom can be unicellular (e.g. yeast) or multicellular eukaryotes (molds). The classification of fungal phylogeny is on the basis of cytology (Taylor, 1978), cell ultra structure (Heath, 1986), cell wall composition (Bartnicki-Garcia, 1970), morphology and metabolism (Vogel, 1964). The body of organisms (except yeast) among this kingdom is made up ofthin thread-like hyphae which form a network called mycelium. The hyphae of some organisms have cross walls, while in others there is absence of true cell wall with continuous cytoplasm and thus possess many nuclei and are called coenocytic hyphae. The cell wall of fungus is mainly made of chitin. The mode of nutrition is heterotrophic and they obtain the nourishment by absorbing the solution of organic material from its inhabiting environment like soil, sea water, fresh water, plant or animal host. Most of the organisms are saprophytes e.g. yeast, while others are parasites e.g. *Puccinia*. They can reproduceby different methods i.e. vegetative, asexual and sexual methods. The large multicellular fungi i.e. Mushrooms, may look like plants, but unlike plants they do not carry out photosynthesis. The major groups of kingdom fungi are Phycomycetes (*Mucor, Rhizopus*), Ascomycetes (*Aspergillus*), Basidiomycetes (*Agaricus, Puccinia*) and Deuteromycetes or imperfect fungi (*Colleterium, Alternaria*).

Yeasts are single celled fungi and most of them reproduce by budding (*Saccharomyces cerevisiae*) and others may divide by fission (*Schizosaccharomyces pombe*). Most of the yeasts are placed under phyla Ascomycota, however few of them are under Basidiomycota. The genome sequences of yeast species resulted in advancement in our understanding of evolutionary mechanisms in eukaryotes (Dujon, 2010).The highly simplicity of this unicellular eukaryote make it an important vehicle in genetic engineering for the expression of multicellular eukaryotic genes and for the improved production of industrially relevant strains (Kavscek *et al.*, 2015). The second member of kingdom fungi is mold, which generally grows in the form of multicellular filaments, called hyphae and generally grow by apical extensions. Hyphae can be septate or aseptate and they show absorptive mode of nutrition. Most of the molds come under Phycomycetes and Ascomycetes.Mold can produce both sexual as well as asexual spores and many of these spores are colored in nature. Most of the molds are involved in spoilage of foods (Saranraj and Geetha, 2012) and also cause diseases (Mendell *et al.*, 2011). The toxins produced by molds are called as mycotoxins. Mushrooms are third member of kingdom fungi, which are fleshy, spore bearing fruiting body of fungus and produced on above ground of soil and they are high calorie food. They are placed under Basidiomycetes and many species of mushrooms appear overnight, growing or expanding rapidly. Mushrooms possess many medicinal (antibacterial, antiviral, antiparasitic, antiinflamatory and antidiabetic) and psychoactive properties. The secondary metabolites produced by many varieties of mushrooms are toxic in nature.

**Classification on the basis of Ecological Niche**

On the basis of ecological niche, microorganisms are classified into two main categories i.e. terrestrial and aquatic (freshwater and marine).

***Terrestrial Biodiversity***

The most abundant and important group of terrestrial biodiversity (grassland, savannah and tropical forests) involves arbuscular mycorrhizal (AM) fungi, the ecto-mycorrhizal (EM) fungi and the ericoid mycorrhizal (ERM) fungi. Among all the mycorrhizal fungi, AM fungi are abundant in terrestrial ecosystem and associate with many grasses, herbs, tropical trees and shrubs (Van der Heijen *et al.*, 1998; Read and Moreno, 2003). EM fungi are abundant in temperate and boreal forests and in some tropical forests. They show association with 6000 tree species (Alexander and Lee, 2005). EM fungi are most abundant in heath land where they associate with members of the Ericaceae (Smith and Read, 1997). Mycorrhizal fungi and nitrogen fixing bacteria are also responsible for nitrogen and phosphorous fixation. Approximately 5-20% (grassland and savannah) to 80% (temperate and boreal forests) of all nitrogen, and up to 75% of phosphorus, that is acquired by plants annually is fixed by these microorganisms. Some of the important biological activities like plant productivity, crop yield, regulation of plant pathogens etc. are regulated by the soil inhabiting microorganisms through the mineralization, competition and regulation of invasion of exotic species (Van der Heijden *et al.*, 2008; Ali *et al.*, 2015).

Grassland ecosystems have limited water availability with annual precipitation between 150-1200 mm and mean annual temperature between 0-25°C. The order of biodiversity in grassland ecosystem is bacteria>fungi>nematodes>protozoa>macroarthropods>microarthropods (Sala *et al.*, 2001). Globally, forests cover nearly one third of the land area with 80% of terrestrial biodiversity.Bacteria and fungi present in forest ecosystem is mainly involved mineral cycling with nutrient enrichment by resource stoichiometry influencing microbial growth rates (Rousk and Baath, 2007 a,b), substrate use efficiency (Sinsabaugh *et al.*, 2013) and the production of extracellular enzymes that degrade soil organic matter (Redmile-Gordon *et al.*, 2015). Mycorrhizal fungi plays an important role in forest biodiversity by nutrient recycling, increased water uptake by plants under drought condition (Treseder, 2004; Lehto and Zwiazek, 2011; Smith*et al.*, 2015). Desert ecosystem constitute the most extensive terrestrial biome which is characterized by lack of moisture with annual rainfall of 254 mm and it covers one-third of the Earth's continental surface. The dominant biodiversity of desert soil includes *Archangium, Cystobacter, Myxococcus, Polyangium, Sorangium, Cyanobacteria* and *Stigmatella* and sub-dominant forms comprise *Acinetobacter, Bacillus, Micrococcus, Proteus and Pseudomonas* (Bhatnagar and Bhatnagar, 2005; Pointing and Belnap, 2012).

***Aquatic Biodiversity***

The difference between freshwater and marine systems is not limited to the concentration of NaCl, but it also considers a wide range of biological, physical and chemical factors. The most dominant phyla in freshwater lakes are Actinobacteria and they can contribute approximately 50% of the bacteria in the surface waters (epilimnion) (Glockner *et al.*, 2000) but their abundance often decreases with increase in depth when the oxygen concentration decreases (Allgaier, and Grossart. 2006; Taipale *et al.*, 2009). Viruses play an important role in the aquatic environment with regulation of aquatic ecosystems, from microscale microbial processes to global biogeochemical cycling (Weinbauer, 2004; Suttle, 2007). A general overview of viral abundance and ecology in pelagic, benthic and wetland ecosystems with a potential differences in the role of viruses between different marine and freshwater habitats was provided by Wilhelm and Matteson (2008), Clasen *et al.* (2008), Danovaro *et al.* (2008) and Jackson and Jackson (2008).

Most of the important bioactive compounds are produced by marine microbes. They also possess the potential of bioremediation, which helps in the decomposition of organic matter and cycling of nutrients. Marine microbes also serve as food for some bottom-living organisms. Many bacteria, viruses, actinomycetes and fungi are found in the marine ecosystem. Marine bacteria are further classified into sulphate-reducing bacteria (*Desulfomonas, Desulfovibrio*), methanogenic bacteria (*Methanococcus, Methanosarcina, Methanomicrobium),* Halophilic bacteria (*Haloarcula, Halobacterium, Haloferax),* nitrifying Bacteria (*Nitrosococcus, Nitrococcus)* and luminous bacteria (*Photobacteriumleiognathi, Photobacteriumphosphoreum, Vibrio fischeri)* (Das *et al.*, 2006). Viruses show important effects on microbial loop dynamicsand biogeochemical cycling of organic matter mainly carbon by the lysis of bacteria and phytoplankton (Haabe and Middelboe, 2009). Pearman *et al.* (2010) reported the presence of fungal species i.e. *Acremomium strictum, Basidiomycete sp., Cosmospora vilior, Discomycete sp., Fusarium sp., Kirschsteiniothelia sp., Orbilia sp., Peziza sp., Neonectria lucida, Scolecobasidium salinum, Trichoderma sp., Xylaria sp., Zopfiella sp.* in the aquatic habitat (freshwater and marine).

Recently, from the metagenomic study of Sundarban mangrove, 2746 species of microorganisms are recorded. These microorganisms belong to 33 different phyla revealing the dominance of Proteobacteria, Firmicutes, Chloroflexi, Bacteroidetes, Acidobacteria, Nitrospirae and Actinobacteria respectively (Basak *et al.*, 2015). A total number of 24 bacteria, 4 actinomycetes and 8 fungi were also isolated from the marine samples collected from Vizhinjam and Mulloor coast of South India. The best five bacterial isolates showed inhibitory activity against many pathogens like *Klebsiella pneumonia* KU1, *Pseudomonas aeruginosa* VL3, *Salmonella enterica typhimurium* MTCC 98, *Escherichia coli* MTCC 40, *Micrococcus luteus* MTCC 105, *Staphylococcus simulans* MTCC 3610, *Proteus vulgaris* MTCC 426, *Vibrio fluvialis, Vibrio sp.* P3a and *Vibrio sp.* P3b (Sinimol *et al.*, 2016).

**Classification on the basis of Nutrition Requirement**

On the basis of nutritional requirement, microorganisms can be classified as autotrophs or heterotrophs, depending on whether they can synthesize their own food or not (Ebeling *et al.*, 2006; Aislabie and Deslippe, 2013).

***Autotrophs***

Autotrophic microorganisms are able to synthesize their own organic food by utilizing inorganic substances as raw material. They can utilize hydrogen sulphide ($H_2S$) or ammonia ($NH_{3)}$ or hydrogen ($H_2$) as the source of hydrogen and the main source of carbon is $CO_{2.}$ The source of energy in autotrophs is light or other reduced inorganic molecule. Autrotrophic microorganisms can be obligate autotrophs (obtain their carbon from $CO_2$ like algae) or they can be facultative autotrophs (they can live as autotrophs and utilize carbon from $CO_2$). Autotrophs can be phototoautotrophs (*Nostoc*) or chemoautotrophs (*Nitrosomonas, Nitrobacter* and *Thiobacillus)*. The genus *Nitrosomonas* are able to utilize carbon of $CO_2$ and obtain sufficient energy by oxidizing the ammonia into nitrite. All the photosynthetic bacteria are divided into 35 groups and out of these, 10 groups contains anoxygenic photosynthetic bacteria (purple bacteria, green bacteria) and the rest 11 groups belong to oxygenic phototrophic bacteria (Cyanobacteria and Prochlorophytes). Along with bacteria, algae are also phototrophs and contain many photosynthetic pigments to manufacture their food.

***Heterotrophs***

Heterotrophic microorganisms use reduced and preformed organic compounds like sugar, protein and lipids as sources of carbon and energy. The source of hydrogen is usually water and oxygen, obtained from atmosphere or from water where it is found in dissolved state. Amyl alcohol, paraffin and rubber are utilized as a carbon source by the common soil bacteria. Another bacteria i.e. *Burkholderia cepacia* can utilize 100 different carbon sources as a carbon source. Heterotrophs can be photoheterotrophs (*Rhodopseudomonas*) or chemoheterotrophs (*Pseudomonas*).

## Classification on the basis of Environmental Conditions

There are many abiotic factors (physical and chemical) in the environment which affect microbial diversity, which are water availability, salinity, oxic/anoxic conditions, temperature, pH, pressure, chemical pollution, heavy metals, pesticides, antibiotics etc. (Karki and Aryal, 2014). These environmental variations result in a shift in the diversity profile in different ways and to different degrees (Fakruddin and Mannan, 2013). The microbial diversity under these conditions is discussed below.

### *Based on Oxygen Requirement*

Oxygen and carbon dioxide are the two principal gases that affect the growth of microorganisms. Microorganisms fall into four different groups with respect to the effect of oxygen on their growth and metabolism (Ivanov, 2010).Obligate aerobic microorganismsrequire air oxygen (21%) as electron acceptor for their growth. These microbes have respiratory enzymes and most of these microbes lack the capacity for fermentation. e.g. *Pseudomonas sp.* Obligate anaerobic microorganismsdo not need or utilize $O_2$ as electron acceptor and $O_2$ is even toxic for their growth. Some anaerobes are nonstringent or tolerant anaerobes (can tolerate low levels of oxygen) and others are stringent or strict anaerobes (cannot tolerate even low levels of oxygen). Strict anaerobes are also involved in fermentation. e.g. *Clostridium sp.*Facultative anaerobic organismscan switch between aerobic and anaerobic types of metabolism. These organisms are not inhibited by the presence of oxygen. Under anaerobic conditions (in absence of $O_2$), they grow by fermentation or anaerobic respiration, but in the presence of $O_2$ they switch to aerobic respiration. Both the aerobic and facultative organisms have developed protective mechanism (superoxide dismutase, catalase and peroxidase) against the toxic form of oxygen. e.g *Escherichia sp., Enterococcus sp.*Aerotolerant anaerobesdo notrequire oxygen for their growth, but they can tolerateits presence. Their metabolism remains fermentative and do not use oxygen. e.g. *Streptoccocus pyogenes.* Microaerophiles require oxygen for their growth, but less than that present in the air. Therefore, microaerophiles grow best under modified oxygen conditions. e.g. *Campylobacter.*

### *Based on Temperature Requirement*

Temperature has high influence on the growth of microbes because the rate of metabolic reaction is highly influenced by temperature. The temperature range at which particular organism grow best is called optimum temperature. There are three groups of microorganisms as regard to the temperature i.e. psychrophile, mesophile and thermophile (Ivanov, 2010; Fakruddin and Mannan, 2013). Psychrophiles are able to grow at 0° C or lower, but the best temperature for their growth is higher. The optimum temperature for the growth of psychrophiles is 15° C with maximum temperature of 20° C. The examples of psychrophiles are *Candida sp., Vibrio sp., Yersinia enterocolitica, Alcaligenes, Alteromonas, Aquaspirillum, Arthobacter, Bacillus, Bacteroides*. Mesophilesare able to grow best within the temperature range of 20° C to 40° C. All the pathogenic organisms of human are mesophiles because most of the disease causing microbes grow best at about body temperature (37° C). Thermophilesgrow best at a higher temperature of 50°-70° C. Some facultative thermophilescan grow into mesophilic range, but othertrue thermophiles, obligate thermophiles or stenothermophiles cannot grow into mesophilic range. e.g. *Bacillus stearothermophilus, Thermus aquaticus.* Extremothermophiles or hyperthermophilesgrow best at temperatures higher than 70□C. The optimum pH for the growth of acidophilic hyperthermophiles is below 3.0. *Sulfolobus, Sufurococcus, Desulfurolobus* and *Acidianus* produce sulphuricacid from the oxidation of elemental sulphur or sulphidic oresin Yellowstone National Park. A few thermophilic fungi belonging to Ascomycetes (*Chaetomium thermophile, Thermoascus aurantiacus, Dactylomyces thermophilus, Melanocarpus albomyces, Talaromyces thermophilus, T. emersonii, Thielavia terrestris*), Basidiomycetes (*Phanerochaete chrysosporium*), Hyphomycete (*Acremonium alabamensis, A. thermophilum, Myceliophthora thermophila, Thermomyces lanuginosus, Scytalidium thermophilum, Malbranchea cinnamomea*) and Zygomycetes (*Rhizomucor miehei, R. pusillus*) have been isolated from composts, soils, nesting materials of birds, wood chips,hot water springs and many other sources by different researchers (Tansey and Brock, 1978).

***Based on pH Requirement***

pH has an important role on the growth of microorganisms because every microbe requires a specific pH for its growth and other metabolic activities. The range of pH over which an organism grows is defined by three cardinal points: minimum pH (below which the organism cannot grow), maximum pH (above which the organism cannot grow) and optimum pH (at which the organism grows best).

Microbes can be acidophiles (pH 2-5) like *Sulfolobus*, neutrophiles (pH 5.5-8.5) like *Leptothrix ochracea* oralkalophile (9-10.5) like *Bacillus alkalophilus*. For most bacteria, the optimum pH for growth lies between 6.5-7.5, means most of the bacteria are neutrophilic in nature. There can be decrease in the pH of medium with time due to production of organic acids (Quinto *et al.*, 2014; Anitha and Devi, 2016). The presence of salt of organic acid (sodium malate) may result in increase in pH of the medium. Hence, under these conditions only those microorganisms are able to survive which have a potential to grow under the respective range of pH. Geothermal areas are characterizedby high or low pH and in these areas, the increase in the pH of soil during alkaline condition is due to microbial ammonification and sulphate reductionand by water derived from leached silicate minerals. Due to limited buffering capacity of these areas, the pH fluctuates considerably and therefore, alkalitolerant microbesare more abundant in these habitats than alkaliphiles. The alkalophilic microbes possess widespread importance in the epidemiology of pathogenic bacteria, in remediation and industrial settings, as well as in marine, plant-associated and extremely alkaline ecological niches (Padan *et al.*, 2005). The best studied and most stable example of such an alkaline environment issoda lakes and soda deserts (Satyanarayan *et al.*, 2005).

***Based on Osmotic Pressure Tolerance***

The majority of microorganisms in the microbial diversity can survive at a high concentration of salts (30 g/L). Some groups of microorganisms are adapted to high osmotic pressure by reducing the cell osmosis and such microorganisms are called as obligate or extreme halophiles. Some organisms can grow at low concentration of NaCl (>15%) and they are called as facultative halophiles. Other microorganisms, which require a very high concentration of NaCl (15-30%) are called as extreme halophiles. The microbes which can grow under dry conditions or in the absence of water are called as Xerophiles. Such a kind of adaptation in halophiles and xerophiles is due to their ability for intracellular accumulation of such low molecular weight hydrophilic osmoprotectors as polyols, oligosaccharides and aminoacids.At a high salt concentration (1-3.5 M NaCl), green algaeof the genus *Dunaliella* (*D. salina*, *D. parva*, *D. viridis*) are ubiquitous and they use polyols ascompatible solutes (e.g., glycerol in *D. salina*). Some species of diatoms (*Amphora coffeaeformis* and *Nitzschia* and *Navicula)* accumulate proline and oligosaccharides for osmoregulation and have been found at a high concentration of salt (2 M NaCl). Protozoa (*Porodon utahensis*and *Fabrea salina)* and halotolerant yeast (*Debaryomyces hansenii)* have been described from saline environments. *Cladosporium glycolicum* wasfound growing on submerged wood in the Great Salt Lake (Das Sarma and Arora, 2001; Oren, 2006).

## METHODS FOR ANALYZING MICROBIAL DIVERSITY

Microbial diversity consists of very different and taxonomically diverse group of communities. There is a significant difference in morphology, physiology and phylogeny among all the members or groups or taxa. Polyphasic taxonomy (Phenotypic methods and Genotypic methods) is commonly used to study microbial diversity of natural habitats.

**Phenotypic Techniques**

These methods have been used successfully to estimate the microbial diversity of microbial communities in contaminated sites (Konopka *et al.*,

1998), plant rhizospheres (Grayston *et al.*, 1998), soils treated with herbicides (Fantroussi *et al.*, 1999) and arctic soils (Derry *et al.*, 1999). The phenotypic characterization of microbes mainly include morphological characteristics and chemotaxonomic profiles. Different morphological characteristics (colour, shape, pigmentation, production of slime etc.), features of cell (size, shape, Gram reaction, presence of capsule, flagella, endospore and inclusion bodies), biochemical and physiological features (temperature pH, salinity and atmospheric conditions, production of various enzymes, growth in the presence of different carbon and nitrogen sources) are used for the characterization of microbes in microbial diversity (Tindall *et al.*, 2010). Numerical taxonomy is another method to generate meaningful relationship amongst a large number of microorganisms using computer programmes generating data matrices between each pair of isolate according to degree of similarity. From these similarity data, the overall pattern of similarity or dissimilarity is studied based on dendrograms (Sneath, 1984). The other phenotypic methods used for analyzing microbial diversity are cell wall composition (Schleifer and Ludwig, 1989), fatty acid analysis (Tindall *et al.*, 2010) and isoprenoid quinones (Collins and Jones, 1981). The chemical composition of bacterial cells, metabolites and its relation to microbes from which these are obtained, is determined by using some advanced analytical techniques such as Pyrolysis Mass Spectrometry, Fourier Transform Infrared Spectroscopy and UV Resonance Raman Spectroscopy (Goodacre and Kell, 1996).

**Genotypic Techniques**

Genetic methods greatly influence the modern taxonomy and it has been used for the classification and identification for the specific gene sequences. 16S/18S rRNA sequencing is found to be a universal tool for the phylogenetic tree and interrelationship among the organisms. Due to its highly conserved nature, it gives more information than DNA molecule. Hence by using this method measure of similarity between the organisms can be determined, but at a level even beyond that of species (Vandamme *et al.*, 1996). Some curated databases [ARB (www.arb-home.de), RDP (http://rdp.cme.msu.edu/), SILVA (www.arb-silva.de) and LTP (www.arb-silva.de/projects/livingtree/)] are used for alignment of genome sequence with high quality sequence data. However, other multiple alignment programmes (CLUSTAL X, CLUSTAL W, CLUSTAL X2, CLUSTAL W2, MEGA, T-COFFEE, MUSCLE) can also be used for alignment with manual editing (Tindall *et al.*, 2010). Another classical method for the establishment of genomic content is determination of moles percent of guanine (G) and cytosine (C) to establish taxonomic position of organism. The G+C content within genera ranges to 10%, however within species it ranges to 3% (Stackebrandt and Liesach, 1993). Overall, in bacteria, the G+C content ranges from 24-76%(Sarethy *et al.*, 2014). DNA-DNA hybridization is an indirect measurement of sequence similarity between genomes and for the establishment of species, a cutoff value of 70% similarity is considered for the time (Vandamme *et al.*, 1996). DNA microarrays and DNA hybridization, Denaturing and Temperature Gradient Gel Electrophoresis (DGGE and TGGE), Single Strand Conformation Polymorphism (SSCP), Terminal Restriction Fragment Length Polymorphism (T-RFLP), Ribosomal Intergenic Spacer Analysis (RISA) and Automated Ribosomal Intergenic Spacer Analysis (ARISA) are some molecular methods used to study soil microbial diversity (Fakruddin *et al.*, 2013). The newer genotypic methods to characterize a taxon are RFLP(Restriction Fragment Length Polymorphism), RAPD (Random Amplified Polymorphic DNA), AFLP (Amplified Fragment Length Polymorphism), ARDRA (Amplified Ribosomal DNA Restriction Analysis), Ribotyping, REP-PCR (Repetitive Element Polymerase Chain Reaction), MLST (Multi Locus Sequence Analysis) (Sarethy *et al.*, 2014).

As 99% of the microbial population is considered to be uncultivable, therefore for the identification of uncultured microorganisms metagenomics with Next Generation Sequencing (NGS) has emerged as a promising field of interest (Land *et al.*, 2015). The most widely used NGS technologies are Roche 454 pyrosequencing and Illumina (Zinger *et al.*, 2012; Kistler *et al.*, 2015). However, processing of huge amount of data obtained from the community is the major limitation involved in analyzing microbial diversity by metagenomics. Therefore, some statistical methods are incorporated to improve the efficiency of analysis programmes (Abdo *et al.*, 2006). For binning and improved taxonomic estimation of metagenome sequences, bioinformatics tools like Metagenome Analyzer (MEGAN), CARMA or sequence ortholog based approach can be used (Simon and Daniel, 2011). Another approach gaining popularity for assessing microbial diversity is DNA bar coding (Valentini *et al.*, 2009). In bioinformatics, some distance matrices are available for sequence aligment, which are used for clustering the OTUs (Operational Taxonomic Units) using programmes such as MOTHUR (Schloss *et al.*, 2009). However, for the sequencing of eukaryotic microbes very limited datasets are available. According to International Committee on Taxonomy of Viruses (ICTV), the taxonomical details required for viral texa are dsDNA, ssDNA, rtDNA, rtRNA, dsRNA, ssNRNA, ssPRNA, SAT (Satellites), VIR (Viroids),UN (unassigned).

## UTILITY OF MICROBIAL DIVERSITY

A huge amount of commercial products are produced by microorganisms like enzymes, amino acids, antibiotics, alcohols, organic acids etc. Some of these products are produced during their growth (log phase) and therefore, are called as primary metabolites, such as enzymes, amino acids and vitamins. On the other hand, some other products are not used for the growth of microbe such as organic acids, antibiotics, alcohols etc. and these products are called as secondary metabolites. These secondary metabolites are produced during the stationary phase of growth. Some of these products are produced extracellularly, while others are produced intracellularly. Various products produced from microorganisms are presented in table 7.2. The microbial enzymes, which are commercially important are usually extracellular in nature and these products are marketed in crude form. A list of important enzymes produced from different microorganisms is given in table 7.3. In addition, different types of interactions are found between the microorganisms that exist in nature like commensalism, cooperation, mutualism and symbiosis (Zamioudis and Pieterse, 2012; Kowalski *et al.* 2015). Many heterotrophic soil microbes are also involved in regulating the annual $CO_2$ flux of the atmosphere (Pold and DeAngelis, 2013). Microorganisms are involved in metabolism of different substrates which regulate the recycling of animal and plant remains, food chain and food web. All of these microbial activities provide essential nutrients for the growth of plants (Bhat, 2013).

**Table 7.2: Industrial application of microorganisms**

| Microorganism | Product | References |
|---|---|---|
| (1) | (2) | (3) |
| **Bacteria** | | |
| *Bacillus natto* | Natto | Okamoto *et al*., 1995 |
| *Lactobacillus bulgaricus*<br>*Streptococcus thermophilus* | Yogurt | Childs and Drake, 2008 |
| *Bacillus firmus* AZ-78B<br>*Streptomyces halstedii*, AZ- 8A) | Vitamin B12 | Atta *et al*., 2008 |
| *Gluconobacter sp.* | Vinegar | Stasiak and B³azejak, 2009 |
| *Streptomyces fradiae* NCIM *2418*. | Neomycin | Vastrad and Neelagund, 2011 |
| *Bacillus thuringiensis* | Bioinsecticide | Marzban, 2012 |
| *Leuconostoc mesenteroides* | Dosa | Ghadge and Prasad, 2012 |
| *Amycolatopsis mediterranean* MTCC 14 | Rifamycin B | Vastrad and Neelagund, 2012 |
| *Corynebacterium glutamicum* | L-glutamate | Ahmed *et al*., 2013 |
| *Leuconostoc mesenteroides* | Idli | Das *et al*., 2013 |
| *AzotobacterPhosphobacter* | Biofertilizers | Amutha *et al*., 2014 |
| *Streptomyces speibonae* OXS1 | Oxy Tetracycline | Ezejiofor *et al*., 2015 |
| *Brevibacterium flavum* | L-Lysine | Irshad *et al*., 2015 |
| **Fungi** | | |
| *Clostridium aceticum*<br>*C. thermoaceticum*<br>*C. formicoaceticum*<br>*Acetobacterium woodii* | Acetic acid | Cheryan, 2001 |
| *Aspergillus niger* | Citric acid | Majumder *et al*., 2010 |

(Table Contd...)

| (1) | (2) | (3) |
|---|---|---|
| *Lactobacillus casei L. delbrueckii* | Lactic acid | Mudaliyar *et al.*, 2012 |
| *Trichoderma viride* | Biopesticide | Khandelwal *et al.*, 2012 |
| *Asprgillus sojae*<br>*A. oryzae* | Shoyu (soya sauce) | Wan *et al.*, 2013 |
| *Asprgillus oryzae* | Gluten soy sauce | Ma *et al.*, 2014 |
| **Yeast** | | |
| *Candida tropicalis* | Xylitol | Rao *et al.*, 2008 |
| *Saccharomycese cerevisiae* | Wine | Guleria, 2014 |
| *Saccharomyces pastorianus* | Beer | Dezelak *et al.*, 2014 |
| strain TUM 34/70 | | |
| *Saccharomyces cerevisiae* | Ethanol | Singh *et al.*, 2014 |
| **Algae** | | |
| *Spirulina maxima* | Single Cell Protein | Gabriel *et al.*, 2014 |

**Table 7.3: Production of microbial enzymes and their applications**

| Microorganism | Enzyme | Applications | Reference |
|---|---|---|---|
| (1) | (2) | (3) | (4) |
| *Bacillus sp.*<br>*Lactobacillus bulgaricus*<br>*Aspergillus niger*<br>*A. foetidus*<br>*A.phoenecia*<br>*Candida pseudotropicalis*<br>*Kluyveromyces lactis* | Lactase (beta-galactosidases) | Dairy Industry | Kardel *et al.*, 1995;<br>Mahoney, 1997;<br>Carminatti, 2001;<br>Prasad *et al.*, 2013 |
| *Aspergillus versicolor*<br>*Rhizopus stolonifer* | Glucose oxidase | Food Industry, Pharmaceutical and Clinical, Fruit and Fruit Juices, Eggs, Flavours, Carbonated beverages | Sandholm *et al.*, 2002;<br>Sumaiya and Ratna, 2015 |
| *Candida sp.*<br>*Aspergillus sp.*<br>*Penicillium sp.*<br>*Rhizopus sp.*<br>*Mucor sp.* | Lipase | Detergent, Dairy Industry Pharmaceutical and Clinical, Dry Cleaning, Laundry | Pandey *et al.*, 1999;<br>Reddivari *et al.*, 2002;<br>Mahmoud *et al.*, 2015 |
| *Bacillus sp.*<br>*Erwinia sp.*<br>*Aspergillus sp.*<br>*Rhizopus sp.*<br>*Trichoderma sp.*<br>*Sporotrichum thermophile*<br>*Penicillium viridicatum* RFC3<br>*Pseudomonas sp.*<br>*Fusarium sp.*<br>*Kluyveromyces sp.* | Pectinase | Food Industry, Brewing Industry, Coffee Industry, Fruit and Fruit juices | Kashyap *et al.*, 2003;<br>Kaur *et al.*, 2004;<br>Silva *et al.*, 2005;<br>Uenojo and Pastore, 2007;<br>Palaniyappan *et al.*, 2009;<br>Maciel *et al.*, 2013;<br>Meena *et al.*, 2015 |

(Table Contd...)

| (1) | (2) | (3) | (4) |
|---|---|---|---|
| *Streptomyces* sp. CH7<br>*Bacillus licheniformis* | Glucose isomerase | Food industry | Chanitnun and Pinphanichakarn, 2012; Nwokoro, 2015 |
| *Thermoactinomyces thalophilusBacillus* sp.<br>*Humicola insolens* | Xylanase | Baking and Milling, Brewing Industry, Confectionery Industry, Distilled Beverages, Dry Cleaning, Laundry, Paper, Starch and Syrup, Pharmaceutical and Clinical, Textile Industry, Paper Industry | Vikari *et al.*, 1994; Pandey *et al.*, 1999; Nigam and Pandey, 2009; Irfan *et al.*, 2012; Du *et al.*, 2013; Chaturvedi *et al.*, 2015 |
| *Steccherinum ochraceum*<br>*Polyporus versicolor*<br>*Panus tigrinus* | Ligninase | Bioremediation, Textile Industry | Nigam *et al.*, 1987; Robinson *et al.*, 2001; Dwivedi *et al.*, 2010; Gorska *et al.*, 2014; Duangporn and Siripong, 2015 |
| *Polyporus* sp.<br>*Pleurotus* sp.<br>*Trichoderma* sp.<br>*Aspergillus* sp.<br>*Bacillus brevis*<br>*Bacillus sp.* Y3 | Cellulase | Pharmaceutical and Clinical, Pulp and Paper Industry | Nigam *et al.*, 1987; Nigam and Prabhu, 1988; Hardiman *et al.*, 2010; Bajaj *et al.*, 2014; Fatema and Manchur, 2015; Lugani *et al.*, 2015 |
| *Aspergillus awamori*<br>*Rhizopus delemar*<br>*Endomyces sp.*<br>*Mucor pussilus*<br>*Trichoderma viride*<br>*Humicola insolens* | Amylase | Food and Textile Industry, Wine Miscellaneous | Nguyen *et al.*, 2002; Aquino *et al.*, 2003; Asghar *et al.*, 2007; Atinuke and Samuel, 2015 |
| *Kluyveromyces marxianus*<br>*Aspergillus niger*<br>*A. oryzae*<br>*Bacillus amyloliquifaciens*<br>*B. stearophilus*<br>*Mucor miehei*<br>*M. pussilus* | Inulinase<br>Protease | High fructose corn syrup Photographic, Textile, Milk and Brewing industry | Singh *et al.*, 2007 Melo *et al.*, 2002; Josephine *et al.*, 2012; Anbu *et al.*, 2015 |

Microbes are also involved in the production of useful industrial products such as cheese, yoghurt, enzymes, amino acids, vitamins, alcohol, antibiotics, organic acids, bioinsecticides and biopesticides. Microbes are also involved in bioremediation and biofortification (Hasan *et al.*, 2013; Karman *et al.*, 2015). The microbial diversity has trendous applications, which are discussed below.

**Biogeochemical Role**

Soil is a reservoir for the growth of vast variety of microorganisms and their metabolic versatility is involved with the degradation of a vast variety of complex organic compounds.A diverse range of biota present in soil including micro-fauna (e.g., nematodes and protozoa), meso-fauna (e.g., Collembola, mites and acari) and macro-fauna (e.g., earthworms, molluscs and termites). Darwin's pioneering work has revealed the impact of invertebrates on soil organic matter turnover (Darwin 1881). The beneficial affects of microarthropods due to activities of microorganisms for organic matter processing in soil has been proved well known (Edwards 2000). Microorganisms are involved in recycling of mineralssuch as carbon, nitrogen, potassium, phosphorous, oxygen, sulphur etc. for more accurate and more sustainable management of agroecosystems (Groenigen *et al.*, 2015).

**Microbial Products for Agriculture**

The broad application of microbes in sustainable agriculture is due to the genetic dependency of plants on the beneficial functions provided by symbiotic cohabitants present in the soil (Noble and Ruaysoongnern, 2010). There are many indirect positive effects of microorganisms on plants like population density, dynamics and metabolicactivities of soil-borne pathogens, mainly through competition, antibiosis, lysis andhyperparasitism. However, rhizosphere microorganisms exhibit many direct positive effects on plants through phytostimulation and biofertilization of plants; these processes are involved in production of phytohormones, non-symbiotic nitrogen fixation and the increase of availability of phosphate and other nutrients in the soil (Lugtenberg and Kamilova, 2009; Bhattarai *et al.*, 2015). Currently, attention has been paid to the development of agriculture in which high productivities of plants and animals are ensured within their natural habitat with minimal disturbance to the environment (Noble and Ruaysoongnern, 2010). Tolerance of plants in adverse conditions such as salinity (Zawoznik *et al.*, 2011) and drought (Arzanesh *et al.*, 2011) conditions has also been associated with the microbes present in the soil.

**Biodegradation of Xenobiotics**

The principal xenobiotics include alkanes, polycyclic aromatic hydrocarbons (PAHs), antibiotics, synthetic azo dyes, pesticides, fuels, solvents, pollutants (dioxins and polychlorinated biphenyls), polyaromatic, chlorinated and nitro-aromatic compounds (Sinha *et al.*, 2009). These create a deleterious effect on the public health (Agrawal and Shahi, 2015). Most of themicroorganisms, particularly bacteria playan important role in transformation of toxic contaminants in non-hazardous or less hazardous substances (Tropel and Van der Meer, 2004). Many aerobic (*Pseudomonas, Gordonia, Bacillus, Moraxella, Micrococcus, Escherichia, Sphingobium, Pandoraea, Rhodococcus)* and anaerobic bacteria (*Pelatomaculum, Desulphovibrio, Methanospirillum, Methanosaeta desulfotomaculum, Syntrophobacter, Syntrophus)* are involved in the degradation of xenobiotic compounds by mineralization, transformation or immobilization of pollutants (Chowdhury *et al.*, 2008; Hamsavathani *et al.*, 2015). Other than bacteria, fungi and actinobacteria also plays an important role in degradation of xenobiotics. The degradation of bonny light crude oil by fungi like *Aspergillus niger, Gliocladium deliquescence* and *Penicillium italicum* was reported by Ekundayo *et al.* (2012).

**Industrial Applications**

The practical definition of biotechnology is "it is application of power of micorbe's biosynthetic capabilities to manufacture high-value products that are too complex for chemical synthesis by economically viable processes, resulting in value addition and financial gains". A large number of microbes are extracted from soil and used in industrial production of various kinds as food processing and production, development of biocides, biocontrol agents, medicines and other natural products. The microbes used for industrial applications could be a naturally occurring or even it could be genetically engineered through human ingenuity. Pharmaceutical companies spend millions of dollars annually on screening soil and litter for useful microorganisms (Vibha and Neelam, 2012).

***Applications in Food Industry***

Bacteria, yeasts and fungi possess highly diversified applications in the food sector. Most of the products of food industry, such as alcoholic beverages, ethyl alcohol, dairy products and organic acids are mainly produced by fermentation (Pai, 2003). During the past four decades, with the advancement of biotechnology, there is rapid development of enzyme industries in the food sector for the production of cheese, beer, wine and vinegar (Kirk *et al.*, 2002). The antimicrobial metabolite, nisin (a bacteriosin), produced by lactic acid bacteria shows promising applications in industrially processed foods and nutraceuticals (Gupta *et al.*, 2014).Microorganisms are used for the production of many products like yogurt, cheese, sour cream, buttermilk and other fermented milk products from the very ancient time at home level. Yeasts are used in production of beer, wine, ethanol and leavening of bread. Some other bacteria are involved in the manufacture of fermented foods like soy sauce, sauerkraut, dill pickles, olives, salami, cocoa and black teas (Jay *et al.*, 2005; Lynn *et al.*, 2013;Gavilan *et al.*, 2015; Zwietering *et al.*, 2016). The use of inulinase for high fructose corn syrup (Singh *et al.*, 2007) has also been established. Various industrial enzymes and their applications are presented in Table 7.3.

***Applications in Medical and Pharmaceutical Industries***

In recent years, microbialenzyme technology has grown to a multimillion dollar industry and exploration of microbial strain for discovering enzymes with novel properties as well as indiscovery and production of other useful pharmaceutical products (Vibha and Neelam, 2012). Many microbial natural products or their derivatives are used as antitumour drugs and the approved products deserving special attention are actinomycin D, anthracyclines (daunorubicin, doxorubicin, epirubicin, pirirubicin and valrubicin), bleomycin, mitosanes (mitomycin C), anthracenones (mithramycin, streptozotocin and pentostatin), enediynes (calcheamycin), taxol and epothilones (Gupta *et al.*, 2014). Various microbial products can be used as immune-suppresants, such as cyclosporin A, produced by the mold, *Tolypocladium nivenum* (originally classified as *Trichoderma polysporum* and later as *Tolypocladiuminflatum*), used in heart, liver and kidney transplants (Viaud *et al.*, 2013). Tacrolimus (FK506) is another immune-suppresants produced by *Streptomyces tsukubaensis and* it is approximately 100 times more active as an immunosuppressive than cyclosporin A. Microbes are also suggested to be utilized for the treatement of many diseases, such as anaemia (Kassinen *et al.*, 2007; Scarpignato, 2008), obesity (Liou *et al.*, 2013; Ohtani *et al.*, 2014; Mekkes *et al.*, 2014), diabetes (Hossain *et al.*, 2007; Gupta *et al.*, 2013), atopic dermatitis (Winkler *et al.*, 2007; Thomsen, 2014), crohn disease (Gevers *et al.*, 2014) and allergies (Gupta *et al.*, 2014; Cao *et al.*, 2014). The probiotic nature of microbes also make them an important source for different medical applications.

***Applications in other Industries***

Microbial cells and their purified products like enzymes are also used in some other industrial sectors such as detergent, textiles, paper and pulp, poultry, pork and caprine feeding (Hewitt *et al.*, 2006; Subramaniumet and Prema, 2002; Gupta *et al.*, 2003; Hmidet *et al.*, 2009; Mishra *et al.*, 2011; Nigam, 2013; Adrio, J.L and Demain, 2014; Patel and Savanth, 2015).The use of other enzymes like cellulase (Lugani *et al.*, 2015) and xylose reductase (Sooch and Lugani, 2015) for diverse applications has been investigated recently.

## CONSERVATION OF MICROORGANISMS

There are many threats for the existence of microbial diversity in their natural habitat due to environmental changes like overexploitation, environment pollution, habitat loss or land use change and invasion by exotic species (Malmqvist and Rundle, 2002; Postel and Richter, 2003; Revenga *et al.*, 2005; Machovina *et al.*, 2015). Due to the crisis of this precious heritage, the main focus of humans, nations and government is towards the conservation and management of this biodiversity. The main effect of decline in this biodiversity was assumed in fresh waters ecosystem than those of terrestrial ecosystems.

There are two ways for the conservation of microorganisms for biological diversity i.e. *in situ* and *ex situ* programmes. In situ preservation involves on site conservation of microbial flora by conserving the ecosystems and natural habitats. Various types of diverse microenvironments and unique ecosystems such as different soil orders, boiling waters, springs, deep sea vents, salt pans, acid mine drainage, cold environments are present in India that are home to diverse populations of microorganisms. Western ghat and the North-eastern region are two hotspot regions in India's biodiversity, which is tectonically active with approximately 17% of a set of 2500 species due to large nutrients efflux (Bhat, 2013).Ashok *et al.* (2015) described 42 species of fungi belonging to 16 genera from coastal area of Tuticorin Dt., Tamil Nadu, India in the year of 2012-2013. Among them Deuteromycetes were represented by 97.62% and Phycomycetes were 2.38%. In a similar study, 22 species of marine fungi comprising 13 ascomycetes, 1 basidiomycete and 8 asexual fungi were identified from decaying animal substrates collected from the beaches along west coast of India. Among them, Matsusporium tropicalis (14.63%) and Trichocladium achrasporum (12.20%) were the most frequently found (Nambiar and Raveendran, 2015). However, *ex situ* conservation is the most effective and efficient mechanism for conserving biodiversity by gene banks, culture collections and microbial resource centers.Due to availability of very little information about the microbial diversity, relatively rapid evolution and adaptability of microbes with the environmental conditions,it is difficult to assess the effectiveness of *in situ* conservation of microorganisms. The maintenance of microbial population is essential to avoid strain deterioration and contamination during growth of these strains. Different methods are available for the preservation of microbial strain like lyophilization, paraffin method, silica gel storage, freeze drying and cryopreservation. The main choice of method for bacterial culture is freeze drying, which gives excellent recovery and it is easy to distribute the ampoules under simple storage conditions. With some isolates of fungi, change in physiology and genetic stability are found, so there is a need to establish certain optimal preservation protocols. Many pathogenic strains can also be preserved with the pathogenic tissue. Yeasts can be preserved by a number of preservation methods due to its robust nature, tolerance of unfavorable conditions, nutritionally undemanding nature and readily management in industries.Various government and non government organizations are making efforts to preserve the microbial diversity by establishing microbial culture depositories. A list of major microbial culture depositories along with type of culture in India is given in Table 7.4.

There are many threats to biodiversity such as soil erosion, pesticidesand climate change (Sandilyan, 2013; Veresoglou *et al.*, 2015). Many attempts have been made to preserve microbial diversity, such as (a) prevention of soil erosion (b) preservation and improvement of soil (c) reclamation of waste land (d) Improvement in the methods of cultivation including dry farming practices and extensionof cultivation (e) Construction of earth and masonry works in fields, gullies and ravines (Bhat, 2013).

**Table 7.4: Culture Collection Centers in India**

| Sl. No. | Culture Collection Center | State | Cultures Preserved |
|---|---|---|---|
| (1) | (2) | (3) | (4) |
| 1. | Anaerobic Bacterial Resource Center, University of Hyderabad | Andhra Pradesh | More than 210 bacterial strains |
| 2. | Microbial Type Culture Collection and Gene Bank (MTCC), Institute of Microbial Technology (IMTECH), Chandigarh | Chandigarh | Bacteria: 1124<br>Fungi: 1245<br>Yeasts: 575<br>Plasmids: 85 |
| 3. | Goa University Fungus Culture Collection and Research Unit | Goa | Algae: 01<br>Bacteria: 200<br>Fungi: 1000<br>Yeasts: 300<br>Archaea: 30 |
| 4. | National Collection of Dairy Cultures National Dairy Research Institute, Karnal | Haryana | Bacteria: 400<br>Fungi: 15<br>Yeasts: 20<br>Dairy Starter Cultures: 25 |
| 5. | NII Microbial Culture Collection NIICC, National Institute for Interdisciplinary Science and Technology (CSIR), Trivandrum | Kerala | Bacteria: 294<br>Fungi: 78<br>Yeast: 07 |
| 6. | Culture Collection, Microbiology and Cell Biology Laboratory Institution, Indian Institute of Science, Bangalore | Karnatka | Bacteria: 214<br>Fungi: 78<br>Yeasts: 43<br>Cell lines: animal:10<br>Viruses: animal: 3<br>Viruses: bacteria: 11 |
| 7. | Food and Fermentation Technology Division, University of Mumbai | Maharashtra | Bacteria: 35<br>Fungi: 20<br>Yeasts: 05<br>Algae: 03 |
| 8. | Microbial Culture Collection National Centre for Cell Science, University of Pune, Pune | Maharashtra | Bacteria: 135488<br>Fungi: 41 |
| 9. | National Collection of Industrial Microorganisms, National Chemical Laboratory (NCL) (CSIR), Pune | Maharashtra | Algae: 15<br>Bacteria: 1400<br>Fungi: 950<br>Yeasts: 600 |
| 10. | Maharashtra Association for the Cultivation of Science, Aghargar Research Institute, Pune | Maharashtra | Bacteria: 256<br>Fungi: 08 |
| 11. | National Fungal Culture Collection of India, Agharkar Research Institute, Pune | Maharashtra | Fungi: 2800 |
| 12. | Indian Type Culture Collection, Division of Plant Pathology, Indian Agricultural Research Institute | New Delhi | Total strains: 3800 |

(Table Contd...)

| (1) | (2) | (3) | (4) |
|---|---|---|---|
| 13. | Delhi University Mycological Herbarium | New Delhi | Fungus |
| 14. | National Facility for Marine Cyanobacteria Bharatidasan University, Tiruchirappalli | Tamil Nadu | Marine Cyanobacteria |
| 15. | National Bureau of Agriculturally Important Microorganisms (NBAIM), Indian Council of Agricultural Research (ICAR), Kushmaur | Uttar Pradesh | Bacteria, filamentous fungi, yeasts, Actinomycetes |
| 16. | Visva-Bharti Culture Collection of Algae, Visva Bharti Central University, Santiniketan | West Bengal | Algae: 50 |

Government of India Ministry of Environment, Forests and Climate Change in annual report (2014-15) has focused on conservation of microbial diversity by environmental conservation and management (MoEF, 2015). Monitoring and Modeling of Marine Ecosystem (MMME) under Ministry of Earth Sciences (2015) has focused on identification of microbes and other organisms for the extraction of bioactive compounds (MMME, 2015). The ninth report of Committee on Estimates, Ministry of Agriculture (2015-16) has focused on role of biodiversity in soil. The need for patenting of novel microbes has been also recommended by the committee (MoA, 2015).All India Coordinated Project on capacity Building in Taxonomy (AICOPTAX)) has recommended "Enhancement of country's capabilities for inventorying, monitoring, conserving, community participation in assessment and utilizing biodiversity as well as for establishing leadership in the field of taxonomy at regional and global level with collection and maintenance of collections of taxonomic groups for which no information is available." The implementing agencies for achieving quality milestone of this scheme are Botanical Service of India and Zoological Service of India.

Microbial diversity has a significant role in tremendous applications in diversefields, hence, there is a need for the conservation of microorganisms by in situ and ex situ programmes.

## *REFERENCES*

Abdo, Z., Schuette, U.M., Bent, S.J., Williams, C.J., Forney, L.J. and Joyce P. (2006): Statistical Methods for Characterizing Diversity of Microbial Communities by Analysis of Terminal Restriction Fragment Length Polymorphisms of 16S rRNA Genes. Environ. Microbiol., 8(5): 929-38.

Adrio, J.L. and Demain, A.L. (2014): Microbial Enzymes: Tools for Biotechnological Processes. Biomolecules, 4(1): 117-139.

Agrawal, N. and Shahi, S.K. (2015): An Environmental Cleanup Strategy - Microbial Transformation of Xenobiotic Compounds. Int. J. Curr. Microbiol. App. Sci., 4(4): 429-461.

Ahmed, Y.M., Khan, J.A., Abulnaja, K.A. and Al-Malki, A.L. Production of Glutamic Acid by *Corynebacterium glutamicum* using Dates Syrup as Carbon Source. Afr. J. Microbiol. Res., 7(19): 2071-2077.

Aislabie, J. and Deslippe, J.R. (2013): Soil Microbes and their Contribution to Soil Services. In: Ecosystem Services in New Zealand: Conditions and Trends. Dymond, J.R. (ed.). Manaaki Whenua Press, New Zealand: p. 143-161.

Alexander, I.J. and Lee, S.S. (2005): Mycorrhizas and Ecosystem Processes in Tropical Rain Forest: Implications for Diversity. In: Biotic Interactions in the Tropics. Burslem, D., Pinard, M. and Hartley, S. (eds.). Cambridge University Press: pp. 165-203.

Ali, N.S., Hassan, W.F. and Janno, F.O. (2015): Soil Iron and Nitrogen Availability and their uptake by Maize Plants as Related to Mineral and Bio Nitrogen Fertilizers Application. Agric. Biol. J.N. Am., 6(5): 118-122.

Allgaier, M. and Grossart H.P. (2006): Seasonal Dynamics and Phylogenetic Diversity of Freeliving and Particle-associated Bacterial Communities in Four Lakes in Northeastern Germany. Aquat.Microb. Ecol., 45(2): 115-128.

Amutha, R., Karunakaran, S., Dhanasekaran, S., Hemalatha, K., Monika, R., Shanmugapriya, P. and Sornalatha, T. (2014): Isolation and Mass Production of Biofertilizers (Azotobactor and Phosphobacter). Int. J. latest Res. Sci. Technol., 3(1): 79-81.

Amura, P.K. and Marneedi, S. (2015): Bio Aerosols and its Relation with Bioterrorism. J. Microbiol. Biotechnol., 4(1): 1-9.

Anbu, P., Gopinath, S.C.B., Chaulagain, B.P., Tang, T.H. and Marimuthu Citartan, M.(2015): Microbial Enzymes and their Applications in Industries and Medicine 2014. BioMed Res. Int., 2015: 1-3.

Anitha, S. and Devi, S.N.P. (2016): Efficiency of Aspergillus Terreus to Solubilize Insoluble form of Phosphorous into Soluble form under Cultural Conditions. Int. J. Pharm. Bio. Sci., 7(1): 120-126.

Aquino, A.C. Jorge, J.A., Terenzi, H.F.and Polizeli, M.L. (2003): Studies on a Thermostable α-amylase from the thermophilic fungus *Scytalidium thermophilum*. Appl. Microbiol. Biotechnol., 61(4): 323-328.

Arzanesh, M.H., Alikhani, H.A., Khavazi, K., Rahimian, H.A. and Miransari, M. (2011). Wheat (*Triticum aestivum* L.) Growth Enhancement by *Azospirillum sp*. Under Drought Stress. World J. Microbiol. Biotechnol., 27: 197-205.

Asghar, M., Asad, M.J., Rahman, S.U. and Legge, R.L. (2007).A thermostable α-amylase from a moderately thermophilic *Bacillus subtilis* strain for starch processing. J. Food. Eng., 79(3): 950-955.

Ashok, G., Senthilkumar, G. and Panneerselvam, A. (2015). Diversity and Seasonal Variation of Soil Fungi Isolated from Coastal Area of Tuticorin Dt., Tamil Nadu, India. Int.J.Curr.Microbiol.App.Sci., 4(10): 161-178.

Atinuke, O.A. and Samuel, F. (2015): Production of Bacterial Amylases and Cellulases using Sweet Potato (*Ipomoea batatas*.(L.) Lam.) Peels. Afr. J. Biochem. Res., 9(9): 104-109.

Atta, H.M., Arafa, R.A., Salem, M.S. and El-Meleigy, M.A. (2008): Microbiological Studies on the Production of Vitamin B12 from Two Mixed Cultures Under Solid-state Fermentation Condition. J. Appl. Sci. Res., 4(11): 1463-1477.

Bajaj, B.K., Sharma, M. and Rao, R.S. (2014): Agricultural Residues for Production of Cellulase from *Sporotrichum thermophile* LAR5 and its Application for Saccharification of Rice Straw. J. Mater. Environ. Sci., 5(5): 1454-1460.

Bartnicki-Garcia, S. (1970). Cell Wall Composition and Other Biochemical Markers in Fungal Phylogeny, In: Phytochemical Phylogeny. J.B. Harbone (ed.). London Academic Press: p. 81-103.

Basak, S.K., Ali, M.M., Islam, M.S. and Shaha, P.R. (2015): Aquatic Weeds of Haor Area in Kishoregonj District, Bangladesh: Availability, Threats and Management Approaches. Int. J. Fish. Aquat. Stud., 2(6): 151-156.

Bhargava, D., Bhargava, K., Sabri, I., Siddharth, M., Dave, A., Jagadeesh, H.G. and Goel, M. (2011): Bioterrorism - "My Role as a Dentist." J. Ind. Acad. Forensic Med., 33(3): 254-257.

Bhat, A.K. (2013): Preserving Microbial Diversity of Soil Ecosystem: A Key to Sustainable Productivity. Int. J. Curr.Microbiol. App. Sci., 2(8): 85-101.

Bhatnagar, A. and Bhatnagar, M. (2005): Microbial Diversity in Desert Ecosystems. Curr. Sci., 89 (1): 91-100.

Bhattarai, A., Bhattarai, B. and Pandey, S. (2015): Variation of Soil Microbial Population in Different Soil Horizons. J. Microbiol. Exp., 2(2): 1-4.

Cao, S., Feehley, T.J. and Nagler, C.R. (2014): The Role of Commensal Bacteria in the Regulation of Sensitization to Food Allergens. FEBS Lett., 588(22): 4258-4266.

Carminatti, C.A. (2001): Ensaios de hidrolise enzimática da lactose em reator a membrana utilizando beta-galactosidase e Kluyveromyces lactis. Dissertacao (Mestrado em Engenharia Química) – Universidade Federal de Santa Catarina, Florianopolis.

Chamaille-Jammes, S., Massot, M., Aragon, P. and Clobert, J. (2006): Global Warming and Positive Fitness Response in Mountain Populations of Common Lizards *Lacerta vivipara*. Global. Change Biol., 12: 392-402.

Chanitnun, K. and Pinphanichakarn, P. (2012): Glucose (xylose) Isomerase Production by *Streptomyces sp*. CH7 Grown on Agricultural Residues. Braz. J. Microbiol., 43(3): 1084-1093.

Chaturvedi, S., Kohli, K.U., Rajni, S. and Khurana, S.M.P. (2015): Statistical Optimization of Medium Composition for Xylanase Production by Solid State Fermentation using Agroresidues. Am. J. Microbiol. Res., 3(2): 85-92.

Cheryan, M. (2000): "Acetic Acid Production". Encyclopedia of Microbiology. Vol. 1. 2nd edn. Academic Press: p. 13-17.

Childs, J. and Drake, M. (2008): Sensory Properties of Yogurt Powders. Poster Presentation, IFT Annual Meeting, June 2008. Abstract: 048-09.

Chowdhury, A., Pradhan, S., Saha, M. and Sanyal, N. (2008): Impact of Pesticides on Soil Microbiological Parameters and Possible Bioremediation Strategies. Ind. J. Microbiol., 48(1): 114-127.

Clarholm, M. (1994). The Microbial Loop in Soil. In: Beyond the Biomass. Ritz, K., Dighan, J. and Giller, K.E. (eds.). John Wiley Publs, Chichester: pp. 221-230.

Clasen, J.L., Brigden S.M., Payet, J.P. and Suttle, C.A. (2008). Evidence that Viral Abundance Across Oceans and Lakes is Driven by Different Biological Factors. *Freshw. Biol.*, 53(6): 1090-1100.

Collins, M.D. and Jones, D. (1981): Distribution of Isoprenoid Quinine Structural Types in Bacteria and their Taxonomic Implications. Microbiol. Rev., 45(2): 316-354.

Corliss, J.O. (2002): Biodiversity and Biocomplexity of the Protists and an Overview of their Significant Roles in Maintenance of our Biosphere. Acta. Protozool., 41: 199-219.

Danovaro, R., Corinaldesi, C., Filippini, M., Fischer, U.R., Gessner, M.O., Jacquet, S., Magagnini, M. and Velimirov, B. (2008): Viriobenthos in Freshwater and Marine Sediments: a Review. Freshw. Biol., 53(6): 1186-1213.

Darwin, C. (1881): The Formation of Vegetable Mould through the Action of Worms, with Observations of their Habits. John Murray Publs, London.

Das, S., Lyla, P.S. and Khan, S.A. (2006): Marine Microbial Diversity and Ecology: Importance and Future Perspectives. Curr. Sci., 90(10): 1325-1335.

Das, A., Raychaudhuri, U. and Chakraborty, R. (2013): Effect of Wheatgrass for Enhancing the Nutritional, Textural, Total Antioxidant and Sensory Characteristics of 'Idli' – An Indian Steamed Rice Cake. J. Food Technol., 11(3): 67-74.

Das Sarma, S. and Arora, P. (2001): Halophiles. Encyclopedia of Life Sciences. Nature Publishing Group: 1-9.

Derry, A.M., Staddon, W.J., Kevan, P.G. and Trevors, J.T. (1999): Functional Diversity and Community Structure of Micro-organisms in Three Arctic Soils as Determined by Sole-carbon Source-utilization. Biodivers. Conserv., 8(2): 205-221.

Dezelak, M., Zarnkow, M., Becker, T. and Kosir, I.J. (2014): Processing of Bottom-fermented Gluten-free Beer-like Beverages based on Buckwheat and Quinoa Malt with Chemical and Sensory Characterization. J. Inst. Brew., 120(4): 360-370.

Du, Y., Shi, P., Huang, H., Zhang, X., Luo, H., Wang. Y. and Yao, B. (2013): Characterization of Three Novel Thermophilic Xylanases from *Humicola insolens* Y1 with Application Potentials in the Brewing Industry. Bioresour. Technol., 130: 161-167.

Duangporn, P. and Siripong, P. (2015): Selection of Ligninolytic Basidiomycetes Fungi from a Dry Dipterocarp Forest in Thailand. Aus. J. Basic Appl. Sci., 9(20): 210-219.

Dubey, R.C. and Maheswari, D.K. (2005): A Text Book of Microbiology. D.K Maheswari (ed.). S. Chand Publs. p. 74.

Dujon, B. (2010): Yeast Evolutionary Genomics. Nat. Rev. Genet., 11(7): 512-524.

Dwivedi, P., Vivekanand, V., Pareek, N., Sharma, A. and Singh, R.P. (2010): Bleach Enhancement of Mixed Wood Pulp by Xylanase-laccase Concoction Derived Through Co-culture Strategy. Appl. Biochem. Biotechnol., 160(1): 255-268.

Ebeling, J.M., Timmons, M.B. and Bisogni, J.J. (2006): Engineering Analysis of the Stoichiometry of Photoautotrophic, Autotrophic, and Heterotrophic Removal of Ammonia–nitrogen in Aquaculture Systems. Aquacult., 257(1-4): 346-358.

Edwards, C. (2000): Soil Invertebrate Controls and Microbial Interactions in Nutrient and Organic Matter Dynamics in Natural and Agroecosystems. In: Invertebrates as Webmasters in Ecosystems. Coleman D, Hendrix P (eds.) CAB International, Wallingford Publs, UK: p. 141-159.

Ekundayo, F.O., Olukunle, O.F. and Ekundayo, E.A. (2012): Biodegradation of Bonnylight Crude Oil by Locally Isolated Fungi from Oil Contaminated Soils in Akure, Ondo State Malaysian. J. Microbiol., 8(1): 42-46.

Ezejiofor, T.I.N., Duru, C.I., Asagbra, A.E.,Ezejiofor, A.N., Orisakwe, O.E., Afonne, J.O. and Obi, E. (2015):Waste to Wealth: Production of Oxytetracycline using *Streptomyces sp.* from Household Kitchen Wastes of Agricultural Produce. Afr. J. Biotechnol.,11(43): 10115-10124.

Fakruddin, M., Shahnewaj, K. and Mannan, B. (2013): Methods for Analyzing Diversity of Microbial Communities in Natural Environments. Ceylon J. Sci. (Biol. Sci.), 42(1): 19-33.

Fakruddin, Md. and Mannan, K.S.B. (2013): Methods for Analyzing Diversity of Microbial Communities in Natural Environments. Ceylon J. Sci. (Bio. Sci.), 42(1): 19-33.

Fantroussi, S., Verschuere, L., Verstraete, W. and Top, E.M. (1999): Effect of Phenylurea Herbicides on Soil Microbial Communities Estimated by Analysis of 16S rRNA Gene Fingerprints and Community-level Physiological Profiles. Appl. Environ. Microbiol., 65(3): 982-988.

Fatema, K. and Manchur, M.A. (2015): Isolation, Identification and Cellulase Production by *Bacillus brevis* from the Acacia Forest Soil. Int.J. Res. Agric. Forest., 2(9): 14-22.

Gabriel, A., Victor, N. and James, C.P. (2014): Cactus Pear Biomass, a Potential Lignocellulose Raw Material for Single Cell Protein production (SCP): A Review. Int. J. Curr. Microbiol. App. Sci, 3(7): 171-197.

Gavilan, C.G.R., Fernandez, M., Hudson, J.A. and Korpela, R. (2015): Role of Microorganisms Present in Dairy Fermented Products in Health and Disease. BioMed Res. Int., 2015: 1-2.

Gevers, D., Kugathasan, S., Denson L.A., Vázquez-Baeza Y., Van Treuren, W.,Ren, B., Schwager, E., Knights, D., Song, S.J., Yassour, M., Morgan, X.C., Kostic, A.D., Luo, C., Gonzalez A., McDonald, D., Haberman, Y., Walters, T., Baker, S., Rosh, J., Stephens, M., Heyman, M., Markowitz, J., Baldassano, R., Griffiths, A., Sylvester, F., Mack, D., Kim, S., Crandall W., Hyams, J., Huttenhower, C., Knight, R.andXavier, R.J. (2014): The treatment-naive microbiome in new-onset Crohn's disease. Cell Host Microbe, 15(3): 382-392.

Ghadge, P.N. and Prasad, K. (2012): Some Physical Properties of Rice Kernels Variety PR-106. J. Food Process. Technol., 3(8): 1-5.

Glockner, F.O., Zaichikov, E., Belkova, N., Denissova, L., Pernthaler, J., Pernthaler, A. and Amann, R. (2000): Comparative 16S rRNA Analysis of Lake Bacterioplankton Reveals Globally Distributed Phyogenetic Clusters including an Abundant Group of Actinobacteria. Appl. Environ. Microbiol., 66(11): 5053-5065.

Goodacre, R. and Kell, D.B. (1996): Pyrolysis Mass Spectrometry and its Applications in Biotechnology. Curr. Opin. Biotechnol., 7(1): 20-28.

Gorska, E.B., Jankiewicz, U., Dobrzynski, J., Galazka, A., Sitarek, M., Gozdowski, D., Russel, S. and Kowalczyk, P. (2014). Production of Ligninolytic Enzymes by Cultures of White Rot Fungi Polish. J. Microbiol., 63(4): 461-465.

Grayston, S.J., Wang, S., Campbell, C.D. and Edwards, A.C. (1998): Selective Influence of Plant Species on Microbial Diversity in the Rhizosphere. Soil Biol. Biochem., 30(3): 369-378.

Groenigen, J.W., Huygens, D., Boeckx, P., Kuyper, T.W., Lubbers, I.M., Rutting, T. and Groffman, P.M. (2015): The Soil N Cycle: New Insights and Key Challenges. Soil, 1: 235-256.

Guleria, A. (2014): Production of Grape Wine by the Use of Yeast, *Saccharomyces cerevisiae*. Global J. Res. Anal., 3(6): 1-5.

Gupta, C., Prakash, D. and Gupta, S. (2013): Role of Microbes in Functional Foods for the Treatment of Diabetes. World J. Pharm. Pharm. Sci., 2(6): 4626-4638.

Gupta, C., Prakash, D. and Gupta, S. (2014): Natural Useful Therapeutic Products from Microbes. J. Microbiol. Exp., 1(1): 1-8.

Gupta, C., Prakash, D., Garg, A.P. and Gupta, S. (2014): Nutraceuticals from Microbes. In: Phytochemicals of Nutraceutical Importance. Prakash D. and Sharma, G (eds.), CABI International Publishers, UK: p. 79-102.

Gupta, R. Gigras, P., Mohapatra, H., Goswami, V.K. and Chauhan, B. (2003): Microbial α Amylases: A Biotechnological Perspective. Proc. Biochem., 38(11): 1599-1616.

Haabe, J. and Middelboe, M. (2009): Viral Lysis of *Phaeocystis pouchetii*: Implications for Algal Population Dynamics and Heterotrophic C, N and P cycling. ISME J., 3(4): 430-441.

Hamsavathani, V., Aysha, O.S. and Valli, S. (2015): Biodegradation of Xenobiotics: A Review on Petroleum Hydrocarbons and Pesticide Degradation. World J. Pharm. Pharm. Sci., 4(11): 1791-1808.

Hardiman, E., Gibbs, M., Reeves, R. and Bergquist, P. (2010). Directed Evolution of a Thermophilic beta-glucosidase for Cellulosic Bioethanol Production. Appl. Biochem. Biotechnol.,161(1-8): 301-312.

Harpole, W. (2010): Neutral Theory of Species Diversity. Nat. Educ. Knowl., 1(8): 31.

Hassan, M.M., Alam, M.Z. and Anwar, M.N. (2013): Biodegradation of Textile Azo Dyes by Bacteria Isolated from Dyeing Industry Effluent. Int. Res. J. Biol. Sci., 2(8): 27-31.

Heath, I.B. (1986): Nuclear Division: A Marker for Protist Phylogeny. Prog. Protistol., 1: 115-162.

Hewitt, L.M., Parrott, J.L. and McMaster, M.E. (2006): A Decade of Research on the Environmental Impacts of Pulp and Paper mill Effluents in Canada: Sources and Characteristics of Bioactive Substances. J. Toxicol. Environ. Health Part B. Crit. Rev., 9(4): 341-356.

Hmidet, N., Ali, N.E.H., Haddar, A., Kanoun, S., Alya, S.K. and Nasri, M. (2009): Alkaline Proteases and thermostable α-amylase Co-produced by *Bacillus licheniformis* NH1: Characterization and Potential Application as Detergent Additive. Biochem. Eng. J., 47(1-3): 71-79.

Hossain, P., Kawar, B. and Nahas, M.E. (2007): Obesity and Diabetes in the Developing World – A Growing Challenge. N. Engl. J. Med., 356: 213-215.

http://164.100.47.134/lsscommittee/Estimates/16_Estimates_9.pdf (Accessed- 12-02-2016).

http://envfor.nic.in/division/research-development (Accessed- 12-02-2016).

http://envfor.nic.in/sites/default/files/Environment%20Annual%20Report%20%20Eng..pdf (Accessed- 10-02-2016).

http://moes.gov.in/programmes/monitoring-and-modeling-marine-ecosystems-mmme (Accessed- 10-02-2016).

Irfan, M., Nadeem, M., Syed, Q. and Baig, S. (2012): Effect of Medium Composition on Xylanase Production by *Bacillus subtilis* using Various Agricultural Wastes. American-Eurasian J. Agric. Environ. Sci., 12 (5): 561-565.

Irshad, S., Faisal, M., Hashmi, A.S., Javed, M.M., Baber, M.E., Awan, A.R. and Anjum, A.A. (2015): Mass Production and Recovery of L-lysine by Microbial Fermentation using *Brevibacterium flavum*. J. Anim. Plant Sci., 25(1): 290-294.

Ivanov, V. (2010): Microbiology of Environmental Engineering Systems. In: Handbook of Environmental Engineering Vol. 10. Wang, L.K., Ivanov, V., Tay, J.H., Hung, Y.T. (eds.). Springer Science Publs: pp. 19-79.

Jackson, E.F. and Jackson, C.R. (2008): Viruses in Wetland Ecosystems. Freshw. Biol., 53 (6): 1214-1227.

Jammes, S.C., Massot, M., Aragon, P. and Clobert, J. (2006): Global Warming and Positive Fitness Response in Mountain Populations of Common Lizards *Lacerta vivipara*. Glob. Change Biol., 12(2): 392-402.

Jay, J.M., Loessner, M. J. and Golden, D.A. (2005): Modern Food Microbiology. 7th ed. Springer Science Publs, USA: pp. 17-54.

Josephine, F.S., Ramya, V.S., Devi, N., Ganapa, S.B., Siddalingeshwara, K.G., Venugopal, N. and Vishwanatha, T. (2012): Isolation, Production and Characterization of Protease from *Bacillus sp.* Isolated from Soil Sample. J. Microbiol. Biotech. Res., 2(1): 163-168.

Kardel, G., Furtado, M.M. and Neto, J.P.M.L. (1995). Lactase na Indústria de Laticínios (Parte 1). Revista do Instituto de Laticínios "Candido Tostes". Juiz de Fora, 50(294):15-17.

Karki, G. and Aryal, S. (2014): Microbial Diversity and Ecosystem Functioning. Int. J. Microbiol. All. Sci., 1(2): 92-97.

Karman, S.B., Diah, S.Z.M. and Gebeshuber, I.C. (2015): Raw Materials Synthesis from Heavy Metal Industry Effluents with Bioremediation and Phytomining: A Biomimetic Resource Management, Approach. Adv. Mater. Sci. Eng., 2015: 1-21.

Kashyap, D.R., Soni, S.K. and Tewari, R. (2003): Enhanced Production of Pectinase by *Bacillus sp.* DT7 using Solid State Fermentation. Bioresour. Technol.,88(3): 251-254.

Kassinen A., Krogius-Kurikka, L., Makivuokko, H., Rinttila, T., Paulin, L., Corander, J., Malinen, E., Apajalahti, J. and Palva, A. (2007): The Fecal Microbiota of Irritable Bowel Syndrome Patients Differs Significantly from that of Healthy Subjects. Gastroenterol., 133(1): 24-33.

Kaur, G., Kumar, S. and Satyarnarayana, T. (2004): Production, Characterization and Application of a Thermostable Polygalactouronase of a Thermophilic mould *Sporotrichum thermophile Apinis*. Bioresour. Technol., 94(3): 239-234.

Kavscek, M., Strazar, M., Curk, T., Natter, K. and Petrovic, U. (2015): Yeast as a Cell Factory: Current State and Perspectives Microb. Cell Fact., 14(94): 1-10.

Khandelwal, M., Datta, S., Mehta, J., Naruka, R., Makhijani, K., Sharma, G., Kumar, R. and Chandra, S. (2012): Isolation, Characterization and Biomass Production of *Trichoderma viride* using Various Agro Products - A Biocontrol Agent. Adv. Appl. Sci. Res., 3(6): 3950-3955.

Kirk, O., Borchert, T.V. and Furlerng, C.C. (2002): Industrial Enzyme Applications. Curr. Opin. Biotechnol., 13(4): 345-351.

Kistler, J.O., Pesaro, M and Wad, W.G. (2015): Development and Pyrosequencing Analysis of an *in-vitro* Oral Biofilm Model. BMC Microbiol., 15(24): 1-10.

Konopka, A., Oliver, L. and Turco, R.F. Jr. (1998): The Use of Carbon Source Utilization Patterns in Environmental and Ecological Microbiology. Microb. Ecol., 35: 103-115.

Kowalski, K.P., Bacon, C., Bickford, W., Braun, H., Clay, K., Leduc-Lapierre, M., Lillard, E., McCormick, M.K., Nelson, E., Torres, M., White, J.and Wilcox, D.A. (2015): Advancing the Science of Microbial Symbiosis to Support Invasive Species Management: A Case Study on *Phragmites* in the Great Lakes. Front. Microbiol., 6(95): 1-14.

Lal, R. (2007): Microbial Diversity, Systematic Research and Microbial Culture Collection Facility in India. Ind. J. Microbiol., 47: 1-2.

Land, M., Hauser, L., Jun, S., Nookaew, I., Leuze, M.R., Ahn, T.H., Karpinets, T., Lund, O., Kora, G., Wassenaar, T., Poudel, S. and Ussery, D.W. (2015): Insights from 20 Years of Bacterial Genome Sequencing. Funct. Integr. Genomics, 15(2): 141-161.

Lehto, T. and Zwiazek, J.J. (2011): Ectomycorrhizas and Water Relations of Trees: A Review. *Mycorrhiza*,21(2): 71-90.

Liou, A.P., Paziuk, M., Luevano, J.M., Machineni, S., Turnbaugh, P.J. and Kaplan, L.M. (2013): Conserved Shifts in the gut microbiota due to gastric bypass reduce Host Weight and Adiposity. Sci. Trans. Med., 5(178): 1-11.

Littlechild, J.A. (2015): Archaeal Enzymes and Applications in Industrial Biocatalysts. Archaea, 2015: 1-10.

Lugani, Y., Singla, S. and Sooch, B.S. (2015). Optimization of Cellulase Production from Newly Isolated *Bacillus sp.* Y3. Bioproc. Biotech., 5(11): 1-6.

Lugtenberg, B. and Kamilova, F. (2009): Plant-growth-promoting rhizobacteria. Annu. Rev. Microbiol., 63: 541-556.

Lynn, T.M., Aye, K.N. and Khaing, K.M. (2013): Study on the Production of Fermented Soybean Sauce by using *Aspergillus oryzae* and *Aspergillus flavus*. J. Sci.Innov. Res., 2(2): 320-239.

Ma, C., Sun, J., Luo, H., Li, S. and Xue, W. (2014): Primary Processing Technology on gluten soy sauce with Low-salt and Solid-state Fermentation. J. Chem. Pharm. Res., 6(5): 1182-1186.

Machovina, B., Feeley, K.J. and Ripple, W.J. (2015): Biodiversity Conservation: The Key is Reducing Meat Consumption. Sci. Total Environ., 536(1): 419-431.

Maciel, M., Ottoni, C., Santos, C., Lima, N., Moreira, K. and Motta, C.S. (2013): Production of Polygalacturonases by *Aspergillus Section Nigri* Strains in a Fixed Bed Reactor. Molecules, 18(2): 1660-1671.

Mahmoud, G.A., Koutb, M.M.M., Morsy, F.M., Bagy, M.M.K. (2015): Characterization of Lipase Enzyme Produced by Hydrocarbons Utilizing Fungus *Aspergillus terreus*. Eur. J. Biological Res., 5(3): 70-77.

Mahoney, R.R. (1997): Lactose: Enzymatic Modification. In: Advanced Dairy Chemistry. Lactose, Water, Salts and Vitamins.Vol. 3.2$^{nd}$ edn. Fox, P.F. (ed.). Chapman and Hall Publs, London: pp. 77-125.

Majumder, L., Khalil, I., Munshi, M.K., Alam, K., Rashid, H.O., Begum, R. and Alamet, N. (2010): "Citric Acid Production by *Aspergillus niger* using Molasses and Pumpkin as Substrates." Eur. J. Biol. Sci., 2(1): 1-8.

Malmqvist, B. and Rundle, S. (2002): Threats to the Running Water Ecosystems of the World. *Environ. Conserv.*, 2: 134-153.

Marzban, R. (2012): Midgut pH Profile and Energy Differences in Lipid, Protein and Glycogen Metabolism of *Bacillus thuringiensis* Cry1Ac Toxin and Cypovirus-infected *Helicoverpa armigera* (Hubner) (Lepidoptera: Noctuidae). J. Entomol. Res. Soc., 14(2): 45-53.

McLain, J.E.T. (2004): Aechea. In: Encyclopedia of Soils in the Environ. Elsevier Ltd., Oxford Publs, UK: pp. 88-94.

Meena, K.K., Jaipal, M.K. and Singh, U. (2015): Production Kinetics and Characterization of Pectinase Enzyme from *Aspergillus niger*. South Asian J. Food Technol. Environ., 1(2): 131-135.

Mekkes, M.C., Weenen, T.C., Brummer, R.J. and Claassen, E. (2014): The Development of Probiotic Treatment in Obesity: A Review. Benef. Microbes, 5(1): 19-28.

Melo, A.C., d'Avila-Levy, C.M., Branquinha, M.H. and Vermelho, A.B. (2002): Crithidia guilhermei: gelatin- and haemoglobin-degrading Extracellular Metalloproteinases. Exp. Parasitol., 102(3-4): 150-156.

Mendell, M.J., Mirer, A.G., Cheung, K., Tong, M. and Douwes, J. (2011): Respiratory and Allergic Health Effects of Dampness, Mold, and Dampness Related Agents: A Review of the Epidemiologic Evidence. Environ. Health Perspect., 119(6): 748-756.

Meynecke, J.O. (2004): Effects of Global Climate Change on Geographic Distributions of Vertebrates in North Queensland. Ecol. Model, 174(4): 347-357.

Mishra, S., Kumar, P., Malik, A. and Satya, S. (2011): Adulticidal and Larvicidal Activity of *Beauveria bassiana* and *Metarhizium anisopliae* against House Fly, *Musca domestica* (Diptera: Muscidae), in Laboratory and Simulated Field Bioassays. Parasitol. Res., 108(6):1483-1492.

Mudaliyar, P., Sharma, L. and Chandrashekhar Kulkarni, C. (2012): Food Waste Management-Lactic Acid Production by *Lactobacillus sp.* Int. J. Adv. Biol. Res., 2(1): 34-38.

Nambiar, G.R. and Raveendran, K. (2015): Frequency of Marine Fungi on Animal Substrates Along West Coast of India. Curr. Res. Environ. Appl. Mycol., 5(4): 394-397.

Nguyen, Q.D., Rezessy-Szabo, J.M., Claeyssens, I.S. and Hoschke A. (2002). Purification and Characterization of Amylolytic Enzymes from Thermophilic Fungus *Thermomyces langinosus* Strain 3426. Enz.Microb. Tech., 31: 345-352.

Nigam P., Pandey A. and Prabhu K.A. (1987): Cellulase and Ligninase Production by Basidiomycetes Culture in Solid-state Fermentation. Biol. Wastes, 20(1): 1-9.

Nigam, P. and Prabhu, K.A. (1988). Thermal Activation and Stability of Cellulases Derived from Two Basidiomycetes. Biotechnol.Lett., 10(12): 919-920.

Nigam, P.S. and Pandey, A. (2009): Solid-state Fermentation Technology for Bioconversion of Biomass and Agricultural Residues. In: Biotechnology for Agro-Industrial Residues Utilization. Nigam, P.S. and Pandey, A. (eds.). Springer Publs, Netherlands: pp. 197-221.

Nigam, P.S. (2013): Microbial Enzymes with Special Characteristics for Biotechnological Applications. Biomolecules, 3: 597-611.

Noble, A.D. and Ruaysoongnern S. (2010): The Nature of Sustainable Agriculture. In: Soil Microbiology and Sustainable Crop Production. Dixon, G.R. and Tilston, E.L. (eds.). Springer Science and Business Media Publs, Germany: p. 1-25.

Nwokoro, O. (2015): Studies on the Production of Glucose Isomerase by *Bacillus licheniformis*. Pol. J. Chem. Technol., 17(3): 84-88.

Ohtani, N., Yoshimoto, S. and Hara, E. (2014): Obesity and Cancer: A Gut Microbial Connection. Cancer Res., 74(7): 1885-1889.

Okamoto, A., Hanagata, H., Kawamura, Y. and Yanagida, F. (1995). Anti-hypertensive Substances in Fermented Soybean, Natto. Plant Foods Human Nutr., 47: 39-47.

Oren, A. (2006): Life at High Salt Concentrations. The Prokaryotes, 2: 263-282.

Padan, E., Bibi, E., Ito, M. and Krulwich, T.A. (2005): Alkaline pH Homeostasis in Bacteria: New insights. Biochimica et Biophysica Acta, 1717(2): 67-88.

Pai, S.J. (2003): Applications of Microorganisms in Food Biotechnology. Ind. J. Biotechnol., 2: 382-386.

Palaniyappan, M., Vijayagopal, V., Viswanathan, R. and Viruthagiri, T. (2009): Screening of Natural Substrates and Optimization of Operating Variables on the Production of Pectinase by Submerged Fermentation using *Aspergillus niger* MTCC 281. Afr. J. Biotechnol., 8(4): 682-686.

Pandey, A., Benjamin, S., Soccol, C.R., Nigam, P., Krieger, N. and Soccol, V.T. (1999): The Realm of Microbial Lipases in Biotechnology. Biotechnol. Appl. Biochem, 29(2): 119-131.

Pandey, A., Selvakumar, P., Soccol, C.R. and Nigram, P. (1999): Solid State Fermentation for the Production of Industrial Enzymes. Curr. Sci., 77(1): 149-162.

Patel, S.J., Savanth, V.D. (2015): Review on Fungal Xylanases and their Applications. Int. J. Adv. Res., 3(3): 311-315.

Pearman, J.K., Taylor, J.E. and Kinghorn, J.R. (2010): Fungi in Aquatic Habitats Near St Andrews in Scotland. Mycosphere, 1: 11-21.

Pelczar, M.J (Jr.), Chan, E.C.S. and Kreig, N.R. (1993): Microbiology Concept and Application. 1st ed. McGraw-Hill Publs, USA.

Pointing, S.B. and Belnap, J. (2012): Microbial Colonization and Controls in Dryland Systems. Nat. Rev. Microbiol., 10(8): 551-562.

Pold, G. and DeAngelis, K. (2013): Up Against the Wall: The Effects of Climate Warming on Soil Microbial Diversity and the Potential for Feedbacks to the Carbon Cycle. Divers., 5(2): 409-425.

Postel, S. and Richter, B. (2003): Rivers for Life: Managing Water for People and Nature. Island Press, Washington D.C., U.S.A.

Prasad, L.N., Ghosh, B.C., Sherkat, F. and Shah, N.P. (2013): Extraction and Characterisation of β-galactosidase Produced by *Bifidobacterium animalis spp. lactis* Bb12 and *Lactobacillus delbrueckii spp. bulgaricus* ATCC 11842 Grown in whey. Int. Food Res. J., 20(1): 487-494.

Quinto, E.J., Jiménez, P., Caro, I., Tejero, J., Mateo, J. and Girbes, T. (2014): Probiotic Lactic Acid Bacteria: A Review. Food Nutr. Sci., 5: 1765-1775.

Rao, R.S., Jyothi, C.P. and Rao, L.V. (2008): Biotechnological Production of Xylitol by Mutant Candida Tropicalis OMV5: Process Optimization using Statistical Approach. Ind. J. Biotechnol., 7(2): 218-224.

Read, D.J. and Moreno, J.P. (2003): Mycorrhizas and Nutrient Cycling in Ecosystems- A Journey Towards Relevance? New Phytol.,157(3): 475-492.

Reddivari, M., Chirumamilla, R. and Nigam, P. (2002): Understanding Lipase Stereoselectivity. World J. Microbiol. Biotechnol. 18: 81-97.

Redmile-Gordon, M.A., Evershed, R.P., Hirsch, P.R., White, R.P. and Goulding, K.W.T. (2015): Soil Organic Matter and the Extracellular Microbial Matrix Show Contrasting Responses to C and N availability. Soil Biol. Biochem., 88: 257-267.

Revenga, C., Campbell, I., Abell, R., de Villiers, P. and Bryer, M. (2005): Prospects for Monitoring Freshwater Ecosystems Towards the 2010 Targets. Phil. Trans. R. Soc. Lond. B Bio. Sci., 360(1454): 397-413.

Robinson, T., McMullan, G., Marchant, R. and Nigam, P. (2001) Remediation of dyes in Textile Effluent: A Critical Review on Current Treatment Technologies with a Proposed Alternative. Bioresour. Technol., 77(3): 247-255.

Rousk, J. and Baath, E. (2007a): Fungal Biomass Production and turnover in Soil Estimated using the Acetate-in-ergosterol Technique. Soil Biol. Biochem., 39(8): 2173-2177.

Rousk, J. and Baath, E. (2007b): Fungal and Bacterial Growth in Soil with Plant Materials of different C/N ratios. FEMS Microbiol. Ecol., 62(3): 258-267.

Sala, O.E., Austin, A.T. and Vivanco, L. (2001): Temperate Grassland and Shrubland Ecosystem Terms. Encyclop. Biodiver., 5: 627-635.

Sandholm, T.M., Myllärinen, P., Crittenden, R., Mogensen, G., Fonden, R. and Saarela, M. (2002): Technological Challenges for Future Probiotic Foods. Int. Dairy J.,12(2-3): 173-182.

Sandilyan, S. (2013): Emu bird-Potential Threat to the Biodiversity and Agriculture Productivity of Western Ghats, Southern India. J. Pure Appl. Zool., 1(2): 193-195.

Saranraj, P. and Geetha, M. (2012): Microbial Spoilage of Bakery Products and its Control by Preservatives. Int. J. Pharm. Biol. Arch., 3(1): 38-48.

Sarethy, I.P., Pan, S. and Danquah, M.K. (2014): Modern Taxonomy for Microbial Diversity. In: Biodiversity - The Dynamic Balance of the Lanet. Oscar Grillo (ed.). Intech Publs, India: pp. 51-68.

Satyanarayana, T., Raghukumar, C. and Shivaji, S. (2005): Extremophilic Microbes: Diversity and Perspectives. Curr. Sci. 89(1): 78-90.

Scarpignato, C. (2008): NSAID-induced Intestinal Damage: are Luminal Bacteria the Therapeutic Target? Gut, 57(2): 145-148.

Schleifer, K.H. and Ludwig, W. (1989): Phylogenetic Relationships Among Bacteria. In: The Hierarchy of Life. Fernholm, B., Bremer, K. and Jornvall, H. (eds.). Amsterdam: Elsevier Science Publs B.V, Netherland: pp. 103-117.

Schloss, P.D., Westcott, S.L., Ryabin, T., Hall, J.R., Hartmann, M., Hollister, E.B., Lesniewski, R.A., Oakley, B.B., Parks, D.H., Robinson, C.J., Sahl, J.W., Stres, B., Thallinger, G.G.,Van Horn, D.J. and Weber, C.F. (2009): Introducing Mothur: Open-source, Platform-independent, Community-supported Software for Describing and Comparing Microbial Communities. Appl. Environ. Microbiol.,75(23): 7537-7541.

Shapiro, J.A. (1988): Bacteria as Multicellular Organisms. Sci. Am., 1988: 82-89.

Silva, D., Tokuioshi, K., Martins, E. S., da Silva, R. and Gomes, E. (2005): Production of Pectinase by Solidstate Fermentation with *Penicillium viridicatum* RFC3. Proc. Biochem., 40(8): 2885-2889.

Simon, C. and Daniel, R. (2011): Metagenomic Analyses: Past and Future Trends. Appl. Environ. Microbiol., 77(4): 1153-1161.

Singh, A.K., Rath, S., Kumar, Y., Masih, H., Peter, J.K., Benjamin, J.C., Singh, P.K. and Singh, D.P. (2014): Bio-ethanol Production from Banana Peel by Simultaneous Saccharification and Fermentation Process using Cocultures *Aspergillus niger* and *Saccharomyces cerevisiae*. Int. J. Curr. Microbiol. App. Sci., 3(5): 84-96.

Singh, R.S., Sooch, B.S. and Puri, M. (2007): Optimization of Medium and Process Parameters for the Production of Inulinase from a Newly Isolated *Kluyveromyces marxianus* YS-1. Biores. Technol, 98(13): 2518-2525.

Sinha, S., Chattopadhyay, P., Pan, I., Chatterjee, S., Chanda, P., Bandyopadhyay, D., Das, K. and Sen, S.K. (2009): Microbial Transformation of Xenobiotics for Environmental Bioremediation. Afr. J. Biotechnol., 8(22): 6016-6027.

Sinimol, S., Sarika, A.R. and Nair, A.J. (2016): Diversity and Antagonistic Potential of Marine Microbes Collected from South-west Coast of India. 3 Biotech, 6(7): 1-9.

Sinsabaugh, R.L., Manzoni, S., Moorhead, D.L. and Richter, A. (2013). Carbon Use Efficiency of Microbial Communities: Stoichiometry, Methodology and Modelling. Ecol. Lett., 16(7): 930-939.

Smith, P., Cotrufo, M.F., Rumpel, C., Paustian, K., Kuikman, P.J., Elliott, J.A., McDowell, R., Griffiths, R.I., Asakawa, S., Bustamante, M., House, J.I., Sobocka, J., Harper, R., Pan, G., West, P.C., Gerber, J.S., Clark, J.M., Adhya, T., Scholes, R.J. and Scholes, M.C. (2015): Biogeochemical Cycles and Biodiversity as Key Drivers of Ecosystem Services provided by Soils. Soil, 1: 665-685.

Smith, S.E. and Read, D.J. (1997): Mycorrhizal Symbiosis. New Phytol., 137( 3): 563-568.

Sneath, P.H.A. (1984): Genus Chromobacterium Bergonzini 1881, 153[AL]. In: Bergey's Manual of Systematic Bacteriology. Krieg, N.H. and Holt, J.G. (eds.), Vol. 1, Williams and Wilkins Publs, Baltimore: pp. 580-582.

Stackebrandt, E. and Liesack, W. (1993): Nucleic Acids and Classification. In: Handbook of New Bacterial Systematic. Goodfellow, M. and O'Donnell. A.G. (eds.). Academic Press Ltd., London: pp. 151-194.

Stasiak, L. and B³azejak, S. (2009). Acetic Acid Bacteria- Perspectives of Application in Biotechnology- A Review. Pol. J. Food Nutr. Sci., 59(1): 17-23.

Subramanium, S. and Prema, P. (2002): Biotechnology of Microbial Xylanases: Enzymology, Molecular Biology and Application. Crit. Rev. Biotechnol., 22(1): 33-64.

Sumaiya, A.S. and Trivedi, R. (2015): A Review on Glucose Oxidase. Int. J. Curr. Microbiol. App. Sci., 4(8): 636-642.

Suttle, A. (2007): Marine Viruses- Major Players in the Global Ecosystem. Nat. Rev. Microbiol., 5: 801-812.

Taipale, S., Kankaala, P., Hamalainen, H. and Jones, R.I. (2009): Seasonal Shifts in the Diet of Lake Zooplankton Revealed by Phospholipid Fatty Acid Analysis. Freshw. Biol., 54(1): 90-104.

Tansey, M.R. and Brock, T.D. (1978): Microbial Life at High Temperatures: Ecological Aspects. In: Microbial Life in Extreme Environments. D.J. Kushner (ed.). Academic Press, London: p.159-194.

Taylor, F.J. (1978): Problems in the Development of an Explicit Hypothetical Phylogeny of the Lower Eukaryotes. BioSystems, 10(1-2): 67-89.

Telemeco, R.S., Elphick, M.J. and Shine, R. (2009): Nesting Lizards (*Bassiana duperreyi*) Compensate Partly, but not Completely, for Climate Change. Ecol., 90(1): 17-22.

Thomsen, S.F. (2014): Atopic Dermatitis: Natural History, Diagnosis, and Treatment. ISRN Allergy, 2014: 1-7.

Tindall, B.J., Mora, R.R., Busse, H.J., Ludwig, W. and Kampfer, P. (2010): Notes on the Characterization of Prokaryote Strains for Taxonomic Purposes. Int. J. Syst. Evol. Microbiol., 60(1): 249-266.

Tortora, G.J., Funke, B.R., Case, C.L. (2006): Microbiology An Introduction. 8$^{th}$ ed. Dorling Kindersley Publs, India.

Treseder, K.K. (2004): A Meta-analysis of Mycorrhizal Responses to Nitrogen, Phosphorus, and Atmospheric $CO_2$ in Field Studies. New Phytol., 164(2): 347-355.

Tropel, D. and Van der Meer, J.R. (2004): Bacterial Transcriptional Regulators for Degradation Pathways of Aromatic Compounds. Microbiol. Mol. Biol. Rev., 68(3): 474-500.

Uenojo, M. and Pastore, G. (2007): "Pectinases: Aplicações Industriais e Perspectivas". Quim. Nova, 30(2): 388-394.

Valentini, A., Pompanon, F. and Taberlet, P. (2009): DNA Barcoding for Ecologists. Trends Ecol. Evol., 24(2): 110-117.

Van der Heijden, M.G.A., Klironomos, J.N., Ursic, M., Moutoglis, P., Streitwolf, E.R., Boller, T., Wiemken, A. and Sanders, I.R. (1998): Mycorrhizal Fungal Diversity Determines Plant Biodiversity, Ecosystem Variability and Productivity. Nature, 396: 69-72.

Van der Heijden, M.G., Bardgett, R.D.and van Straalen, N.M. (2008): The Unseen Majority: Soil Microbes as Drivers of Plant Diversity and Productivity in Terrestrial Ecosystems. Ecol Lett., 11(3): 296-310.

Vandamme, B., Pot, B., Gillis, M., de Vos, P., Kersters, K. and Swings, J. (1996): Polyphasic Taxonomy, a Consensus Approach to Bacterial Systematics. Microbiol. Rev., 60(2): 407-438.

Vastrad, B.M. and Neelagund, S.E. (2011): Optimization and Production of Neomycin from Different Agro Industrial Wastes in Solid State Fermentation. Int. J. Pharma. Sci. Drug Res., 3(2): 104-111.

Vastrad, B.M. and Neelagund, S.E. (2012): Optimization of Process Parameters for Rifamycin B Production under Solid State Fermentation from *Amycolatopsis mediterrane* MTCC 14. Int. J. Curr.Pharm. Res., 4(2): 101-108.

Veresoglou, S.D., Halley, J.M. and Rillig, M.C. (2015). Extinction Risk of Soil Biota. Nat. Commun., 6(8862): 1-10.

Viaud, S., Saccheri, F., Mignot, G., Yamazaki, T., Daillere, R., Hannani, D., Enot, D.P., Pfirschke, C., Engblom, C., Pittet, M.J, Schlitzer, A., Ginhoux, F., Apetoh, L., Chachaty, E., Woerther, P.L., Eberl, G., Berard, M., Ecobichon, C., Clermont, D., Bizet, C., Gaboriau-Routhiau, V., Cerf-Bensussan, N., Opolon, P., Yessaad, N., Vivier, E., Ryffel, B., Elson, C.O., Dore, J., Kroemer, G., Lepage, P., Boneca, I.G., Ghiringhelli, F. and Zitvogel, L. (2013): The Intestinal Microbiota Modulates the Anticancer Immune Effects of Cyclophosphamide. Sci., 342(6161): 971-976.

Vibha, B. and Neelam, G. (2012): Importance of Exploration of Microbial Biodiversity. J. Biol. Sci., 1: 78-83.

Viikari, L., Kantelinen, A., Sundquist, J. and Linko, M. (1994): Xylanases in Bleaching: From an Idea to the Industry. FEMS Microbiol. Rev.,13(2-3): 335-350.

Vincent,W.F. (2009): Protists, Bacteria and Fungi: Planktonic and Attached- Cyanobacteria. In: Plankton of Inland Waters. Vol. 3. G Likens (ed.). Elsevier Publs: pp. 226-232.

Visser, M.E. and Both, C. (2005): Shifts in Phenology due to Global Climate Change: The Need for a Yardstick. Proc. R. Soc. B, 272: 2561-2569.

Vogel, H.J. (1964): Distribution of Lysine Pathways Among Fungi: Evolutionary Implications. Am. Nat., 98(903): 435-446.

Wan, S., Wu, Y., Wang, C., Wang, C., Hou, L. (2013): The Development of Soy Sauce from Organic Soybean. Agric. Sci., 4(5B): 116-121.

Watve, M.G., Shete, A.M., Jadhav, N., Wagh, S.A., Sheetal, S.P., Chakraborti, S.S., Botre, A.P. and Kulkarni, A.A. (1999): Myxobacterial Diversity of Indian Soils- How many Species do we have? Curr. Sci., 77(8): 1089-1095.

Weinbauer, M.G. (2004): Ecology of Prokaryotic Viruses. *FEMS Microbiol. Rev.,* 28(2): 127-181.

Wilhelm, S.W. and Matteson, A.R. (2008): Freshwater and Marine Virioplankton: A Brief Overview of Commonalities and Differences. Freshw. Biol., 53(6): 1076-1089.

Willey, J.M., L.M. Sherwood, L.M. and C.J. Woolverton, C.J. (2008): Prescott, Harley and Kleins's Microbiology. 7th ed. McGraw-Hill Publs.

Winkler, D.W., Dunn, P.O. and McCulloch, C.E. (2002): Predicting the Effects of Climate Change on Avian Life-history Traits. Proc. Natl. Acad. Sci. U.S.A, 99(21): 13595-13599.

Winkler, P., Ghadimi, D., Schrezenmeir, J. and Kraehenbuhl, J.P. (2007): Molecular and Cellular basis of Microflora-host Interactions.J. Nutr.,137(3): 756-772.

Woese, C. (1998): The Universal Ancestor. Proc. Natl. Acad. Sci. U.S.A, 95(12): 6854-6859.

Woese, C.R. and Fox, G.E. (1977): Phylogenetic Structure of the Prokaryotic Domain: The Primary Kingdoms. Proc. Natl. Acad. Sci. USA. 74(11): 5088-5090.

Zamioudis, C. and Pieterse, C.M. (2012): Modulation of Host Immunity by Beneficial Microbes. *Mol. Plant Microbe Interact.,* 25(2): 139-150.

Zawoznik, M.S., Ameneiros, M., Benavides, M.P., Vázquez, S. and Groppa, M.D. (2011). Response to Saline Stress and Aquaporin Expression in *Azospirillum* Inoculated Barley Seedlings. Appl. Microbiol. Biotechnol., 90(4): 1389-1397.

Zinger, L., Gobet, A. and Pommier, T. (2012): Two Decades of Describing the Unseen Majority of Aquatic Microbial Diversity. Mol. Ecol., 21(8): 1878-1896.

Zwietering, M.H., Jacxsens, L., Membre, J.M., Nauta, M. and Mats Peterz, M. (2016): Relevance of Microbial Finished Product Testing in Food Safety Management. Food Control, 60: 31-43.

Pages: 167-198

**FOREST AND BIODIVERSITY CONSERVATION**
*Edited by:* **Dr. Alka Chauhan** and **Dr. Pawan Kumar 'Bharti'**
**ISBN: 978-93-5056-873-6**
***Edition:* 2017**
***Published by:* Discovery Publishing House Pvt. Ltd., New Delhi (India)**

# 8 Baseline Status of Flora and Fauna at Tehsil Neem Ka Thana District Sikar, Rajasthan and Impact due to Riverbed Bajri Mining

*Dr. Ashok Kumar Rathoure*

## INTRODUCTION

Rajasthan is the largest State in India, occupying an area of about 3,42,239 $Km^2$ nearly about 11 percent of the total geographical area (TGA) of India, and lies between 23° 30′ and 30° 12′ North latitude and 69° 30′ and 78° 17′ East longitude. Rajasthan is bordered by Pakistan in the west and northwest, the Indian States of Punjab, Uttar Pradesh and Haryana lie in the north and northeast, Madhya Pradesh in the southeast and Gujarat in the southwest. Administratively, Rajasthan is divided into 33 districts (Ajmer, Alwar, Banswara, Baran, Barmer, Bharatpur, Bhilwara, Bikaner, Bundi, Chittorgarh, Churu, Dausa, Dholpur, Dungarpur, Hanumangarh, Jaipur, Jaisalmer, Jalore, Jhalawar, Jhunjhunu, Jodhpur, Karauli, Kota, Nagaur, Pali, Pratapgarh, Rajsamand, Sawai Madhopur, Sikar, Sirohi, Sri Ganganagar, Tonk and Udaipur). Rajasthan is a unique State which shows great variation from one area to another and is noticeable in respect of climate, altitude and vegetation. Rajasthan has three major physiographic regions, *viz*. the western desert (Thar Desert), the Aravalli hills and the south-eastern plateau. The most striking geographical feature is the Aravalli range, the oldest folded mountain range in the world, which intersects the State diagonally end to end north-east to south-west into three-fifth north-western desertic zone and two-fifth eastern semi-arid region. The elevation of Aravalli range gradually decreases in north-east direction, as it is 1,772 m at Mt. Abu (Gurushikar), 1100 m at Bijapur, 913 m at Harshanath and 792 m at Khetri; the elevation further decreases to 335 m at Delhi beyond the boundaries of the State in north-east direction. The total forest area of the State is 16,036 $km^2$, which occupies 4.69% of the total geographical area (FSI, 2009). The vegetation

Vardan EnviroNet, Gurgaon (HR), (India)

delineation depends on spatial, spectral and temporal resolution of the satellite sensor on one hand and the spatial extent and degree of homogeneity of the species assemblages on the other hand. The forest class is subdivided into mixed species forest types, gregarious species forest types, locale specific types, degraded types based on composition and location specific distribution controlled by physiographic, edaphic and disturbance conditions.

The biodiversity we see today is the fruit of billions of years of evolution, shaped by natural processes. The vast array of interactions among the various components of biodiversity makes the planet habitable for all species, including humans. There is a growing recognition that, biological diversity is a global asset of tremendous value to present and future generations. At the same time, the threat to species and ecosystems has never been as great as it is today. Species extinction caused by human activities continues at an alarming rate. Protecting biodiversity is in our self-interest. Ecological impact assessment (EcIA) is used to predict and evaluate the impacts of development activities on ecosystems and their components, thereby providing the information needed to ensure that ecological issues are given full and proper consideration in development planning. Environmental impact assessment (EIA) has emerged as a key to sustainable development by integrating social, economic and environmental issues in many countries. EcIA has a major part to play as a component of EIA but also has other potential applications in environmental planning and management (Kumar, 2014). Mineral resources of the nation reflect in terms of potential economic growth of the country at large. Our natural mineral wealth has been exploited considerably during the past 50 years. Floristic and Faunistic pattern of the area was studied based on opportunistic survey (personal observation), inquiries from the local people and forest officials and secondary data. The study area falls under 3 districts of Rajasthan and 1 district of Hayrana State *viz*. Sikar, Jhunjhunu, Jaipur (Rajasthan) and Mahendragarh (Haryana). The mining activity will be done at Neem Ka Thana Tehsil in Siker district only. The mining will be done at dry river bed, and the rivers of this area are completely dry. Only rainwater comes during heavy rain. Kind of trees found in this area are Babul, Khejari, Neem, Sheesham, Mango, Pipal, Vad, Mahua, Khajur, Imili, Jungle-jalebi, Ber, etc. There is only protected forest which is mountainous range with *Prosopus juliflora* and *Acacia nilotica* as scrub falling in study area and there is no any wild life sanctuary within 10 Km radius.

## BASELINE STUDY AREA AND PERIOD

The baseline study was conducted for the evaluation of the floral and faunal biodiversity of the terrestrial environment of the study area (10 Km radius from the lease mine area-Refer figure 8.1 a, b & c) and it comprises of total 88 villages and its nearby area of District Sikar, Jaipur, Jhunjhunu (Rajasthan) and Mahendragargh (Hayrana). Total 53 villages of District Sikar, 11 villages of District Jaipur, 11 villages of District Jhunjhunu and 13 villages of Mahendragarh (Haryana) were surveyed for the present study.

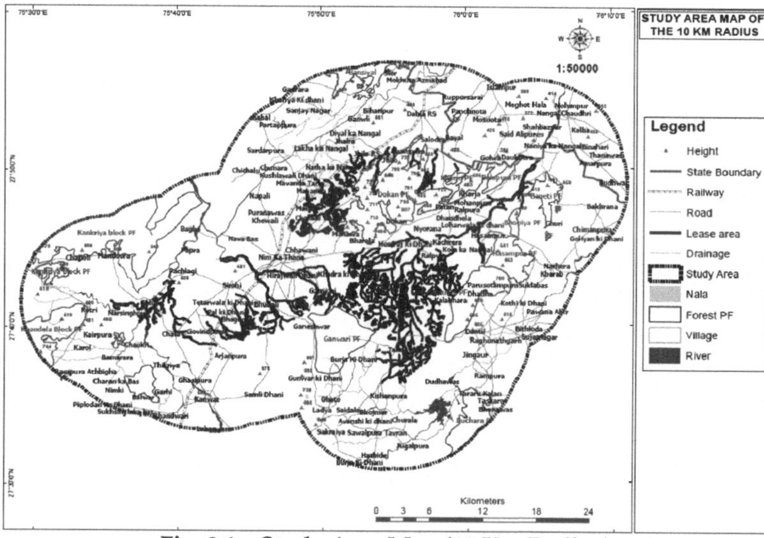


Fig. 8.1a: Study Area Map (10 Km Radius)

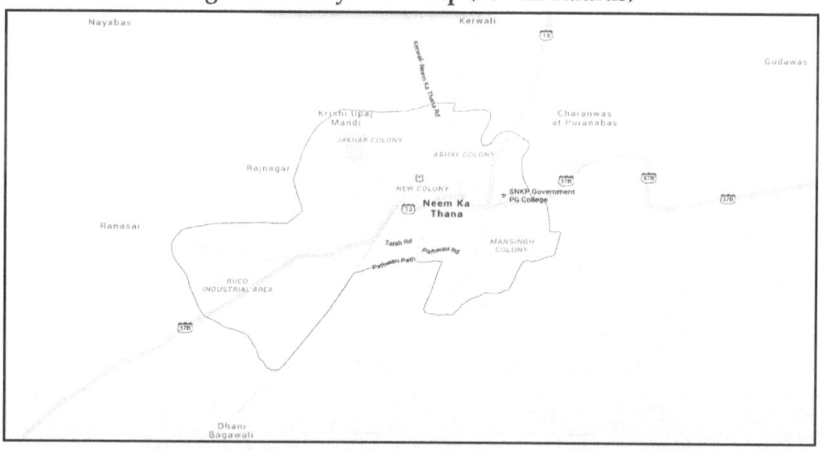


Fig. 8.1b: Google Map of Showing Tehsil Boundary

Fig. 8.1c. Google Map of Study Area

The buffer area comprises of 251334.63 hectares falls in state Rajasthan and Haryana (interstate boundary) and lease mining area is 3150.07 hectares in Teh.-Neem Ka Thana, District-Sikar. The study area comprises of protected forest (rocky terrain) and agricultural land. The village list is given in table 8.1. The baseline study has been conducted on 20th, 21st and 22nd June, 2015.

## METHODOLOGY FOR TERRESTRIAL ECOLOGY

The primary objective of survey was to describe the floral and faunal communities within the study area. The sampling plots for floral inventory were selected randomly in the suitable habitats (Anderson, 1867; Jain and Rao, 1983). The methodology adopted for faunal survey involve random survey, opportunistic observations, diurnal bird observation, active search for reptiles, faunal habitat assessment, active search for scats and foot prints, animal call, and review of previous studies. The aim was to set baselines in order to monitor and identify trends after the commissioning of the mining activity. Emphasis has been placed on presence of endemic species, threatened species if any present in the study area. Desktop literature review was conducted to indentify the representative spectrum of threatened species, population and ecological communities listed by IUCN, WCMC, ZSI, BSI and Indian Wild life Protection Act, 1972 (Bentham and Hooker, 1862-1883; Hunter, 1879; Dixit, 1984; Ghosh *et al.*, 2004; Lushington, 1915; Wilson and Reeder, 1993; BirdLife International, 2000; BirdLife International, 2004a, b; Wilson and Reeder, 2005; BirdLife International, 2010; Kumar and Srivastava, 2012; Kumar, 2013; Kumar *et al.*, 2013; Kumar and Aggarwal, 2013a, b). The status of individual species was assessed using the revised IUCN/SSC category system (WCMC, 1988; IUCN, 1994; WCMC, 2000; IUCN, 2001, 2003, 2008, 2010). The villages covered for baseline study are given in the table 8.1.

**Table 8.1: List of villages for baseline study**

| Sl.No. | Village Name | Sl.No. | Village Name |
|---|---|---|---|
| **Sikar** | | 12. | Dayal Ka Nangal |
| 1. | Baleshwar | 13. | Dhandhela 1 & 2 |
| 2. | Ballupura | 14. | Dilpura |
| 3. | Banethi | 15. | Dhokan |
| 4. | Bhasudi Khurd | 16. | Fatehpura |
| 5. | Bhudoli | 17. | Ganeshwar |
| 6. | Birhampur | 18. | Ganvadi |
| 7. | Bopia | 19. | Ghursali |
| 8. | Chak Mandi | 20. | Guhala |
| 9. | Chala | 21. | Hemrajpura |
| 10. | Chapar | 22. | Harjanpura |
| 11. | Dabla | 23. | Jhilo |

(Table Contd...)

| Sl.No. | Village Name | Sl.No. | Village Name |
|---|---|---|---|
| 24. | Kairwali | 57/4 | Dada |
| 25. | Kakad ki Tibara | 58/5 | Datil |
| 26. | Kanwat | 59/6 | Dwarikapuri |
| 27. | Keetpura | 60/7 | Khadeb |
| 28. | Khandela | 61/8 | Narheda |
| 29. | Khurdia | 62/9 | Pabnera |
| 30. | Kola ki Nangal | 63/10 | Purushottampura |
| 31. | Kotda | 64/11 | Shukla ka Bas |
| 32. | Kotdi | **Jhunjhunu** | |
| 33. | Kotrak | 65/1 | Babai |
| 34. | Lakha Ka Nangal | 66/2 | Bagholi |
| 35. | Manda | 67/3 | Dalolpura |
| 36. | Mavda | 68/4 | Hardia |
| 37. | Moduka | 69/5 | Jahaj |
| 38. | Nanagwas | 70/6 | Jhadaya |
| 39. | Napawali | 71/7 | Mandvara |
| 40. | Narsinghpura | 72/8 | Mavta |
| 41. | Natha Ka Nangal | 73/9 | Nathuwala |
| 42. | Naya Bas | 74/10 | Pachlangi |
| 43. | Neem ka thana | 75/11 | Tal |
| 44. | Nimu | **Mahendragarh** | |
| 45. | Patan | 76/1 | Amarpura |
| 46. | Pritampuri | 77/2 | Bayal |
| 47. | Puranabas | 78/3 | Binneri |
| 48. | Ram Singhpura | 79/4 | Budhwal |
| 49. | Rampura | 80/5 | Deota |
| 50. | Sirohi | 81/6 | Amarpura |
| 51. | Syalodra | 82/7 | Lujota |
| 52. | Thoi | 83/8 | Mushanta |
| 53. | Toda | 84/9 | Nangal Chaudhary |
| **Jaipur** | | 85/10 | Nangal Durg |
| 54/1 | Banaar | 86/11 | Nangal Nunia |
| 55/2 | Beri | 87/12 | Pashata |
| 56/3 | Chhardaha | 88/13 | Rupar Sarai |
| | | – | |

## TERRESTRIAL FLORAL AND FAUNAL COMPONENTS OF THE STUDY AREA

The area for the present biological baseline study falls under 88 villages of 4 districts from 2 states. The plantation on road side and domesticated plants in villages were scattered. There is dry deciduous forest falling in the study area. The study area belongs to plain, undulating, fallow land and some grazing land; the thick vegetation cover observed in the south to west with scrub. The major trees were Khejri *(Prosopis cineraria)*, Babool (*Acacia nilotica*) and few shrubs of Bilayati baool *(Prosopis juliflora)* as dominant vegetation. The people were engaged in Maize, Peanuts and Pearl millet cultivation during the study period. The crop is depending on rain, as there is no other means of water for irrigation. Some part of the study area has bore/tube wells, but the water table is more than 100 m.

**Fig. 8.2: Aquatic Habitat of the Study Area**

**Fig. 8.3: Terrestrial Habitat of the Study Area**

Villages are small and scattered in between the large patches of agriculture lands and rocky terrain. The tree cover in the study area is scanty restricted only in the habituated areas of the village and few along the boundary of the agricultural fields and road sides. The almost village pond were dry during study period and these village talabs used in rain water harvesting. The water from pond is used by local villagers for various purposes. In some part of South, people were taking water from nearby area/village where other source of water or water tanker available. Some people were engaged in poultry farming in this area.

**Fig. 8.4: Agriculture Land of Study Area**

**Fig. 8.5. Non-agriculture Land of Study Area**

The approx 22% of the study area was occupied by protected forest (rocky terrain), 20% of the area is follow land, 13% is barren, 16% is pasture, approx 2% is settlement, 2% river sand and 25% of the study area is agricultural land. Major agricultural land is in the north while in the west and south, it is occupied by rocky terrain with protected dry deciduous forest. There are patches of small rocks having scrub vegetation. The tree species, herbs and shrubs and major crops, were documented during this base line study. The list of floral species documented in the study area is enlisted in tables 8.2-8.6.

## FLORAL DIVERSITY OF THE STUDY AREA

The objective of this floral inventory of the study area is to provide necessary information on floristic structure in the study area for formulating effective management and conservation measures. The climatic, edaphic and biotic variations with their complex interrelationship and composition of species, which are adapted to these variations, have resulted in different vegetation cover, characteristic of each region (Ohasi, 1975). The tree species, herbs, shrubs, climbers and major crops, were documented during this base line study (Jain, 1968; 1991). The list of floral species documented in the study area (core and buffer zone) is enlisted in tables 8.2-8.5. The tree species observed in the study area is enlisted in the table 8.2.The undergrowth during this summer season was almost in dry state. The shrubs observed in the study are documented in the table 8.3. Herbs and climbers in the study area are represented in table 8.4 and table 8.5 respectively.

**Fig. 8.6: River Bed Area where Sand Mining in Operation**

**Fig. 8.7: Scrub Area**

**Fig. 8.8a: Grazing Area**

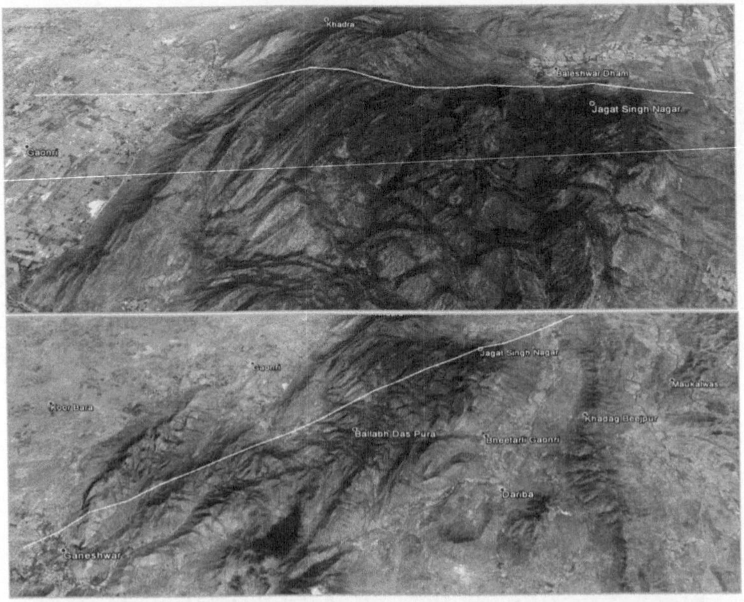


**Fig. 8.8b: Google Image showing Elevation of Mountainous Area (Protected Forest)**

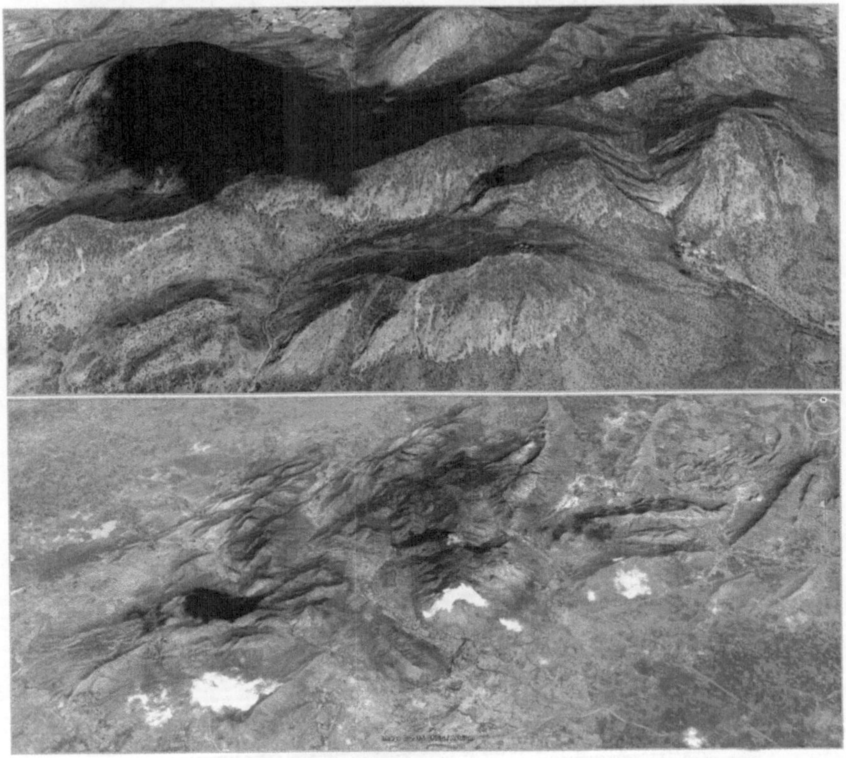

**Fig. 8.9: Google Image Showing Protected Forest Range**

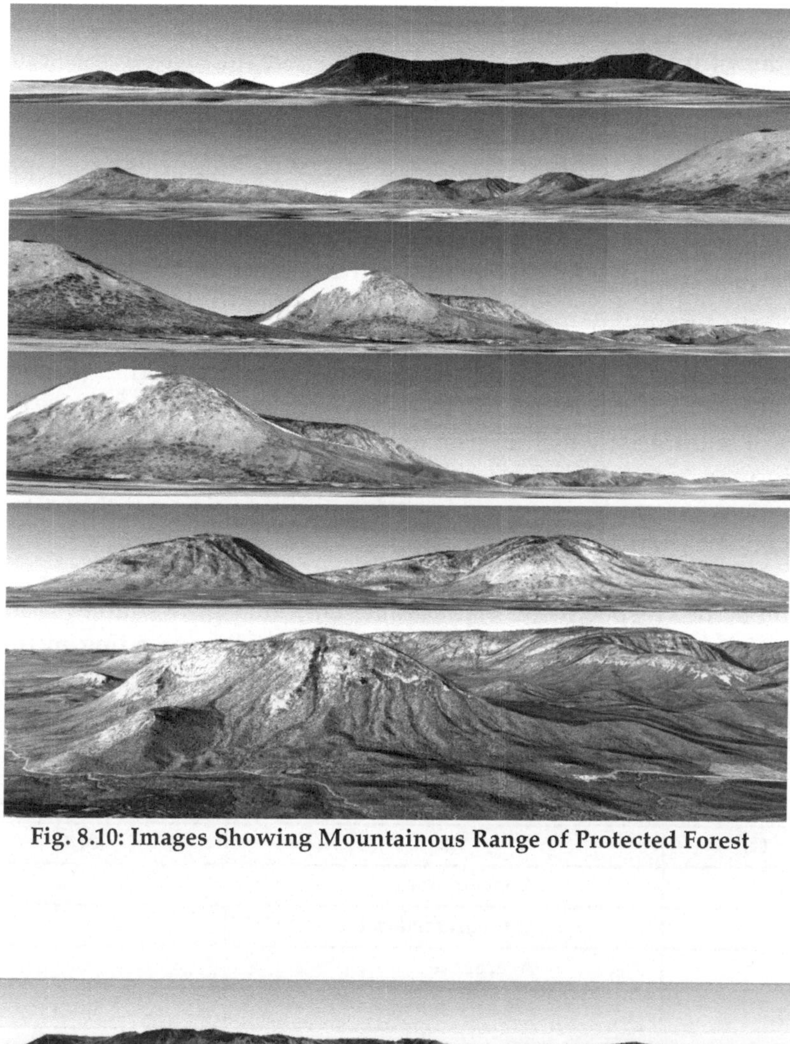

**Fig. 8.10: Images Showing Mountainous Range of Protected Forest**

**Fig. 8.11: Image Showing Plain Area and Mountainous Range at Bhudoli**

**Trees:** The dominant trees in the study area are Khejari *(Prosopis cineraria)*, Babool *(Acacia nilotica)*, *Azadirachta indica* (Neem), *Mangifera indica* (Aam). Total 31 species of trees belong to 14 families are enumerated from the study area.

Scrub is a vegetation cover predominantly occupied by shrubs or poor tree growth chiefly of small or stunted trees with crown density less than 10%. Desert dune scrub is unique to sandy parts of desert on partially stabilised dunes and on shifting dunes. It is the dominant scrub type of Rajasthan State and of this area. Thorn scrub is generally seen in the fringes of thorn forests, hill tops and nearby settlements. Dry Deciduous scrub has been subjected to more degradation and frequently found in and around dry deciduous forests. Calotropis scrub is specifically found in long fallow areas and bordering crop fields in desert region. Euphorbia (*E. caducifolia* and *E. tirucalli*) scrub is unique to rocky and badly eroded areas of rocky terrain of south-east which is part of Ganwari Protected Forest. It is a very open formation in which *Euphorbia caducifolia* predominates. *Prosopis juliflora* and *Lantana camara* L. are worst invasive alien species and threat to native biodiversity (Reddy, 2008). *Prosopis juliflora* and *Lantana camara* being aggressive colonizers, form dense thickets referred as Prosopis scrub and Lantana scrub, respectively. *Prosopis juliflora* often grows along road sides, canals and degraded thorn forest lands and rapidly spreading in this area. *Lantana camara* prefers openings and fringes of dry deciduous forests and sub-humid tracts of broad leaved hill forests.

**Table 8.2: Trees in the study area**

| Sl.No. | Family and Scientific Name | Vernacular Name |
|---|---|---|
| (1) | (2) | (3) |
| 1 | **Anacardiaceae** | |
| 1/1 | *Mangifera indica* L. | Aam |
| 2 | **Arecaceae** | |
| 2/1 | *Phoenix sylvestris* | Kajoor |
| 3 | **Apocynaceae** | |
| 3/1 | *Plumeria rubra* L. | Champa |
| 4 | **Caesalpiniaceae** | |
| 4/1 | *Delonix regia* (Boj.) Raf. | Gaulmor |
| 5/2 | *Cassia siamea* Lam. | Amaltas |
| 6/3 | *Peltophorum pterocarpum* | Sonmukhi |
| 7/4 | *Tamarindus indica* | Imli |
| 5 | **Caricaceae** | |
| 8/1 | *Carica papaya* L. | Papaya |

(Table Contd...)

| (1) | (2) | (3) |
|---|---|---|
| 6 | **Fabaceae** | |
| *9/1* | *Dalbergia sisoo* | Shisam |
| *10/2* | *Acacia catachu* | Khair |
| 7 | **Malvaceae** | |
| *11/1* | *Thespesia populnea* | Paras pipal |
| 8 | **Meliaceae** | |
| *12/1* | *Azadirachta indica* A.Juss | Neem |
| *13/2* | *Melia azadirachta* L. | Bakain |
| 9 | **Mimosaceae** | |
| *14/1* | *Acacia nilotica* | Babool |
| *15/2* | *Leucaena leucocephala* (Lam.) De | Pardesi Baval |
| *16/3* | *Pithecellobium dulce* (Roxb.) Bth. | Jungle jalebi |
| *17/4* | *Prosopis cineraria (L.)* | Khejari |
| *18/5* | *Acacia senegal* (L.) Willd, | Babool |
| *19/6* | *Acacia leucophloea* (Roxb.) Willd. | – |
| *20/7* | *Acacia tortilis* (Forssk.) Hyene. | – |
| 10 | **Moraceae** | |
| *21/1* | *Ficus benghalensis* L. | Bargad |
| *22/2* | *Ficus religiosa* L. | Pipal |
| 23/3 | *Ficus glomerulata* | Goolar |
| 24/4 | *Morus alba* | Shahtoot |
| 11 | **Myrtaceae** | |
| 25/1 | *Eucalyptus sp.* | Nilgari |
| 26/2 | *Syzygium cumini (L.) Skeels.* | Jamun |
| 12 | **Papilionaceae** | |
| 27/1 | *Pongamia pinnata* (L.) Pierre | Karanj |
| 13 | **Rhamnaceae** | |
| 28/1 | *Zizyphus mauritiana* | Ber |
| 29/2 | *Zizyphus vulgaris* | Ber |
| 30/3 | *Zizyphus xylopyrus* | Jugnle Ber |
| 14 | **Rutaceae** | |
| 31/1 | *Aegle marmelos* | Bel |

**Shrubs:** Shrubs encountered during the present survey are given in the Table 8.3. Total 21 shrub species belong to 15 families are enumerated from the study area. The dominant shrub community in this area was represented by *Prosopis juliflora* (Bilayati babool), *Calotropis procera, C. gigantea* (Akoda), Kaner (*Thevetia peruviana), Ipomoea fistulosa* and *Abutilon indicum,* etc.

**Table 8.3: List of shrubs in the study area**

| Sl.No. | Family and Scientific Name | Vernacular Name |
|---|---|---|
| **1** | **Apocynaceae** | |
| 1/1 | *Nerium indicum* | Lal Kaner |
| 2/2 | *Thevetia peruviana* Merr. | Pili Kaner |
| **2** | **Asclepiadaceae** | |
| 3/1 | *Calotropis gigantea* (L.) R. Br | Akoda |
| 4/2 | *Calotropis procera* (Ait.) R.Br | Akoda |
| **3** | **Balanitaceae** | |
| 5/1 | *Balanites aegyptiaca* (L.) Del. | – |
| **4** | **Bignoniaceae** | |
| 6/1 | *Tecoma stans* (L.) H.B. and K. | – |
| **5** | **Cactaceae** | |
| 7/1 | *Cereus peruvianus* | Cactus |
| **5** | **Caesalpiniaceae** | |
| 8/1 | *Cassia auriculata* L | – |
| **6** | **Capparaceae** | |
| 9/1 | *Capparis decidua* (Forsk.) Edgew | – |
| **7** | **Compositae** | |
| 10/1 | *Xanthium strumarium* L. | Gokhru |
| **8** | **Convolvulaceae** | |
| 11/1 | *Ipomoea fistulosa* Mart.ex Choisy | Besharm |
| **9** | **Euphorbiaceae** | |
| 12/1 | *Euphorbia neriifolia L.* | Thor |
| 13/2 | *Jatropha curcas L.* | Ratanjot |
| 14/3 | *Ricinus communis L.* | Arand |
| **10** | **Malvaceae** | |
| 15/1 | *Abelomoschus manihot (L.) Medic.* | Jagali bhindi |
| 16/2 | *Abutilon indicum (L.) Sw.* | – |
| **11** | **Musaceae** | |
| 17/1 | *Musa paradisiaca L.* | Kela |
| **12** | **Mimosaceae** | |
| 18/1 | *Prosopis juliflora* DC | Bilayati babool |
| **13** | **Nyctaginaceae** | |
| 19/1 | *Bougainvillea spectabilis* Willd. | Bougainvelia |
| **14** | **Rhamnaceae** | |
| 20/1 | *Zizyphus nummularia* (Burm.f.) W. and. | Jharbera |
| **15** | **Solanaceae** | |
| 21/1 | *Datura metel* L | Datura |

**Herbs:** The most of the undergrowth was dried up, except near water logged regions and along the periphery of the village ponds. Total 24 herbaceous species belongs to 13 family were recorded from the study area.

**Table 8.4: List of herbaceous species observed in the study area**

| Sl.No. | Family and Scientific Name | Vernacular Name |
|---|---|---|
| **1** | **Acanthaceae** | |
| 1/1 | *Hygrophila auriculata (Schum.)* | Kokilaksha |
| **2** | **Asteraceae** | |
| 2/1 | *Eclipta prostrata* (L.) L. | Bhangra |
| 3/2 | *Echinops echinatus* Roxb | Shulia |
| 4/3 | *Tridax procumbens L* | Pardesi bhangra |
| **3** | **Boraginaceae** | |
| 5/1 | *Trichodesma indicum l.* | Undha fuli |
| 4 | Cyperaceae | |
| 6/1 | *Cyperus bulbosus* Vahl. | – |
| 7/2 | *Cyperus difformis* L. | – |
| 8/1 | *Cyperus stoloniferus* Retz. | – |
| 9/2 | *Cyperus rotundus* L. | – |
| **5** | **Lamiaceae ( Labiatae)** | |
| 10/1 | *Ocimum basilicum* L. | – |
| 11/2 | *Ocimum sanctum* L. | Tulsi |
| **6** | **Nyctaginaceae** | |
| 12/1 | *Boerhavia diffusa* L. | – |
| 13/2 | *Boerhavia chinensis* Druce | – |
| **7** | **Papaveraceae** | |
| 14/1 | *Argemone mexicana* L. | Darudi/Katiaya |
| **8** | **Papilionaceae** | – |
| 15/1 | Cortalaria medicaginea Lam | Ran methi |
| 16/2 | *Indigofera oblongifolia* Forks. | – |
| **9** | **Poaceae (Gramineae)** | |
| 17/1 | *Saccharum munja* | Munja |
| 18/3 | *Cynodon dactylon* Pers. | – |
| 19/4 | *Pennisetum typhoides (Burm.)* | Bajri |
| **10** | **Poligonaceae** | |
| 20/1 | *Poligonum sp.* | – |
| 11 | Pontederiaceae | |
| 21/1 | *Eichhornia crassipes* (Mart.) | Jalkumbhi |
| **12** | **Solanaceae** | |
| 22/1 | *Solanum surattense Burm.* | Bhoringini |
| 23/2 | *Datura metel* | Dhatura |
| **13** | **Zygophyllaceae** | |
| 24/1 | *Tribulus terrestris* L | Gokhru |

**Climbers and Twiners:** The climbers and twiners observed along the agricultural hedges and road side hedges of the study area are given in the table 8.5. Total 5 species of climbers/ twiners belongs to 3 families are recorded from the area.

**Table 8.5. List of climbers observed in the study area**

| Sl.No. | Family and Scientific Name | Vernacular Name |
|---|---|---|
| 1 | **Convolvulaceae** | |
| 1/1 | *Ipomoea obscura* (L.) Ker – Gawl. | Vad fudardi |
| 2 | **Cucurbitaceae** | |
| 2/1 | *Citrulus colocynthis (L)* | Indravarna |
| 3/2 | *Coccinia grandis* (L.) Voigt | Ghiloda |
| 4/3 | *Luffa cylindrica (L.) M.J.Roem* | Galku |
| 3 | **Cuscutaceae** | |
| 5/1 | *Cuscuta chinensis* Lam. | Amarval |

## Cultivated Plants in the Study Area

The prevalent cropping systems of this area are the cumulative results of past and present decisions by individuals; these decisions are usually based on experience, tradition, expected profit, personal preferences and resources, and so on. The crop occupying the highest percentage of the sown area of this region is taken as the major crop and all other possible alternative crops which are sown in this region either as substitutes of the base crop in the same season or as the crops which fit in the rotation in the subsequent season, are considered as minor crop.

(a) **Major Crops:** Mainly people of this area was dependent on rain to cultivate the corps. Major crops in the study area are Wheat (*Triticum aestivum*), Maize (*Zea mays*), Bajra *(Pennisetum glaucum)* and Peanuts (*Arachis hypogaea*).

(b) **Minor crops:** The minor crops of this region are Mustard (Brassica campestris var.), Green gram (*Vigna radiate*), Pigeon Pea (*Punica granatum*) and Black Gram (*Vigna mungo).*

(c) **Major horticultural crops:** Aam (*Mangifera indica* L.), Papaya (*Carica papaya* L.), Banana (*Musa Paradisiaca* L.), Lime (*Citrus aurantifolia*), Guava (*Psidium guajava*), Jack-fruit (*Artocarpus heterophyllus*) and Jujube (*Ziziphus mauritiana*).

(d) **Major Vegetable corps:** The major vegetables grown in the study area were:

1. Bottle gourd: *Lagenaria siceraria.*
2. Brinjal: *Solanum melongena.*
3. Carrot: *Daucus carota.*

4. Chilli: *Capsicum annum.*
5. Coriander: *Coriandrum sativum*
6. Cucumber: *Cucumis sativus*
7. Lady's finger: *Abelmoschus esculentus.*
8. Potato: *Solanum tuberosum.*
9. Pumpkin: *Cucurbita moschata.*
10. Radish: *Raphanus sativus.*
11. Bean: *Dolichos lablab.*
12. Sponge gourd: *Luffa cylindrica.*
13. Tomato: *Lycopersicum esculantum*

(e) **Major Ornamental Plants:** Following is the list of ornamental plants in the study area.

1. Marigold: *Tagates erecta.*
2. China rose: *Hibiscus rosasinensis.*
3. Sunflower: *Helianthus annuus.*
4. Rose: *Rosa indica.*
5. Jasmin: *Jasminum sambac.*

**Rare and Endangered Flora in the Study Area:** The IUCN Red List is the world's most comprehensive inventory of the global conservation status of plant and animal species. It uses a set of criteria to evaluate the extinction risk of thousands of species and subspecies. These criteria are relevant to all species and all regions of the world. With its strong scientific base, the IUCN Red List is recognized as the most authoritative guide to the status of biological diversity. Out of 17000 species of higher plants known to occur in India, nearly 614 higher plant species were evaluated by IUCN. Among them 247 species are under threatened category (IUCN, 2008). Among the enumerated flora in the study area, none of them were assigned any threat category by Red data book of Indian Plants (Jain and Sastry, 1984; Nayar and Sastry, 1987; 1988; 1990; Oldfield *et al.*, 1998; Kholia and Bhakuni, 2009) and Red list of threatened Vascular plants (IUCN, 2010).

**Endemic Plants of the Study Area:** De Candolle (1855), Swiss botanist, first used the concept of Endemic, which is defined as an area of a taxonomic unit, especially a species which has a restricted distribution or habitat, isolated from its surrounding region through geographical, ecological or temporal barriers. Out of 17000 species of known flowering plants of India nearly 5000 species are said to be endemic. Nearly 58 genera and 1932 taxa are found to be endemic to peninsular India (Nayar, 1980; Ahmedullah and Nayar, 1986; 1987; Jain 1992; Nayar, 1996; Vijaya Shankar *et al.*, 2005; Nautiyal *et al.*, 2009a,b; Shendage *et al.*, 2010). Among recorded plant species none can be assigned the status of endemic plant of this region.

**Status of the Forest, Their Category in Study Area:** No any reserve forest was observed in the study area except protected forest of Dry Deciduous forest, Thorn forest (*Prosopis cineraria* (L.) Druce., *Acacia senegal* (L.) Willd, *Acacia nilotica* (L.) Willd. ex Del, *Acacia leucophloea* (Roxb.) Willd., *Acacia tortilis* (Forssk.) Hyene.and *Zizyphus mauritiana* Lam) and *Prosopis cineraria* (L.) Druce forest with few other scrub species and grazing lands with thin vegetation cover.

## FAUNAL BIODIVERSITY OF STUDY AREA

For the documentation of the faunal biodiversity of the study area with respect to birds, reptiles, amphibians, and butterfly species, a baseline survey had been conducted. The study area falls under two states Rajasthan and Haryana (interstate boundary).

**Birds:** The sighting of bird species was very lass during the study period during June 2015. The most commonly spotted bird species of this area were; Cattle Egret, Intermediate Egret, Red-wattled Lapwing, Rock Pigeon, Eurasian Collared-Dove, Spotted Dove, Chestnut-headed Bee-eater, Bank Myna and Common Myna. The Indian Peafowl was observed which is listed as schedule - I as per IWPA, 1972 and others listed as schedule IV as per IWPA, 1972. List of schedule - 1 as per Wild life Protection Act 1972, species is given in the table 8.6. Systematic account of the birds in the study area with the status of occurrence is given in the table 8.7.

**Table 8.6: Schedule – I Bird(s) of study area**

| Species | As IWPA 1972 | IUCN | CITES |
|---|---|---|---|
| Indian Peafowl (*Pavo cristatus*) | Schedule I | Least Concern ver 3.1 | Not listed |

**Table 8.7: Systematic lists of birds in the study area with its distribution and migratory status**

| Old Common Name | New Common Name | Scientific Name | Dist. |
|---|---|---|---|
| (1) | (2) | (3) | (4) |
| **I. ORDER: APODIFORMES** | | | |
| **Family: Apodidae (swifts)** | | | |
| Common Swift | Common Swift | *Apus apus* | R |
| House swift | Little Swift | *Apus affinis* | R |
| **II ORDER: BUCEROTIFORMES** | | | |
| **Family: Upupidae** | | | |
| Hoopoe | Hoopoe | *Upupa epops* | R |
| **III ORDER: FALCONIFORMES** | | | |
| **Family: Accipitridae (Vulture, Sparrow hawk, Eagle, Harrier, Kite and Vulture)** | | | |
| Shikra | Shikra | *Accipiter badius* | R |
| Black-winged Kite | Black-winged Kite | *Elanus caeruleus* | R |

(Table Contd...)

| (1) | (2) | (3) | (4) |
|---|---|---|---|
| **IV ORDER: CICONIIFORMES** | | | |
| **Family: Ardeidae (heron, Egret, Bittern)** | | | |
| Cattle Egret | Cattle Egret | *Bubulcus ibis* | R |
| Median or Smaller Egret | Intermediate Egret | *Mesophoyx intermedia*<br>*Egretta intermedia* | R |
| Little Egret | Little Egret | *Egretta garzetta* | R |
| Pond Heron | Indian Pond-Heron | *Ardeola grayii* | R |
| **Family: Charadriidae (Plover, Stilt, Oystercatcher, Lapwing, Avocet )** | | | |
| Red-wattled Lapwing | Red-wattled Lapwing | *Vanellus indicus* | R |
| **V ORDER: COLUMBIFORMES** | | | |
| **Family: Columbidae (Pigeon, Dove)** | | | |
| Blue Rock Pigeon | Rock Pigeon | *Columba livia* | R |
| Ring Dove | Eurasian Collared-Dove | *Streptopelia decaocto* | R |
| Rufous Turtle Dove | Oriental Turtle-Dove | *Streptopelia orientalis* | R |
| Spotted Dove | Spotted Dove | *Streptopelia chinensis* | R |
| **VI ORDER: CORACIFORMES** | | | |
| **Family: Dacelonidae (Kingfishers)** | | | |
| White breasted Kingfisher | White-throated Kingfisher | *Halcyon smyrnensis* | R |
| Family: Coraciidae (Roller) | | | |
| BlueJay or Roller | Indian Roller | *Coracias benghalensis* | R |
| Family: Meropidae (Bee Eater) | | | |
| Chestnut-headed Bee-eater | Chestnut-headed Bee-eater | *Merops leschenaulti* | R |
| Blue-cheeked Bee-eater | Blue-cheeked Bee-eater | *Merops persicus* | R |
| **VII ORDER: CUCULIFORMES** | | | |
| **Family: Centropodidae (Cocucal)** | | | |
| Crow-Pheasant or Coucal | Greater Coucal | *Centropus sinensis* | R |
| **Family: Cuculidae (cuckoo, Koel)** | | | |
| Koel | Asian Koel' | *Eudynamys scolopacea* | R |
| Indian Drongo Cuckoo | Drongo Cuckoo | *Surniculus lugubris* | R |
| **VIII ORDER: GALLIFORMES** | | | |
| **Family: Phasianidae (Peafowl, Partridge, Quail, Spur fowl, Jungle fowl, Monal)** | | | |
| Common Peafowl | Indian Peafowl | *Pavo cristatus* | R |
| Grey Partridge | Grey Francolin | *Francolinus pondicerianus* | R |
| Common Quail | Common Quail | *Coturnix coturnix* | R |
| Red jungle fowl | Red jungle fowl | *Gallus domesticus* | R |

(Table Contd...)

| (1) | (2) | (3) | (4) |
|---|---|---|---|
| **IX ORDER: GRUIFORMES** | | | |
| **Family: Rallidae (Waterhen, coot, crake water cock, Moorhen, Rail)** | | | |
| White-breasted Water hen | White-breasted Water hen | *Amaurornis phoenicurus* | R |
| Indian Moorhen | Common Moorhen | *Gallinula chloropus* | R |
| **X ORDER: PASSERIFORMES** | | | |
| **Family: Paridae (Tit )** | | | |
| Grey Tit | Great Tit | *Parus major* | R |
| **Family: Corvidae** | | | |
| Raven | Common Raven | *Corvus corax* | R |
| House Crow | House Crow | *Corvus splendens* | R |
| Black drongo- King Crow | Black Drongo | *Dicrurus macrocercus* | R |
| Tree Pie | Rufous Treepie | *Dendrocitta vagabunda* | R |
| **Family: Muscicapidae (Short wing, Chat, Robin, Shama** | | | |
| Indian Robin | Indian Robin | *Saxicoloides fulicata* | R |
| Pied Bushchat | Pied Bushchat | *Saxicola caprata* | R |
| **Family: Nectariniidae (Sun Birds, Flower pecker, Spider hunter )** | | | |
| Purple Sunbird | Purple Sunbird | *Nectarinia asiatica* | R |
| Small Sunbird | Crimson-backed Sunbird | *Nectarinia minima* | R |
| **Family: Passeridae (Avadavat, Pipit, Wagtail, Munia, Snowfinch, Sparrow, Accentor)** | | | |
| House Sparrow | House Sparrow | *Passer domesticus* | R |
| **Family: Pycnonotidae (Bulbul)** | | | |
| Red-whiskered Bulbul | Red-whiskered Bulbul | *Pycnonotus jocosus* | R |
| Red-vented Bulbul | Red-vented Bulbul | *Pycnonotus cafer* | R |
| **Family: Sturnidae (Myna, Starling)** | | | |
| Bank Myna | Bank Myna | *Acridotheres ginginianus* | R |
| Indian Myna | Common Myna | *Acridotheres tristis* | R |
| **Family: Sylviidae (Warbler, Browning, Fulvetta, Babbler, Laughing thrash, Tailor birds)** | | | |
| Common Babbler | Common Babbler | *Turdoides caudatus* | R |
| Jungle Babbler | Jungle Babbler | *Turdoides striatus* | R |
| **XI ORDER: PSITTACIFORMES** | | | |
| **Family: Psittacidae (Parrot and Parakeet)** | | | |
| Rose-ringed Parakeet | Rose-ringed Parakeet | *Psittacula krameri* | R |
| **Family: Ploceidae** | | | |
| Baya | Baya weaver | *Ploceus philippinus* | R |
| **XII ORDER: STRIGIFORMES** | | | |
| **Family: Strigidae (Owl and Owlet)** | | | |
| Owlet | Spotted owlet | *Athene brama* | R |

*Note:* **R** = Widespread Resident, r = Very Local Resident, **W** = Widespread Winter Visitor, w = Sparse Winter Visitor, **RW** =Resident and winter visitor as per the Distribution (**Dist.**) given in WCMC, Check list of Indian Birds

**Butterflies from the study area:** Butterflies from three families observed during the present study are documented in the Table 8.8.

**Table 8.8: Butterflies in the study area**

| Scientific Name and Family | Common Name | Relative Abundance |
|---|---|---|
| **Family Papilionidae** | | |
| *Papilio polytes* | Common Mormon | Common |
| **Family Pieridae** | | |
| *Eurema hecabe* | Common Grass yellow | Very Common |
| *Ixias Marianne* | White orange tip | Common |
| **Family: Nymphalidae** | | |
| *Danaus chrysippus* | Plain Tiger | Common |
| *Phalantha phalantha* | Common Leopard | Fairy Common |
| *Hypolimanas misippus* | Danaid egg fly | Common |
| *Mycalesis perseus* | Common bush brown | Uncommon |

**Herpetofauna:** In amphibian group, the toads were sighted during the study period during June 2015. The reptile, Common Garden Lizard, Common Indian Monitor, House Gecko and Fan-Throated Lizard, Rosebelly Worm-eating Snake and Himalayan Wolf Snake were observed in the region is given in the table 8.9.

**Table 8.9: Reptiles and Amphibian in the Study Area**

| Sl.No. | Common Name | Scientific Name | Schedule as IWPA, 1972 |
|---|---|---|---|
| 1. | Toad | *Bufo bufo* | Not listed |
| 2. | Common Indian Monitor | *Varanus bengalensis* | Schedule I |
| 3. | Common Garden Lizard | *Calotes versicolor* | Not listed |
| 4. | Fan-Throated Lizard | *Sitana ponticeriana* | Not listed |
| 5. | House Gecko | *Hemidactylus flaviviridis* | Not listed |
| 6. | Rose belly Worm-eating Snake | *Trachischium guentheri* | Not listed |
| 7. | Himalayan Wolf Snake | *Lycodon mackinnon* | Not listed |
| 8. | Indian Cobra | *Naja naja* (L) | Schedule II |
| 9. | *Russell's Viper | *Daboia russelii* | Schedule II |

* Not sighted but included as per the secondary information from the villagers.

**Mammals:** The wild mammals observed other than the domesticated ones are given in the table below. Common Mongoose (*Herpestes edwardsii*), Jackal (*Canis aureus*) and Monkey (*Macaca mulatta*) were observed which are protected under schedule II and Nilgai (*Boselaphus tragocamelus*) is Schedule-II animal as per Wildlife Protection Act 1972. Bat (*Rousettus leschenaulti*) and Common House Rat (*Rattus rattus)* are protected under schedule V.

**Table 8.10: Mammals in Study Area**

| Sl.No. | Common Name | Scientific Name | Status as per IWPA 1972 |
|---|---|---|---|
| 1. | Bat | *Rousettus leschenaulti* | Schedule V |
| 2. | Common House Rat | *Rattus rattus* | Schedule V |
| 3. | Common Mongoose | *Herpestes edwardsii* | Schedule II |
| 4. | Five striped Palm Squirrel | *Funambulus pennanii* | Schedule IV |
| 5. | Hare | *Lepus nigrigolis dayanus* | Schedule IV |
| 6. | Jackal | *Canis aureus* | Schedule II |
| 7. | Monkey (Rhesus macaque) | *Macaca mulatta* | Schedule II |
| 8. | Nilgai (Blue Bull) | *Boselaphus tragocamelus* | Schedule-III |

**Fishes:** During the study period (summer), there were no any major pond or river (aquatic body) was observed. The small fishes observed in one village pond along with tadpoles.

**Domestic Animals**

The domestic animals viz. Dog, cow, buffalo, goat, sheep and chicken observed in the study area are listed in the table below. Some people of this area practising poultry farming and some are sheep and goat farming.

**Table 8.11: Domestic animals in study area**

| Sl.No. | English/Hindi Name | Scientific Name |
|---|---|---|
| 1. | Buffalo/Bhains | *Bulbalus bulbalis* |
| 2. | Chicken/Murga | *Gallus gallus domesticus* |
| 3. | Cow/Gai | *Bos primigenius* |
| 4. | Dog/Kutta | *Canis lupus familiaris* |
| 5. | Goat/Bakri | *Capra aegagrus hircus* |
| 6. | Sheep/Bhed | *Ovis aries* |

**Rare and Endangered Fauna of Study Area:** The IUCN Red List is the world's most comprehensive inventory of the global conservation status of plant and animal species. It uses a set of criteria to evaluate the extinction risk of thousands of species and subspecies. These criteria are relevant to all species and all regions of the world. With its strong scientific base, the IUCN Red List is recognized as the most authoritative guide to the status of biological diversity. IUCN, (2008) has evaluated 1976 animal species from India, among them 313 have in recognized as threatened species. Among them one species is considered as extinct, while 44 species are in critically endangered (CR) category, 88 is in endangered category (EN), while 181 is considered as vulnerable (VU). Wild Life (Protection) Act, 1972, amended on 17$^{th}$ January 2003, is an Act to provide for the protection of wild animals, birds and plants and for matters connected therewith or ancillary or incidental thereto with a view to ensuring the ecological and environmental security of the country. Some of the sighted fauna was given protection by the Indian Wild Life (Protection) Act, 1972 by including them in different schedules. Among the birds in the study area, Pea fowl (*Pavo cristatus)* is included in schedule I of Wild life protection Act (1972), while many other birds are included in schedule IV. Among the reptiles, Indian Cobra (*Naja naja*) and Russell's viper were provided protection as per Schedule-II of Wild life Protection Act, (1972). Among mammals; Common Indian monitor (*Varanus bengalensis*) is schedule-I and Common Mongoose (*Herpestes edwardsi)*, Jackal (*Canis aureus* (Linnaeus) and Monkey (*Rhesus macaque*) are a schedule –II animals. Nilgai (*Boselaphus tragocamelus*) is protected as Schedule-III animal and hares and five stripped squirrels are included in schedule IV of Wild Life Protection act 1972.

**Endemic Fauna of the Study Area:** None of the sighted animal species can be assigned endemic species category of the study area.

**Table 8.12: List of schedule-I and II fauna observed during the study**

| Sl. No. | Scientific Name | Local Name | Schedule as per WPA, 1972 | IUCN Category | CITES Listing |
|---|---|---|---|---|---|
| 1. | *Pavo cristatus* | Indian Peafowl | Schedule I | Least Concern ver 3.1 | Not listed |
| 2. | *Varanus bengalensis* | Common Indian monitor | Schedule I | Least Concern ver 3.1 | Appendix I |
| 3. | *Canis aureus* | Jackal | Schedule II | Least Concern ver 3.1 | Appendix II |
| 4. | *Herpestes edwardsi* | Common Mongoose | Schedule II | Least Concern ver 3.1 | Appendix III |
| 5. | *Macaca mulatta* | Rhesus macaque | Schedule II | Least Concern ver 3.1 | Not listed |
| 6. | *Naja naja* | Indian Cobra | Schedule II | Least Concern ver 3.1 | Appendix II |
| 7. | *Vipera/Daboia russelli* | Russell's Viper | Schedule II | Least Concern ver 3.1 | Appendix III |

## ECOLOGICAL IMPACT ASSESSMENT

### Major Impact on Ecological Environment

1. As it is a river bed mining project, mine activities will be confined to core zone only. Thus, no direct impact is foreseen on the flora of the forested area because of mining, whereas activities related to mining as transportation of minerals and passage of workers to and fro from mining area will have an adverse impact on the road side flora.

2. Loud sounds generated by human activities and transportation may have an adverse impact on terrestrial fauna and avifauna.
3. Transportation of sand in the trucks/dumper will disturb the movement of wild animals like jungle cat, jackal, and other reptiles. Fugitive emission from vehicle movement will form a layer in leaves thus reducing the gaseous exchange process. This ultimately affects the growth of plants. Chances of vehicle collisions with wildlife attempting to cross roads are possible.
4. Any human settlement in the mining area will disturb the vegetation cover and reptiles.
5. Indiscriminate mining from active channels of rivers causes many adverse effects on the benthic fauna, which inhabits the bottom sandy substratum. Excessive sand extraction from rivers affects the eco-biology of many terrestrial insects whose initial life history begins in aquatic environments.
6. The Indian peafowl movement is very common in the area; the noise from sand mining will hinder the same.
7. Some scheduled fauna was observed in the study area, the mining activity can hinder their movement.

**Proposed Mitigation Measures**

1. Transportation of sand should be minimise in the morning and evening and cannot be done in night. Access roads will not encroach into the riparian zones.
2. The mining will be restricted to dry bed.
3. All equipment should have sound-control devices no less effective than those provided on the original equipment. Motorized equipment used should be adequately muffled and maintained.
4. No human settlement should be permitted in the lease mining or nearby area. No mining will be carried out during the rainy season to minimize impact on aquatic life.
5. Green belt and community forestry should be encouraged to mitigate the noise level. Plantation will be carried out on approach roads and nearby vicinity at river banks areas.
6. The latest equipment with sound-control devices should be used for sand excavation and loading/unloading, etc. Use of exhaust silencers and optimized acoustical pipe lagging (acoustical wrapping) to minimize compressor noise.
7. No mining will be carried out during the rainy season to minimize impact on aquatic life.
8. Annual bio-monitoring of roadside plants exposed to vehicular pollution will be done to check the dust load and Air Pollution Tolerance Index (APTI).

9. The conservation plan has been prepared along with budgetary provision to implement effectively and will be supervised by Forest department.

**Green Belt Development**

A green belt will be developed along the boundary of the mining lease area. The area for green belt plantation consists of undisturbed soil; hence plantation could be made as in any garden or road side plantation. Green belt is erected not from biodiversity conservation point of view but is basically developed as a screen to check the spread of dust pollution. A green belt, 7.5m in width will be developed around the core zone. Green belt plantation will be started with the beginning of the mining and will be completed within five years from the beginning.

Following precaution will be taken:

- To raise seedlings for plantation in the green belt a nursery will be developed.
- Seedlings of only local species, suitable for green belt plantation will be raised in this nursery.
- All the representative plant species of the region were found to grow in and around the study site.
- Care will be provided against grazing and browsing.
- Timely watering during the initial stages of survival and provision will be made for the allocation of funds as well.
- During the running of mine, flora will be regenerated in different stages and the area having matured Afforestation will be properly fenced so as to avoid cutting, browsing and hacking of branches and pruning of trees
- Creating awareness among villagers residing on the periphery of the mines regarding the use of plantations.
- Plantation of indigenous species, fodder and fruit bearing tree species which can also act as habitats for wild life.
- Plantation of fruits bearing trees like Karonda, Zizyphus, Awala, Gular, Timbru, Lasoda, Aam and other Ficus species will attract sloth bear population.
- For increasing hare population turfing on the ground on both sides of nallahs by grasses will provide a suitable habitat which is most sought food for hares.

**Afforestation Plan**

Under the afforestation plan, plantation in nearby villages and connecting roads will be undertaken. The implementation for development of greenbelt will be of paramount importance as it will not only add up as an aesthetic feature but will also act as a pollution sink. The species to be grown in the areas should be dust tolerant and fast growing species so that a permanent greenbelt is created. Plantation in the barrier zone and roads is necessary as these areas will contain fine particulates resulting from mining operation and vehicle movement. Mining activities will not cause any harm to riparian vegetation cover as the working will not extend beyond the offset left against the banks in the river. Land on both sides is the private agriculture land. Link road from the active zone pass through the areas. It is proposed to have plantation on both sides of the roads as greenbelt to provide cover against dust dissemination. River banks will be strengthened by way of plantation on the banks. Plantation will also be carried out as social forestry programme in villages, school and the areas allocated by the Panchayat/ State authorities. Native plants like Neem, Khejri, Mango and other local species will be planted. A suitable combination of trees that can grow fast and also have good leaf cover shall be adopted to develop the greenbelt.

**Table 8.13: List of species for greenbelt development**

| Sl.No. | Scientific Name | Common Name | Type | Effective in Control |
|---|---|---|---|---|
| 1. | *Azadirachta indica* | Neem | Tree | Dust, air pollution, noise pollution |
| 2. | *Bauhinia variegata* | Kachnar | Tree | Dust |
| 3. | *Tamarindus indica* | Imli | Tree | Air Pollution |
| 4. | *Zizyphus mauritiana* | Ber | Tree | Air Pollution |
| 5. | *Aegle marmelos* | Bel | Tree | Air Pollution, noisepollution |
| 6. | *Polyalthia longifolia* | Ashok | Tree | Dust, Air pollution |
| 7. | *Ficus glomerata* | Gular | Tree | Dust, air pollution,noise pollution |
| 8. | *Acacia nilotica* | Babool | Tree | Air pollution |
| 9. | *Mangifera indica* | Mango | Tree | Dust, air pollution,noise pollution |

*Source*: Guidelines for Greenbelt Development, CPCB, March, 2000.

## CONCLUSION

The study area falls under 3 districts of Rajasthan and 1 district of Hayrana State *viz*. Sikar, Jhunjhunu, Jaipur (Rajasthan) and Mahendragarh (Haryana). The mine lease area is free from the protected forest as per site survey and discussion with client on site. Total 53 villages of District Sikar, 11 villages of District Jaipur, 11 villages of District Jhunjhunu and 13 villages of Mahendragarh (Haryana) were surveyed for the present study. The major trees were Khejri *(Prosopis cineraria)*, Babool (*Acacia nilotica*) and few shrubs of Bilayati baool *(Prosopis juliflora)* as dominant vegetation. The people were engaged in Maize, Peanuts and Pearl millet cultivation during the study period. The crop is depending on rain, as there is no other means of water for irrigation. Total 31 species of trees belong to 14 families are enumerated from the study area. Total 21 shrub species belong to 15 families are enumerated from the study area. The dominant shrub community in this area was represented by *Prosopis juliflora* (Bilayati babool), *Calotropis procera, C. gigantea* (Akoda), Kaner (*Thevetia peruviana), Ipomoea fistulosa* and *Abutilon indicum,* etc. Total 24 herbaceous species belongs to 13 family were recorded from the study area. Total 5 species of climbers/ twiners belongs to 3 families are recorded from the area. Mainly people of this area were dependent on rain to cultivate the corps. Major crops in the study area are Wheat (*Triticum aestivum*), Maize (*Zea mays*), Bajra *(Pennisetum glaucum)* and Peanuts (*Arachis hypogaea*). Among the enumerated flora in the study area, none of them were assigned any threat category by Red data book of Indian Plants. The sighting of bird species was very lass during the study period during June 2015. The most commonly spotted bird species of this area were; Cattle Egret, Intermediate Egret, Red-wattled Lapwing, Rock Pigeon, Eurasian Collared-Dove, Spotted Dove, Chestnut-headed Bee-eater, Bank Myna and Common Myna. The Indian Peafowl was observed which is listed as schedule –I as per IWPA, 1972 and others listed as schedule IV as per IWPA, 1972. In amphibian group, the toads were sighted during the study period during June 2015. The reptile, Common Garden Lizard, Common Indian Monitor, House Gecko and Fan-Throated Lizard, Rosebelly Worm-eating Snake and Himalayan Wolf Snake were observed. Common Mongoose (*Herpestes edwardsii*), Jackal (*Canis aureus*) and Monkey (*Macaca mulatta*) were observed which are protected under schedule II and Nilgai (*Boselaphus tragocamelus*) is Schedule-II animal as per Wildlife Protection Act 1972. During the study period (summer), there were no any major pond or river (aquatic body) was observed. Among the reptiles, Indian Cobra (*Naja naja*) and Russell's viper were provided protection as per Schedule-II of Wild life Protection Act, (1972). Among mammals; Common Indian monitor (*Varanus bengalensis*) is schedule-I and Common Mongoose (*Herpestes edwardsi),* Jackal (*Canis aureus* (Linnaeus) and Monkey (*Rhesus macaque*) are a schedule –II animals for which conservation plan is prepared along with budgetary provision. Transportation of sand will hinder the movement of wild animals and reptiles; hence it is recommended to implement the conservation measures and educate the drivers for the importance of wild life.

## *REFERENCES*

Ahmedullah, M. and M.P. Nayar (1987). Endemic Plants of the Indian Region. Culcutta: Botanical Survey of India. 147 pp.

Ahmedullah, M. and Nayar, M.P. (1986). Endemic Plants of the Indian Region. Vol. 1. Peninsular India. Bot. Surv. of India, Calcutta.

Anderson, T. (1867). An Enumeration of the Indian Species of Acanthaceae. Journal of Linnaean Society 9: 425-454. Gamble, J.S. 1924. The Flora of Presidency of Madras 2. Culcutta: Botanical Survey of India. 743 pp.

APHA (1971). Standard methods for the Examination of Water and Waste Water. American Public Health, Association, New York.

Batten, SD, Clarke R, Flinkman J (2003). CPR Sampling: The Technical Background, Material and Methods, Consistency and Comparability. Progress in Oceanography, 58, 193-215.

Bentham, G. and Hooker, J.D. (1862-1883). Genera Plantarum. L Reeve and Co., London.

BirdLife International (2000). Threatened Birds of the World. Lynx Edicions and BirdLife International, Barcelona and Cambridge, UK.

BirdLife International (2004a). Threatened Birds of the World 2004. CD-ROM. BirdLife International, Cambridge, UK.

BirdLife International (2004b). State of the World's Birds 2004-Indicators for our Changing World. BirdLife International, Cambridge, UK.

BirdLife International (2010). The BirdLife Checklist of the Birds of the World, with Conservation Status and Taxonomic Sources. Version 3. Available from http://www.birdlife.info/docs/SpcChecklist/Checklist_v3_June10.zip

Colebrook, J.M. (1960). Continuous Plankton Records: Methods of Analysis, 1950-59. Bulletins of Marine Ecology, 5, 51-64.

Dixit, R.D. (1984). A Census of the Indian Pteridophytes. Flora of India Series 4. Botanical Survey of India, Howrah (Calcutta).

Edmondson WT (1974). A Simplified method for Counting Phytoplankton. In: A Manual on methods for Measuring Primary Production in Aquatic Environments (Ed. Vollenmeider RE) Balckwell Sci. Pub., Oxford, pp. 14-16.

Ghosh, S.R., Ghosh, B., Biswas, A. and Ghosh, R.K. (2004). The Pteridophytic Flora of Eastern India 1: 1-591. In: Flora of India Series 4, Botanical Survey of India, Kolkata.

Hunter, W.W. (1879). Statlstlcal Account of Assani. Vol II Trubner and Co.

IUCN (1994). IUCN Red List Categories. Prepared by the IUCN Species Survival Commission. IUCN, Gland, Switzerland.

IUCN (2001). IUCN Red List Categories and Criteria: Version 3.1. IUCN Species Survival Commission. IUCN, Gland, Switzerland and Cambridge, UK.

IUCN (2003). Guidelines for Application of IUCN Red List Criteria at Regional Levels: Version 3.0. IUCN Species Survival Commission. IUCN, Gland, Switzerland and Cambridge, UK.

IUCN (2008). Red List of Threatened Species. (www.iucnredlist.org).

IUCN (2010). Guidelines for Using the IUCN Red List Categories and Criteria, Version 8.1 (August 2010), Prepared by the Standards and Petitions Subcommittee of the IUCN Species Survival Commission: on www. http://intranet.iucn.org/webfiles/doc/SSC/RedList/ RedListGuidelines.pdf

Jain, S.K. (1991). Dictionary of Indian Folk Medicine and Ethnobotany. Deep Publications, New Delhi.

Jain, S.K. (1968). Medicinal Plants Nation Book Trust, New Delhi. Jain, S.K. 1983. Rare and Endangered Specles: Observation on Rare, Imperfectly known Endemic Plants. In the Sacred Groves of Western Maharashtra. Calcutta; Bot. Sur of India 169-178.

Jain, S.K. (1992). The Problem of Endangered Species. Concepts, Problems and Solutions. In: Tropical Ecosystems: Ecolosv and Management (Eds. K.P.Singh and J.S.Singh.), Iiley Eastern Limited, New delhi. 69-80.

Jain, S.K. and Rao, R.K. (1983). An Assessment of Threatened Plants of India. Bot. Surv. of India. Calcutta.

Jain, S.K. and Sastry, A.R.K. (1980). Threatened Plants of India - A State of the Alf Report Bot. Surv. of India. New Delhi.

Jain, S.K. and Sastry, A.R.K. (1984). Safeguarding Plant Diversity in Threatened Natural Habitats. In Conservation of Threatened Natural Habitats. (Ed. Anthony V. Hall). African nat. Sci. Prog. Report. 92.

Kholia, B.S. and Bhakuni, K. (2009). Western Himalaya a New Range of Distribution for a Critically Endangered Fern, Dryopsis Manipurensis (Bedd.) Holttum et P.J. Edwards. Nelumbo, Bulletin of the Botanical Survey of India 51: 245-248.

Kumar Ashok (2013). Butterfly (Lepidoptera: Insecta) Diversity from Different Sites of Jhagadia, Ankleshwar, District-Bharuch, Gujarat, Oct. Jour. Env. Res. 1(1): 09-18.

Kumar Ashok (2014). Environmental Management Plan for Chemical Industries Especially Resin Manufacturing Unit, Oct. Jour. Env. Res. 2(3): 262-273.

Kumar Ashok and Aggarwal Savita Goyal (2013a). Ecology and Biodiversity Status of Sachin Gidc and its Surroundings with Special Reference to Conservation Measures for Indian Peafowl (Pavo cristatus) Schedule –I Bird species, Oct. Jour. Env. Res. 2(1): 82-100.

Kumar Ashok and Aggarwal Savita Goyal (2013b). Study of Common Property Resources (Cpr) With Special Reference to Water and Biological Resources at Projected Area Near Village Ninat, Bardoli, District-Surat, Oct. Jour. Env. Res. 1(4): 319-331.

Kumar Ashok and Srivastava Meena (2012). Diversity of Medicinal Plants in Uttarakhand and their Conservation Strategy with special reference to Orchids, In: Proceeding of National Conference on Environementla Health: Challaneges and Management, Jan. 20-21, 2012, Organized by Pt. Deendayal Upadhyay Govt. PG College Rajajipuram, Lucknow. pp. 139-142.

Kumar Ashok, Srivastava Meena and Goyal Savita (2013). The Biodiversity at Sandi Bird Sanctuary, Hardoi With Special Reference to Migratory Birds. Oct. Jour. Env. Res. 1(3): 173-181.

Lackey J B. (1938). The Manipulation and Counting of River Plankton and Changes in Some Organisms due to Formalin Preservation. US Public Health Reports 53: 2081-93.

Lushington, A.W. (1915). Vernacular List of Trees, Shrubs and woody Cl~rnbers of the Madras Presidency. Govt. Press, Madras.

Nautiyal DC, SK Sharma and MK Pandit (2009). Notes on the Taxonomic History, Rediscovery and Conservation Status of Two Endangered Species of Ceropegia (Asclepiadaceae) from Sikkim Himalaya. Journal of Botanical Research Institute Texas 3(2): 815-822.

Nautiyal DC, SK Sharmaand MK Pandit (2009). Notes on the Taxonomic History of Two Rare Species of Begonia (Begoniaceae) from Sikkim Himalaya and their Conservation. Journal of Botanical Research Institute Texas 3(2): 823-830.

Nayar MP and ARK Sastry (1987). Red Data Book of Indian Plants. Vol. I. Botanical Survey of India, Calcutta.

Nayar MP and ARK Sastry (1988). Red Data Book of Indian Plants. Vol. II. Botanical Survey of India, Calcutta.

Nayar MP and ARK Sastry (1990). Red Data Book of Indian Plants. Vol. III. Botanical Survey of India, Calcutta.

Nayar, M.P. (1980). Endemism and Patterns of Distribution of Endemic Genera (Angiosperms) in India. J. Econ. Tax. Bot. I: 99-110.

Nayar, M.P. (1996). Hotspots of Endemic Plants of India, Nepal and Bhutan. Thiruvanathapuram: Tropical Botanical Garden and Research Institute. 204 pp.

Ohasi H (1975). Flora of Eastern Himalaya, Third Report. University Museum of University of Tokyo Bulletin 8: 1-458.

Oldfield, S., Lusty, C. and MacKinven, A. (1998). The World List of Threatened Trees. World Conservation Press, Cambridge.

Shendage, S.M. and S.R. Yadav (2010). Revision of the Genus Barleria (Acanthaceae) in India. Rheedea 20(2): 81-230.

Vijaya Sankar, R., Ravikumar, R. and N.M. Ganesh Babu (2005). On the Collection of a Peninsular Endemic, Barleria Stocksii (Acanthaceae), after a Century. Zoo's Print 20: 1820.

Vollenweider R A (Ed). (1969). A Manual of Methods For Measuring Primary Production in Aquatic Environment. IBP Handbook No. 12, Blackwell Scientific Publications.

Welch F S. (1948). Limnological Methods. McGraw Hill Book Co Inc., New York.

Wilson, D.E. and Reeder, D.M. (eds). (1993). Mammal Species of the World a Taxonomic and Geographic Reference. Second Edition. Smithsonian Institution Press, Washington and London.

Wilson, D.E. and Reeder, D.M. (eds). (2005). Mammal Species of the World. A Taxonomic and Geographic Reference. Third Edition. Johns Hopkins University Press, Baltimore.

World Conservation Monitoring Centre (1988). The Conservation of Biological Diversity. WCMC., I.U.C.N., Cambridge, UK.

World Conservation Monitoring Centre (2000). Global Biodiversity: Earth's Living Resources in the 21st Century. By: Groombridge B. and Jenkins, M.D. World Conservation Press, Cambridge.

# Index

❑ ❑ ❑ ❑ ❑ ❑